UNION RESILIENCE IN TROUBLED TIMES

LABOR AND HUMAN RESOURCES SERIES

LABOR STRUGGLE IN THE POST OFFICE:
From Selective Lobbying to Collective Bargaining
John Walsh and Garth Mangum

MASS IMMIGRATION AND THE NATIONAL INTEREST
Vernon M. Briggs, Jr.

LABOR MARKET INSTITUTIONS IN EUROPE:
A Socioeconomic Evaluation of Performance
Günther Schmid, Editor

UNION RESILIENCE IN TROUBLED TIMES:
The Story of the Operating Engineers, AFL-CIO, 1960–1993
Garth Mangum and John Walsh

UNION RESILIENCE IN TROUBLED TIMES

The Story of the Operating Engineers, AFL–CIO, 1960–1993

GARTH L. MANGUM
JOHN WALSH

M.E. Sharpe
Armonk, New York
London, England

Library of Congress Cataloging-in-Publication Data

Mangum, Garth L.
Union resilience in troubled times: the story of the
operating engineers, AFL-CIO, 1960–1993 /
Garth L. Mangum, John Walsh.
p. cm. —(Labor and human resources)
Includes index.
ISBN 1-56324-452-7. — ISBN 1-56324-453-5 (pbk.)
1. International Union of Operating Engineers—History.
2. Trade-unions—Mechanics (Persons)—United States—History.
3. Trade-unions—Steam engineers—United States—History.
4. Trade-unions—Construction workers—United States—History.
I. Walsh, John, 1925–.
II. Title.
III. Series;: Labor and human resources series.
HD6475.M3M36   1994
331.88′12′009—dc20
94-10047
CIP

Printed in the United States of America
The paper used in this publication meets the minimum
requirements of American National Standard for
Information Sciences—Permanence of Paper for
Printed Library Materials, ANSI Z 39.48-1984.

MV (c)   10   9   8   7   6   5   4   3   2   1
MV (p)   10   9   8   7   6   5   4   3   2   1

TABLE OF CONTENTS

LIST OF PHOTOGRAPHS, TABLES, AND FIGURES

Photographs

Tables

Figures

Map

Acknowledgements

It is a pleasure to acknowledge the assistance that the authors received in the course of researching and writing this book. First and foremost, we are grateful to Frank Hanley, President of the International Union of Operating Engineers, who invested considerable time in answering our questions and providing us with access to all union files and to his entire staff. His thirty-six years of experience in virtually every IUOE initiative during the period 1960–1993 was an extremely valuable resource to the authors.

The cooperation the authors received started with the president but did not end there. Secretary Treasurer Budd Coutts, General Counsel Michael Fanning, and Assistants to the President Jack Weberski, Jim Van Dyke, and Al Lake not only gave their time, but delivered incisive comments that resulted in clear insights into both the successes and failures of the union during the thirty-three-year period. Others on the national staff who were extremely helpful to the authors were Ken Allen, Bud Evans, Ray Pourpore, Howard Brown, Larry Edginton, Bill Smith, Joe Brady, and Dave Treanor. Treanor, who served as the liaison between the writers and the union, answered our requests promptly and always with good cheer, and his comments and suggestions contributed to an improved manuscript.

Dick Griffin and Helen Morgan helped make clear two extremely complicated subjects, the health care battle and the California triumph. Both were vivid examples of the intricacies of National Labor Relations Board proceedings, the vagaries of federal district court decisions, and internecine warfare between AFL-CIO affiliates. Griffin and Morgan reduced both subjects to their essentials and by so doing made them understandable.

The authors were also fortunate in gaining the cooperation of seven outstanding business managers who managed to keep their locals healthy in troubled times. Art Viat and Tom Stapleton in northern California, Bob Fox in southern California, Fred Dereschuk in St Paul, Lionel Gindorf in Chicago, Ron De Juliis in Baltimore, and Peter Babin III in New Orleans provided vivid descriptions of what life is like on the firing line.

A good deal of the history was related to us by those who lived it, including former president Larry Dugan, Reese Hammond, Russ Conlon, Dale Marr, Rowland Hill, Herb Ingram, Jim Biddle, and Peter Babin, Jr., Former Secretary of Labor John Dunlop and Professor Quinn Mills provided valuable insights into the Nixon wage stabilization program and its effect on the construction trades. Two vice presidents of the Associated Builders and Contractors of America, Charles Hawkins and Charlotte Herbert, graciously presented the open shop point of view to writers they suspected were biased the other way. Lane Kirkland, president of the AFL-CIO, described his efforts to establish an IUOE central pension plan when he was an assistant to former IUOE president Joseph Delaney.

Last but far from least, we would like to express our appreciation to the eleven operating engineers who shared with the authors their personal histories and reflections: Billy Hurt, Steve Brown, Lou Previty, Joe Nealy, Nick Mastoris, Orlando Sanchez, Jeanita Martin, Freida Maldonado, Bill Snow, William Harris, Tom Richards, and George McGuire. Our thanks to all of you for your contribution to our understanding of the joys and sorrows of the men and women who operate and maintain heavy equipment and physical plant systems.

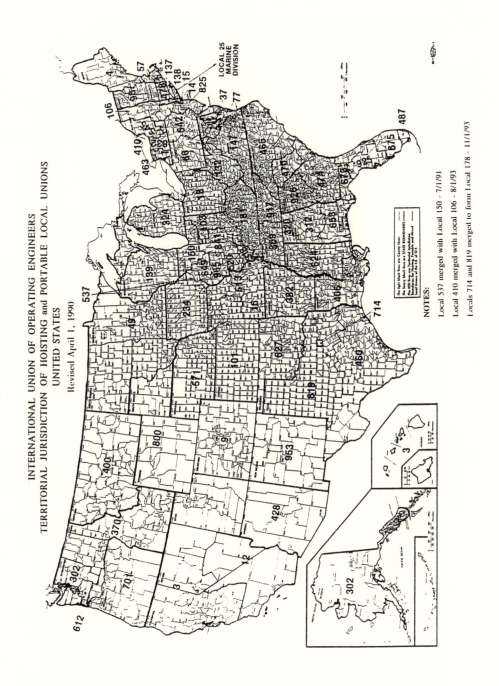

INTERNATIONAL UNION OF OPERATING ENGINEERS
TERRITORIAL JURISDICTION OF HOISTING and PORTABLE LOCAL UNIONS
UNITED STATES

Revised April 1, 1990

LOCAL 25
MARINE
DIVISION

NOTES:

Local 537 merged with Local 150 - 7/1/91

Local 410 merged with Local 106 - 8/1/93

Locals 714 and 819 merged to form Local 178 - 11/1/93

UNION RESILIENCE IN TROUBLED TIMES

INTRODUCTION

In troubled times, despite declining membership, union members, especially those in craft unions, given reasonable choice, maintain allegiance to their organizations. The International Union of Operating Engineers (IUOE), AFL-CIO, is composed of men and women who work as heavy equipment operators and mechanics in construction and related industries, and as the operators and maintainers of physical plant systems in factories, office buildings, hospitals, schools, and other facilities. The former are called "hoisting and portable engineers"; the latter are "stationary engineers." As the quotations below indicate, IUOE members are fully capable of speaking for themselves, not only about their work but also about their union affiliation and the external conditions that affect their working lives. Excerpts from interviews with retirees and operating engineers currently working at the trade provide a vivid picture of the roller coaster ride IUOE members have experienced over the past thirty-three years, as well as what they consider the importance of union representation. As such, they provide an appropriate lead-in to a book that essentially tells their story.

***

Billy Hurt recalled a day thirty years ago when he was twenty-three years old and was just getting started as a crane operator after a five-year apprenticeship as an oiler.

> I was working for a brick contractor on a partially renovated building. At one point I looked up and noticed that there was a wall angling out over my head and that the wall did not look too secure. Since there was nothing over the cab, and since I had safety drilled into me by the union and by my father, who was also an operating engineer, I called over the contractor and told him that I didn't feel too good working under that wall. He looked the situation over and said he didn't see anything wrong with the wall and that I should get back to work.
>
> Well, I had a $500 unpaid grocery bill and I was behind in my rent, my car payments, and everything else, but I was damned if I was going to work under that wall without something over my head, so I told the contractor that I was going to call the union hall. I hadn't got halfway to

the phone before he called me back and said that he'd fix up something. They found a huge, thick door that was metal on the outside, sunk four posts into the ground, and set the door on the posts over the cab.

That was during the lunch hour. About a half-hour later, while I was working, the entire wall came down over me. You say construction work is dangerous? Sure, it's dangerous, and I wouldn't be here today enjoying my union pension if there wasn't some organization with clout to protect me on the job, to intercede with the contractor on my behalf. What would a nonunion worker do in a situation like that? He'd either quit and lose his job or continue operating and maybe lose his life.

I can think of a lot of benefits I received from being a member of the Operating Engineers—good wages, overtime pay, health and welfare protection, and now, a good pension—but I showed you that motorcycle in the shed out back; that's my hobby. Maybe the fact that I'm all in one piece, alive and able to ride that bike, is the most valuable benefit I received from being a union man.

***

Billy Hurt learned his trade on the job; at the time there was no formalized apprenticeship training program for operating engineers. Steve Brown, on the other hand, was a 1972 graduate of Local 77's apprenticeship training program, and one of his teachers was Billy Hurt.

I was just out of high school, married to my high school sweetheart, and working for the Goodyear Tire and Rubber Company. My father-in-law was an operating engineer and suggested that, because I'm mechanically inclined, I should consider becoming an operating engineer. I thought about it and eventually put in an application to become an apprentice engineer.

One day, the apprentice director called me on the job and asked if I was ready to go to work. I said, "Sure I'm ready," and he said, "Okay, you start tonight." I said, "Well, I have to give my company some kind of notice," and he said, "Do you want the job or don't you?" I said, "Yes, I want it." So I went into the office and begged off. They weren't too happy about it, but they understood that it was the best move for me, so they wished me luck.

I worked for a year before I actually started my apprenticeship—six months probation and six months waiting for a new class to start. The program was four years long; the fourth year was 100 percent training on the job. I was lucky. At the time I went through apprenticeship, the D.C.

International Union of Operating Engineers

AFFILIATED WITH THE AMERICAN FEDERATION OF LABOR AND CONGRESS OF INDUSTRIAL ORGANIZATIONS

1125 SEVENTEENTH STREET NORTHWEST ★ WASHINGTON, D. C. 20036

OFFICE OF GENERAL PRESIDENT ● (202) 429-9100

September 29, 1994

MICHAEL J MURPHY
382 HQ STAFF
5305 MANOR LAKE COURT
ROCKVILLE MD 20853

S 0237

Metro was under construction, so there was a lot of work for both operators and apprentices. It's a lot different now. Most of the work around here is going nonunion, so there are far fewer jobs for apprentices.

But let me tell you this: If you are a skilled crane operator or mechanic, you won't be unemployed for long. One crane operator can service over 100 people on the job—carpenters, laborers, iron workers. And one operator doesn't make that much difference in the cost of a project, so skilled operators stay working. Especially nowadays, when the equipment is expensive and complicated and the contractor's liability insurance is going through the roof. Back when Billy started working, there weren't as many people on the streets, and lawsuits were rare. But today—well, let's put it this way—only very competent people are allowed to operate.

Billy Hurt was one of my instructors, and now I teach in the apprenticeship program. I don't do it for the money. I really don't. I enjoy teaching my craft, and I know those apprentices are going to get something out of my teaching. . . . I have turned out quite a few good operators during the short time I have been teaching. They don't come up and tell me that I've done a great job; they probably don't even think about that. But I gave them something—you know—something that they can use down the road, and I enjoy that.

***

Jeanita Martin is unique as an operating engineer, not just because she is a woman, a Navajo, a Job Corps graduate, and an apprenticeship graduate, but because she is alone in being all four. She has the reputation in Local 3 of being an especially skilled engineer, able to operate the full range of highway equipment. Her highway contractor-employer requests her services from the hiring hall at the beginning of each season. She asks:

> How else but through the Job Corps and the IUOE apprenticeship program could a single mother of two gain the skills to earn $40,000 a year, with hospitalization and a pension? After ten years, the work is still exciting and the people are great.

***

Tom Richards still works as the chief engineer in a large Cleveland industrial facility, but he has been around for a long time and is looking forward to retirement in a year or two.

I witnessed the tremendous change that took place in the craft of stationary engineer. I started out working as a switch pitman on a steam-generated power system. I went from there to pitman, boiler operator, and, finally, full-fledged stationary engineer. Later, everything was diesel-driven, and still later, computers controlled the whole operation. Today's stationary engineer works in a high-tech atmosphere and must be trained accordingly. That's where the union performs a great service, by helping the members keep abreast of the trade through training and retraining. But that's not the only thing that a union does. A union is nothing more than a group of workers standing up for the economic health and safety of the individual worker. There is no other way that individuals can get the respect and protection on the job that they need and deserve. And that applies to nonunion workers as well as union members. If there weren't unions around, those nonunion people would become agitators, because their wages would be as close to the minimum as employers could make them.

***

George McGuire, chief engineer at a commercial building in downtown San Francisco, was recognized by the San Francisco Water Department for developing a system that saved 6,000 gallons of water a day during a period when San Francisco and all of California were suffering from one of the worst droughts in history. He is an example of an IUOE-trained stationary engineer who does a lot more than merely put in eight hours a day.

It all has to do with flushing toilets. The building was originally plumbed with two sets of pipes. Drinking water was fed to the fountains, and a well supplied untreated water for flushing toilets. The well failed when BART [Bay Area Rapid Transit] construction changed ground-water availability and the building had to switch to city water for flushing toilets. In the meantime, the building was buying steam from Pacific Gas and Electric for heating; its condensate was then shunted to the sewers.

I came up with the idea to collect the condensate from steam in the building's radiator system. The steam condensate is collected in traps and then goes to a condensate tank. It is finally pumped to a flush tank, where it is used only for flushing the building's toilets. I also installed photocells at the urinals that activate flushing only when somebody stands there, replacing continual flushing. The building uses city water for drinking purposes only now. I don't think we're wasting a drop.

***

Lou Previti's experience was a good deal different from that of most hoisting and portable engineers, in that he was one of the few engineers who worked for only one employer throughout most of his career.

> I was a graduate of Local 77's first apprenticeship program, and it was no pink tea, let me tell you. We had to tear down diesel engines and put them back together again, and if they weren't put together right, you wouldn't get out of apprenticeship until you did do it right.
>
> Before I entered the apprenticeship program and before I went into the army, I had worked as an oiler at the Pentagon and on other jobs around Washington, D.C. But after I graduated from the apprenticeship program, I went to work for an excavating contractor and remained with him for thirty-five years. I worked as an operator for about ten years and then as a superintendent.
>
> Was there a conflict of interest involved in my being a union member and company superintendent? If there had been, I never would have lasted as a company superintendent. Remember, the company kept me on for thirty-five years! Every once in a while, the union would send somebody out who couldn't do the job. I'd give them every chance to perform, but if they couldn't, I'd sit them down and call the union hall and explain the problem. A new guy would come out and the old guy would go back to the union hall. There was never a problem.
>
> I didn't retire willingly. I mean, I could have worked for a few more years. But the company's excavating division went out of business because of the open shop. It was sad. The company kept me on for six months doing nothing. Finally, I had to understand the situation. I knew I had to go. The company was no longer in the excavating business. That was in 1982. It was okay for me, but when you've put so much into a company, it hurts that it is going down. And the situation has gotten a lot worse since. . . . In a way it was our own fault, but I don't have much respect for these guys who are working nonunion and earning wages they never would have gotten if it hadn't been for the union. Some of them are union men from other locals, carrying their union cards in their shoes, but then, they have families; they have to put bread on the table; but it's sad. . . . But there'll be a turnaround; it's already happening. Maybe we pushed the wage rate up too high, but they'll make the opposite mistake, they'll push it down too low and the unions will be back in there.

***

And Freida Maldonado, a graduate of New York City's Local 15 apprenticeship program, relates how the IUOE changed her life.

> I was on public assistance—I was on public assistance for ten years! You can't go to school, you can't get a good job. . . . I came here and they worked with me, they helped me, they were great! I thank them every moment of my life that they got me here. Without them, I couldn't make it. I have four children—how much can you do?

This is the story of Billy Hurt, Steve Brown, Tom Richards, George McGuire, Lou Previti, Jeanita Martin, Freida Maldonado, and thousands of others like them, all members of the International Union of Operating Engineers during the period 1960–93, the period covered by this book. Their comments reflect the success of the IUOE during the first part of the period, their concern about the open shop incursion during the latter part, and their feelings about the role the union plays in their working lives. But the experience of the IUOE is a reflection of the experience of the entire labor movement, especially the building trades, during a period of rapid change—a period that saw a substantial shrinkage in the percentage of the labor force represented by trade unions and an inevitable diminution of the economic and political influence of the labor movement. However, the IUOE experience also indicates that, by making the right moves, a trade-union resurgence is possible. Those right moves include concern for the safety of workers on the job, improving the employability of union members through training and retraining, aggressive organizing activities, and the wisdom to strengthen the competitive position of the employers of union labor.

The book is divided into two parts. Part I traces in five chapters the causes and consequences of the union's rapid growth during the period 1960–75. Chapter 1 provides an overview of the entire period and establishes the theme of the book: success, challenge, and response. The union's early history is summarized in chapter 2. Chapter 3 discusses the economic conditions and collective bargaining initiatives that were the sources of the fifteen-year growth period. The IUOE's venture into apprenticeship and training from a somewhat reluctant beginning to a full-blown policy of "continuous total training" is the subject of chapter 4, while chapter 5 describes the union's legislative and public policy initiatives during the growth years, including its response to the civil rights movement.

Part II covers a period of marked membership decline and the beginnings of recovery during the years 1975–93. Chapter 6 offers an analysis of the causes and extent of the open-shop incursion, which was the major factor in the membership loss. The counterattack at the international level is covered in chapter 7, while chapter 8 zeroes in on the local-level response, including seven case histories of hoisting and portable and stationary locals. Finally, chapter 9 speculates about the union's future.

PART I

THE GROWTH YEARS, 1960-1975

Chapter 1

SUCCESS, CHALLENGE, AND RESPONSE

When the International Union of Operating Engineers gathered for its twenty-sixth convention in Bal Harbour, Florida, on April 1, 1960, it was riding high and was two-thirds of the way through the greatest period of membership growth and economic power in its then sixty-four year history. The union's membership had climbed from less than 60,000 in 1940 to more than 302,000 in 1960, and its net worth had increased from a little over $300,000 to more than $19 million. Although there was no simple measure of its bargaining power, that also had increased apace, as had the wages, fringe benefits, and job security of its membership.

A more subdued convocation gathered in Chicago on April 5, 1993. It was relieved that a membership decline from a peak of 419,000 in 1975 to 360,000 in 1987 had finally been checked and an increase to 368,000 had been accomplished by the end of 1992. There was no lament concerning the difficult period of membership decline, but optimism that aggressive responses in the late 1980s and early 1990s had the union back on the growth track, with renewed ability to serve the needs of its members. Pride in its accomplishments in training and improvement of the skills of its members over the previous three decades and the union's commitment to continue that emphasis was reflected in the theme of the IUOE's 1993 convention—"Training for the Future."

That pattern of success, challenge, and response is the theme that dominates this most recent third of the IUOE's near-century of history. But it is also the story of a substantial part of the U.S. labor movement during those same years. As unionization slipped from 35 percent to 16 percent of the nation's work force (12 percent in the private sector), many unions were victims of overall employment declines in their industries. But for others, it was a shift from union to nonunion employment within growing economic sectors. For the latter, there are lessons to be learned from both the IUOE's successes and failures, as well as from the union's emerging counterattack.

Who Are the Operating Engineers?

The IUOE is composed of the two groups described in the Introduction. Slightly over 70 percent are hoisting and portable engineers—men and women like Billy Hurt, Steve Brown, Jeanita Martin, Freida Maldonado, and Lou Previti—who work mainly in construction. They are the operators and mechanics of heavy equipment—cranes, bulldozers, power shovels, scrapers, clam shells, and the like. They were the major craftsmen of the Panama Canal, San Francisco's Golden Gate Bridge, Toronto's CN Tower and Sky Dome, New York's Statue of Liberty and Empire State Building, Vancouver's Lion Gate Bridge, the Alcan Highway and Alaska Pipeline, and the St. Lawrence Seaway and Hoover Dam.

Stationary engineers like Tom Richards and George McGuire operate and maintain the physical plant systems in commercial and industrial buildings, hotels, hospitals, schools, and other facilities. The distinction between the two groups is not as sharp as it once was. Today, there are many "mixed" locals—that is, locals that consist of both hoisting and portable and stationary engineers—and many supposedly "pure" hoisting and portable locals also include members who are not employed in the construction industry. As for the stationary branch, its base has also broadened. Lionel Gindorf, business manager of Chicago's Local 399, defines stationary engineers as "composite mechanics"—men and women with all the skills necessary to maintain entire buildings. "We do everything," Gindorf says, "including carpentry, electrical work, computer maintenance, shoveling the snow—everything."[1]

The union was founded on December 7, 1896, when eleven locals, the largest having forty members, met in Chicago and joined together to form the National Union of Steam Engineers, the parent organization of today's IUOE. The qualifying term "steam" was adopted solely because steam was the only motive power in use at the time. The new union was granted a charter by the American Federation of Labor (AFL) on May 7, 1897. Near the end of that year, the union's jurisdiction was broadened to include Canadian locals, and its name was changed to the International Union of Steam Engineers. The union's history from its founding until 1959 was covered in Garth L. Mangum's book *The Operating Engineers: The Economic History of a Trade Union* and is summarized in chapter 2.[2] This book covers the thirty-three year period between 1960 and 1993—a period of success, challenge, and response.

The External Environment

The years 1960–93 constituted a tumultuous period for the nation and the world, as well as for the labor movement in general and the IUOE in particular. The 1940–60 growth had been largely the result of the union's responses to World War II, its prosperous aftermath, the Korean conflict and the continuing cold war, and the general expansion of the American economy over those years. The events of 1960–93 were only slightly less dramatic and, in many ways, more complex.

World Events

Just prior to the 1960 convention, the Soviet premier, Nikita Khrushchev, visited the United States and predicted that the Soviet Union would "bury" us. He expressed his disgust with a segment of a movie featuring can-can dancers (supposedly a sign of Western decadence) which he and Madame Krushchev witnessed as guests of a major film studio. During a visit to the United Nations, Khrushchev and the entire Soviet delegation startled that august body by using their shoes to beat out a greeting to Fidel Castro, who had assumed power in Cuba after the collapse of Fulgencio Batista's government. Communist belligerence increased with the building of the Berlin Wall in 1961, and, in 1962, the Cuban missile crisis brought the world to the brink of a nuclear war. American reaction to the apparent advance of communism resulted in the country's long and costly—in terms of dollars, lives, and social cohesion—involvement in Vietnam.

Approximately thirty years later, not long before the 1993 IUOE convention, an amazed world witnessed the disintegration of the Soviet

Union, the collapse of its Eastern European satellites, the destruction
of the Berlin Wall, the reunification of Germany, and the end of the
cold war. The result was not world peace but a decentralization of
strife and a spread of slaughter along ethnic lines at the instigation of
petty tyrants and brigands.

The Domestic Scene

Events on the domestic front were no less tumultuous. During the
1960s and on into the 1980s, the nation reeled from the assassinations
of President John F. Kennedy, his brother Robert, and Martin Luther
King, Jr., and the attempted assassinations of Presidents Gerald Ford
and Ronald Reagan. The country was rocked by riots from Watts to
Washington, D.C., in the sixties; revolt against the Vietnam War and
the Watergate scandal in the 1970s; and the savings and loan debacle,
Iran-Contra, and the Rodney King-Los Angeles riot in the 1980s and
early 1990s. United States post-Vietnam military interventions included the disastrous incursion in Lebanon and the more successful
though no less controversial ventures in Grenada, Panama, the Persian
Gulf, and Somalia. And, in 1993, neither the United States nor Europe
could find an acceptable cure for "ethnic cleansing" in the Balkans.

The era was marked by rapid advances in space exploration and
highway construction, a revolution in communications technology, and
the rise of the environmental movement. New agencies were added to
the federal government, including the Departments of Housing and
Urban Development, Transportation, Energy, and Education; the Environmental Protection Agency; and the Equal Employment Opportunity
Commission. Economic conditions were affected by globalization of
the economy, inflation, "stagflation," a continuing shift of jobs from
the manufacturing to the service sector, and a mounting national debt.
The construction industry experienced periods of boom and bust based
on the demands of warfare, the needs of transportation and economic
growth, and the impact of rising inflation and interest rates—the latter
reaching a record twenty percent in the early eighties.

Labor Trends

The U.S. labor movement, which had risen to unprecedented political
and economic power during the Second World War and its aftermath,

was also facing as yet unforeseen threats. AFL-CIO membership was still rising in 1960 but was slipping as a proportion of the total U.S. labor force. Pressures were mounting that would reduce overall union membership from its historic peak of 35 percent of the labor force in the mid-1950s to 15.8 percent by 1992. Involved would be a sectoral shift away from the industries of historic union power in favor of industries wherein unionization had always been limited. Geography would be a factor—suburbanization and movement of industry toward the nonunion south. Entrance into the work force of previously unorganized women and minorities would add to the organizing challenge. Government deregulation on the one hand and provision by government of benefits and protections that unions might otherwise have pursued through collective bargaining on the other both interfered with and reduced the demand for unionization. Uncontrollable international competition, deterioration of the political alliance that had created the 1930s New Deal and dominated the political scene thereafter, the rise of antiunion national administrations, and a concerted counterattack by employers were other factors in union decline.

By the mid-1970s, historic union-employer relationships began to undergo a strain and, in some cases, break down entirely. This was particularly true in the construction industry, where an increasing amount of the work was being performed in traditionally nonunion areas and in previously unionized areas by nonunion contractors and nonmember workers.

The IUOE was affected less than most unions by these developments —its skilled equipment operators were not easy to replace—but it, along with the other building and construction trades, suffered "the penalties of success." Construction labor costs were driven up during the 1960s and early 1970s until there were incentives and opportunities for an open shop incursion into the organized sectors of the construction industry—the primary cause of substantial membership declines during the 1970s and 1980s among all of the building trades. Although stationary engineers (the IUOE's nonconstruction members) were not affected by the open-shop movement, they too had to alter traditional bargaining patterns because of adverse National Labor Relations Board (NLRB) decisions, changing technologies, and the unique techniques required for organizing in the public sector. The IUOE's response to limit those incursions, reverse the membership decline, and rebuild in a much less favorable atmosphere—perhaps chastened but still effective in pursuing the well-being of its members—is the major accomplishment of this thirty-three year interlude in a near-century of union history.

The fortunes of the IUOE were played out within the historical background described above. Both the 1960 and 1993 conventions were triumphant, but for vastly different reasons. In 1960, the IUOE was in the middle of the greatest growth period in its history. In 1993, it was celebrating the apparent end of a period of decline. In 1960, the union was looking forward to a period of rapid economic growth, presided over by the Kennedy and Johnson administrations. By 1993, it had weathered twelve years of Reagan and Bush and, in the early 1990s, a stagnant economy that had yet to respond to the self-described agent of change, William Jefferson Clinton. Thus the atmosphere at the 1993 convention was a good deal more humble than in 1960, but it was nevertheless confident that the challenge it had been forced to face in the late 1970s and 1980s had been met and that a new period of growth had begun.

Leadership

Five general presidents guided the IUOE during this modern roller coaster ride. For Joseph J. Delaney (1958–62), the primary issue was refurbishing the union's public image after criticisms leveled by a Senate committee in the late 1950s. Hunter B. Wharton (1962–75) wrestled with the strains of continued growth, which, it became increasingly obvious, was carrying with it the seeds of its own destruction. J.C. Turner (1976–85) sought, during a period of increasing antiunion activity, to restore the waning political influence of unions, while Larry J. Dugan (1985–90) began rebuilding the IUOE's neglected organizing program. To Frank Hanley (1990–present) would fall the challenge of getting the union back on a growth track.

In the broader political scene, the book begins during the year in which John F. Kennedy was elected president of the United States, who was then followed by Lyndon Baines Johnson—the leaders of two friendly Democratic administrations. Although the political voice of organized labor became increasingly muted, the administrations of Republicans Richard Nixon and Gerald Ford and Democrat Jimmy Carter were not unfriendly. But they were followed by the avowedly antiunion administrations of Ronald Reagan and George Bush. The book ends with the beginning of the Clinton administration—a new era that

promises to be at least less repressive, if not more propitious, to organized labor than the preceding twelve years of conservative leadership.

A summary of the IUOE's 1960–93 experience will help guide the
reader through the chapters that follow.

The 1960–75 Growth Years

The union's growth during the 1960s and into the early 1970s was due
primarily to expansion in the construction industry. Particularly important for the Operating Engineers was the high proportion of the
nation's construction expenditures invested in highways, airports, reclamation projects, suburban housing sites and industrial parks, and
other earth-moving projects, as contrasted to building activities. These,
in addition to the initial economic consequences of the nation's Vietnam involvement, brought unemployment down to levels not seen
since the Korean conflict and created similar inflationary pressures, but
this time without the benefit of wartime taxes and, for a half-decade,
controls over wages and prices. The combination of deteriorating purchasing power and the bargaining leverage to offset it proved irresist-
ible. Construction wage settlements skyrocketed amidst bitter and
costly strikes and provided a major incentive for the wage stabilization
efforts undertaken by the Nixon administration during 1969–72, as
described in chapter 3.

The upshot for the IUOE was a steady increase in membership and
resources that continued into the mid-1970s. The only serious challenge faced by the union during the 1960s was a result of the civil
rights movement. The IUOE and other craft unions were accused of
discrimination against minorities in apprenticeship and hiring hall operations. Lawsuits were brought against local unions; consent decrees
were obtained; and in a few areas of the country, there was an attempt
to apply hiring quotas to federal construction projects. But the IUOE
responded as realistically as it could, as described in chapter 5, and the
pressures were short-lived.

Leadership for Growth

Joseph J. Delaney took over from William E. Maloney in 1958 and
guided the union until his death in 1962. Maloney, who led the union
for eighteen years (the longest reign of any IUOE president to date),

came up from the ranks in Chicago, fought the attempted infiltration of gangsters into the union (no mean feat in the days of Al Capone), overcame dissension within the ranks of the operating engineers in his home area, and, as International general president, led the union from small membership and near bankruptcy in 1940 to the stellar conditions passed on to Delaney in 1958.

But Delaney also inherited from the Maloney administration what was primarily a public relations problem. Like several other unions, the IUOE had been targeted by the Senate Select Subcommittee on Improper Activities in the Labor-Management Field, better known (after its chairman, Senator John McClellan of Arkansas) as the McClellan committee. The committee censured Maloney for personally investing $11,000 in two oil well ventures (both losers) along with management acquaintances and an alleged union-financed lavish life-style. He was also criticized for "dictatorial practices," primarily because of the number of local unions under international supervision for a variety of reasons discussed in chapter 2.

Delaney emerged from a building trades environment in New York City not unlike Maloney's Chicago experience. He was a contemporary and friend of George Meany, the Bronx plumber who became president of the American Federation of Labor and then merged it with the Congress of Industrial Organizations in 1955 as the AFL-CIO. In the 1920s, Delaney had created from scratch IUOE Local 15 in New York City by organizing a previously ignored diverse group of oilers, helpers, apprentices, mechanics, and welders—many of them doing maintenance work as well as construction on the city's major tunnels. During the thirty-seven years he served as Local 15's business manager, the union's membership increased to three times that of its sister union, Local 14, engaged primarily in building construction and became a power in the New York City labor movement. From that base, Delaney became vice president of the New York State Federation of Labor and was elected IUOE vice president in 1940 and general secretary-treasurer in 1957.

Throughout his international service, he maintained strong ties with New York, where he continued to make his home. As general president, Delaney laid down a policy designed to deal with the "image problem," and adapt to the Labor-Management Reporting and Disclosure Act of 1959 (Landrum-Griffin Act), which was passed in the wake of the McClellan committee investigation.

One of the traditional strengths of building and construction trades unions was the union hiring hall, which supplied contractors with what the unions claimed were the most qualified workers in the industry. To support that claim and control entry into the skilled trades to the extent possible, most of the building trades unions had fostered apprenticeship programs and negotiated with employers for support of, and cooperation with, those programs. However, it was rare for any one contractor to own or use all of the equipment the IUOE considered to be within its wide jurisdiction. Thus, instead of formal apprenticeship, the Operating Engineers had relied on an informal approach to skill development—an approach which became inadequate during a period of rapid growth and economic and technological change.

Having created Local 15 from among those learning the trade by catch-as-catch-can methods, and having made it one of the few locals in the IUOE which, prior to 1960, had instituted an apprentice program, Delaney launched an aggressive promotion to spread the training gospel throughout the international union. The timing was propitious for adding apprenticeship and training to the responsibilities of the union's Department of Research and Organization. Passage, during the same year, of the Manpower Development and Training Act, and thereafter of the Job Corps and other federally financed training programs, provided the IUOE with opportunities to initiate the additional training innovations described in chapter 4.

Another lasting innovation of the Delaney administration was the Operating Engineers' Central Pension Fund, a pet project of Lane Kirkland, former member of the AFL-CIO Social Security Department, later AFL-CIO president but at the time assistant to the IUOE president. Observing that some of the larger consolidated locals of the IUOE were launching multiemployer pension plans that were beyond the reach of the smaller locals, Kirkland designed and barnstormed the locals to sell a centralized plan into which benefit payments negotiated with employers throughout the nation could be invested. The result was one of the most successful of the labor movements multiemployer pension plans.

But Delaney died too soon to see many of his proposed initiatives put into action or bear fruit. His successor, Hunter P. Wharton, was a different type of labor leader, better prepared for the "goldfish bowl" the assignment would become. Wharton also had come up from the ranks, worked at the trade, became active in local union affairs and, eventually, a successful business manager in Pittsburgh, and expanded the jurisdiction of Local 66 to cover all of western Pennsylvania. He did so by extending the jurisdiction of the commercial building-oriented local union into heavy and highway construction, including rural sand and gravel pits, often against the wishes of protectionist forces within his own union. But Pittsburgh was a very different environment from that of either Chicago or New York City. It was controlled by large industry rather than subjected to the diverse and divisive forces of the larger cities. Whereas his two predecessors had to maintain an image as "tough guys" during their local careers, affability was as essential to Wharton's environment. A graduate of Carnegie-Mellon Institute (later University), a rare background for a building tradesman of the 1930s and 1940s, Wharton moved comfortably within all levels of the community.

After twenty years as Local 66's business manager, Wharton was asked to become an International representative and, in that capacity, was assigned by Maloney to supervise the obstreperous Philadelphia Local 542, which fomented a good deal of the McClellan committee criticism. The local had taken advantage of a situation in which the Fairless United States Steel plant was being built outside of the city but within the local's geographic jurisdiction, offering plenty of employment for every member. The local made exorbitant demands of Philadelphia contractors, then struck when they were refused. Since there was ample employment for the local's members outside the city, they continued working, hiring longshoremen to serve as pickets for them. The entire Philadelphia construction industry was shut down, putting other building tradesmen out of work without income loss for the engineers.

Protests to the Building and Construction Trades Department and the AFL-CIO, as well as complaints by employer associations and politicians, forced the IUOE to deal with the situation. Wharton was sent in to take the local union under supervision, remove its elected officers, negotiate a reasonable agreement, and end the strike. The deposed officers took the International to court and appeared before the McClellan committee, protesting the denial of what they saw as the prerogatives of local union democracy.

In that circumstance, Wharton had seen first-hand the chaos that could be created by a local union that tried to exploit to the full the advantages of a temporary economic boom. He had been the focal point of pressures and negotiations, not only between union and employer but between the local, the International, the rest of the building trades and the AFL-CIO, and between the local union and the entire Philadelphia construction industry and city administration, as well as a variety of squabbling groups within the local.

The difference between Wharton and his predecessors was more one of approach than philosophy. Maloney believed in limiting wage demands to those the contractors could profitably live with, often over the objections of vociferous groups of local members, then push wages up as nonunion competition was eliminated. Delaney espoused the same principle when he declared to the 1960 convention:

> As head of a local union in New York, I have constantly preached to the membership the doctrine that "you can't kill the goose that lays the golden egg." My members there over a period of thirty-seven years were told by me that they would be employed only as long as their contractors made money. . . . I was against "featherbedding" and similar practices long before they were condemned by statute and courts. It is wrong—economically and morally.[3]

But Wharton was more likely to seek the same objectives by consensus rather than by confrontation, by negotiation rather than threat. Not that he shied from a fight if there was no other alternative, but with his nonconfrontational style, Wharton came to be viewed by his contemporaries as a labor statesman, ideally suited to meet the challenges of a new and more public era of labor-management relations. Elected to the office of International vice president in 1957, he was named by the general executive board as general secretary-treasurer when Delaney was elevated to the IUOE presidency in 1958, replacing the latter upon his death in office in 1962. In 1965, Wharton became the first IUOE president in sixty-nine years to be elected AFL-CIO vice president and awarded a seat on the summit organization's executive council.

Growth Trends

Together, Delaney and Wharton oversaw a membership growth from 302,000 to 419,000 (see Table 1.1), an average growth of nearly 6,000 per year, compared with 12,000 per year during the Maloney era.

Table 1.1

IUOE Membership Trends, 1959–1992

Year	Total	Increase/Decrease
1959	302,331	—
1963	321,369	19,038
1967	350,204	28,835
1971	402,127	51,923
1975	418,984	16,857
1979	418,805	(175)
1983	382,818	(35,991)
1987	359,252	(23,566)
1992	367,775	8,523

The growth era, however, was not without its problems. Delaney and Wharton contended with jurisdictional battles relating to both the hoisting and portable and stationary memberships, a variety of legislative and regulatory restrictions (including the emergence of equal employment opportunity enforcement), an attack on the craft status of operating engineers, and a Vietnam-era economic stabilization program that put the international union in the unenviable position of mediating between the dictates of the federal government and the demands of its local unions.

Wharton's mediating skills were especially useful as local building- and construction-trades unions (including those of the IUOE) took advantage of Vietnam-era conditions to push for wage and benefit advances, which made them the focal point of the Nixon administration's wage and price stabilization policies detailed in chapter 3. Guided by Professor John T. Dunlop of Harvard University, intellectual "guru" of the construction industry since World War II War Labor Board days and later Secretary of Labor under President Gerald Ford, the stabilization effort, as it applied to the construction industry, would, in effect, have brought a degree of central planning to an otherwise decentralized and often chaotic industry. Unions would have been guaranteed a full partnership role in that tripartite labor/management/government arrangement. Even though the long term initiative failed for political reasons beyond union control, the key roles played by both Hunter Wharton and his assistant and future General President Frank Hanley were important to the IUOE's status in the building and construction trades and to Hanley's visibility and future effectiveness as International president.

The Challenge of the Open Shop

It has been a given of U.S. labor history that there are always forces waiting for any sign of vulnerability to attack and reverse any gains from labor organization. In the 1920s, following the labor gains of the First World War, the employer counterattack was called the American Plan.[4] In the 1970s, for the construction industry, it was called the merit shop, but more descriptively the open or nonunion shop. The failure of the Vietnam-era joint efforts by international unions, employer associations, and the federal government to achieve moderation and stability in the wage-settlement process led to a fracturing of long-term labor-management relationships in the construction industry. That provided a new opening for open shop attack. During the 1969–74 stabilization effort, the international unions, under government fiat, were able to exercise control over the collective bargaining demands of their local constituents, keeping construction wage increases within an acceptable range. During a war without traditional wartime restraints, inflation was rising and prices and profits were under pressure as well as wages, and with less effective controls. When centralized control ended, construction wage rates once again took off, simultaneous with the deepest national recession since the 1930s. The results were incentives to end spiralling construction costs and the creation of a surplus labor force to make that possible—prime conditions for the initiation of an open shop movement.

The prime movers of open shop construction were not the construction contractors, whose basic concern was that labor costs be the same for all bidders, nor even the occasional purchaser of construction services, but large national firms who required the construction of office buildings, mercantile facilities, and factories and oil refineries on a continuing basis across the country. That concern led to the formation of the Business Roundtable, which, in turn, exerted pressure on owners to select open shop contractors wherever possible and on contractors (union or nonunion) to reduce production costs.

Rising unemployment rates in the 1970s forced union members to work nonunion in some areas of the country, and moribund union organizing programs resulted in the loss of union contracts, especially in highway and multiple-family residential construction. As the open shop competition grew, union contractors began "double-breasting," or creating nonunion subsidiaries to compete in markets either where the project owner refused to deal with union contractors or where payment of union wages and benefits would prevent successful bidding. So successful was that customer-led rebellion that the construction industry went from 42 percent to 22 percent union in just twenty years.[5] The IUOE suffered less than the other building and construction trades because its primary source of employment was government-financed heavy and highway, rather than private industrial and building, construction; its job tasks were not as susceptible to performance by lesser-skilled workers; and because its stationary branch did not face the same competitive pressures. Still, its membership decline from 419,000 in 1975 to a low of 359,000 in 1987 would become the primary concern of subsequent international presidents.

Although the revolt of the owners of new construction against soaring costs was the primary problem faced by the IUOE and other construction unions, it was by no means the sole problem they faced. Legal challenges to the stationary engineer jurisdiction, a generally more antiunion attitude in the nation at large, and an intensifying interunion struggle for membership were lesser but still significant problems. Declining union memberships resulted in interunion battles for the already organized and led to a gradual disintegration of traditional union jurisdictions. The American Federation of Labor's philosophy of exclusive jurisdiction had never been fully realized. Prior to the merger of the AFL and CIO, competition between craft and industrial unions threatened all jurisdictional claims, and the 1955 merger did not by any means solve the problem. As union membership declined during and after the 1960s, interunion raiding intensified and led to friction among the crafts as well as among industrial and craft unions. Unions, concerned with their own survival, were out to increase their memberships, regardless of whether their actions resulted in an overall increase in the membership of the AFL-CIO. In that race, the IUOE won more than it lost, especially with respect to its stationary locals and organizational efforts in the public sector.

Leadership for Retrenchment

The weight of membership decline fell on IUOE General Presidents J.C. Turner (1976–85) and Larry J. Dugan (1985–90). Coincidentally, in 1975, the year of maximum membership, Hunter Wharton found it necessary to resign for health reasons. As it turned out, his union career was not over. His health improved, and in 1977 he returned to the less stressful role of director of safety and accident prevention, thus exercising his long-term interest in industrial safety.

The full brunt of the open-shop challenge was felt during the administration of J.C. Turner, former business manager of Washington, D. C.'s hoisting and portable Local 77 and a leading figure in local and national Democratic Party circles. A former intercollegiate boxing champion at The Catholic University of America, Washington, D.C., Turner assumed the union's top office at a time when the fortunes of the IUOE were undergoing a change for the worse, and, as it turned out, most of the membership loss would occur during his administration. His response was to increase the emphasis on organization, release stationary locals to organize outside their historic jurisdiction, and push wage and work-rule concessions to increase the competitiveness of union contractors. He also used his considerable lobbying skills to help override Reagan's vetoes of the Highway Transportation and Clean Water Acts, to defeat attempts to repeal the Davis-Bacon Act, and to secure passage of Superfund legislation (over the opposition of the Reagan administration) that provided $9 billion to begin the job of cleaning up hazardous waste dumps—a bill that was especially important to the Operating Engineers. Nevertheless, these were primarily defensive actions. Major union legislative objectives, such as the Labor Law Reform Act of 1978 (filibustered to death by a junior senator from Utah, Orrin Hatch, despite Democratic control of both the White House and the Congress) were beyond the reach of the best of lobbyists.

The Political Scene

The open shop movement, which gained speed during the late 1970s, accelerated even further during the 1980s. Reagan added substance to his declared anti-union sentiments when he fired 11,400 air traffic controllers for participation in the illegal Professional Air Traffic Controllers (PATCO) strike in 1981. Appointments to the NLRB and the U.S. Department of Labor became "labor unfriendly," and the courts appeared to be equally hostile. Attempts were made to repeal the Davis-Bacon Act, which sets prevailing wages on federally financed construction projects. When that proved unsuccessful, administrative changes designed to lower prevailing wages and distance them from the union scale were undertaken.

Appropriations for management disclosure under the Landrum-Griffin Act were virtually eliminated, whereas the budget allocation to conduct audits of union accounts was doubled.[6] Appropriations for the Occupational Safety and Health Act also were cut to the bone. An attorney for the Associated Builders and Contractors of America (ABC), the voice of the open-shop movement, was appointed deputy under secretary of labor for labor standards, where she would preside over the administration of federal prevailing wage laws, the Fair Labor Standards Act, federal worker's compensation laws, and legislation pertaining to mining and longshore and harbor workers. The Labor Department itself was downgraded with the appointment of political supporters with no previous relevant experience as secretaries of labor, and its virtual removal from responsibilities in the field of industrial relations.

Finally, in what unions hope will be the last act in an era of antilabor politics, President George Bush, just before his defeat in the 1992 election, issued two executive orders that were anathema to labor—one that required all federal contractors to post notices in the workplace advising employees that they had the right to object to paying any portion of their union dues spent on activities not directly related to collective bargaining, and the other barring union-only labor agreements on government contracts.

Both of these orders were rescinded in the early days of the Clinton administration. Clinton also lifted the decade-long employment ban on striking members of PATCO and appointed a commission, under the chairmanship of John Dunlop, to recommend revisions of the nation's labor laws adequate to the changing times yet protective of organized labor. Whether future political trends will support these initially favorable actions remains to be seen.

The IUOE Response

The IUOE did not roll over and play dead in the face of the new challenges, as attested by a resumption in growth after the low ebb of 1987. Had not its leaders reacted quickly to the post-1974 developments, the losses might have been even greater. The times and circumstances were not propitious, yet, in the long run, the repressive atmosphere of the 1980s may prove to have been a boon. The union was forced to face its problems and take action to solve them.

The Counterattack

The IUOE's counterattack in unfavorable times involved aggressive organizing campaigns, intensified training efforts, legal actions, newly cooperative relationships to restore the viability of union contractors, strategic concessions where necessary, renewed attention to the stationary engineer component of its jurisdiction, and an aggressive movement into public-sector employment as the only growing source of union membership.

National agreements, pioneered during the Maloney administration, and project agreements, expanded throughout the construction industry by the Construction Industry Joint Conference, chaired by John Dunlop during the early 1960s, enhanced the ability of union contractors to compete with their open shop counterparts. Local unions, recognizing their precarious positions, became less prone to fight International initiatives and more prone to grant wage and other concessions where they were appropriate. Organization, which had been ignored during the growth years, once again became a union priority.

A technique often used by open shop contractors to lessen labor costs and bypass scarce skilled crafts workers was to subdivide traditional tasks, assigning several semiskilled and unskilled people to work under the direction of one skilled person. However, this technique could not be applied to the operating engineers, whose tasks, because of the one-operator/one-machine nature of the craft, cannot easily be subdivided.

The result of all these factors is that the IUOE suffered far less than its sister building- and construction-trades unions, and the stationary engineers, despite the virtual disappearance of many of the industries in which they traditionally had been employed, continued to grow throughout the entire thirty-three year period.

Organization and Training

In June 1985, J.C. Turner stepped down as IUOE general president and was succeeded by Larry J. Dugan, former business manager of Arizona's Local 428, tenth IUOE vice president, and, at the time of his ascendance to the presidency, assistant to Turner. The son of an operating engineer who was a charter member of Arizona's Local 428, Dugan joined his father's local in 1948 and worked for six years as a crane and bulldozer operator. Eventually he was employed by the local—first as a dispatcher, later as a business agent, district representative, and assistant business manager. He was elected business manager in 1973; six years later he came to Washington as Turner's assistant.

Dugan's major emphasis was on organization. He revamped the union's organizing program and the process through which local unions can qualify for financial assistance. He also expanded the use of national agreements and emphasized fiscal strength.

Dugan retired in 1990 and was succeeded by Frank Hanley, who had served as general secretary-treasurer under both Turner and Dugan. Hanley also came from a family of operating engineers. His father, Simon Hanley, was an Irish immigrant and heavy equipment operator, and his uncle, Ed Hanley, was the business manager of a New York City stationary local. Immediately after graduating from high school, Hanley became a member of the union—first as an oiler and later as a power-shovel operator. After serving in the Marine Corps, where he operated heavy machinery both in the United States and overseas, he entered the University of Notre Dame, and continued to work during summers as a heavy equipment operator. After graduating from Notre Dame, he was hired as an assistant to then General President Delaney in 1958.

Hanley was a unique resource to the union. He had been involved in every IUOE initiative, including jurisdiction, the Vietnam-era wage stabilization program, the Davis-Bacon administration, and negotiation and supervision of national contracts for the intervening thirty-five years. A graduate of the Harvard Trade Union School in 1958, Hanley brought a wealth of administrative experience to the presidency and an in-depth knowledge of the union's strengths and weaknesses. As assistant to three presidents and general secretary-treasurer under two, he had filled in for them during absences and illnesses and had chaired numerous committees for the IUOE, the AFL-CIO Building and Construction Trades Department, and the federal government.

Hanley intensified the organizational effort, reorganized and computerized the International office, expanded the role of local business managers, eliminated international staff from membership on the general executive board, and extended the training emphasis to new and emerging occupations potentially within the IUOE jurisdiction.

During the growth years, 1960–75, organization had been put on the back burner, but when membership began to decline at an alarming rate, organization once again became a top priority. As union membership soared, "top down" organization—that is, the organizing of contractors rather than workers—was the prevailing method. When decline set in, "bottom up" organizing, or the organization of workers at the job site—became a necessity. Under the Dugan and Hanley administrations, the union's organizing program was totally revamped. International and local organizers were trained in the latest methods and new initiatives, including financial incentives to local unions for successful organizing activities, were activated. Forays into the public sector, especially for stationary engineers, were authorized.

Under Hanley, more attention was given to the stationary branch of the union, whose percentage of the total membership began to inch upward during the 1980s. Stationary locals were given the okay to organize outside of the pure "blood lines" of their traditional jurisdiction. Training programs were launched to prepare stationary engineers for future technological challenges, and small stationary locals were merged to increase their effectiveness.

Leadership occurred not only at the international but at the local level as well. The turnaround was due as much to actions taken by such local business managers as Robert H. Fox, Art Viat, Thomas J. Stapleton, and William C. Waggoner in California; Lionel J. Gindorf and William E. Dugan in Chicago; Vincent J. Giblin and Patrick E. Campbell in New Jersey; Fred P. Dereschuk in St. Paul; Joseph E. Beasley in Pennsylvania; Vergil L. Belfi, Jr., in St. Louis; and Peter Babin III in New Orleans. All of the above, with the exception of Fox, who retired in 1992, and the addition of General Secretary-Treasurer N. Budd Coutts of Canada, are members of a strong 1993 general executive board.

These and other local leaders, faced with increased employer opposition and, until 1993, an unfavorable national political environment, were participants in a "numbers game" of interunion competition for workers who were already organized. In that contest, the IUOE was more aggressor than victim. The battle between five AFL-CIO affiliates and two independent unions for 10,500 California public employees is described in chapter 7. Jurisdictional battles between industrial and craft unions multiplied, and the results often were determined by the NLRB or the courts. One such battle, involving the stationary claim to jurisdiction for hospital power plants, took over nine years to settle and is also described in chapter 7. Litigation regarding double-breasting, state right-to-work laws, and jurisdiction, among other subjects, increased through the years and are described in chapters 5 and 7.

Despite being confronted with a host of negative forces, General President Hanley was able to reassure the delegates to the 1993 convention that membership was again on the increase:

> At a time when most unions are suffering devastating losses in membership, the IUOE is growing. While other unions are having to increase dramatically their per capita tax . . . the IUOE is keeping its per capita low and its services high. While other unions see little, if any, hope of growth, the IUOE is positioned to take advantage of the growing trend among underrepresented workers to seek unionization as the only means of achieving decent wages and working conditions.[7]

Continued aggressive organizing was recognized as essential, but training of a skilled membership was cited as the long-run key to survival and a return to substantial growth. The improved political climate combined with the union's success in maintaining its membership and financial strength during periods of adverse economic conditions and virulent antiunion activity promised continued recovery during the remaining years of the twentieth century. Whether that optimism is justified and the implications for the craft union component of the U.S. labor movement are the subjects of the final chapter.

Chapter 2

HISTORICAL PROLOGUE

As our story begins in 1960, the International Union of Operating Engineers was sixty-four years old. Its nature and status at that time were the products of all that had gone before. Hence the union's modern history cannot be understood without some familiarity with preceding events and the forces and reactions of its officers and members to those precedent conditions.[1] It was a union of "engineers," in the sense of those who operate machinery rather than those who design it, and the driving forces of its early history were the nature of the technology and the economics of the industries in which the engineers worked. However, the men and women who made up the union were not automatons; they had discretion in their responses to those technological and economic forces, and they exercised it in determining union policy. The four different titles the union has borne tell much of the story: the National Union of Steam Engineers, 1896; the International Union of Steam Engineers, 1897–1912; the International Union of Steam and Operating Engineers, 1912–28; and the International Union of Operating Engineers thereafter. This chapter summarizes the story of those periods, breaking up the last into the dreary years of the Great Depression and the exhilarating period of growth and prosperity during and after the Second World War and the Korean conflict.

The Steam Engineers

In its early years, the union was largely an organization of men who operated stationary steam engines for the production of heat and refrigeration in breweries, and for heat and electric power in large buildings at a time when each commercial building had its own generating plant. In addition, the organization gathered a small membership among factory employees, marine engineers, and operators of steam-driven hoists, pumps, and compressors in mines and building construction. Industry concerns proved stronger than technological ties in the mining and maritime industries, and steam engineers so employed gravitated to unions based in those industries.

Stationary Engineers

The craft of steam engineer was created in the eighteenth century the moment there were practical steam engines to operate. But a union of steam engineers had to wait until there were enough of them in a geographical area to organize and enough common concerns to make organization attractive. Steam engineers organized on an industrial basis with other brewery employees as early as 1880, but it was developments in the generation of electricity that brought about the first local craft unions of steam engineers, beginning in 1882.

An effective dynamo and a practical arc light were developed in 1876, but the electrical industry had its real birth with Edison's electric lamp in 1879. This was followed in the next decade by the electric motor. The general acceptance of electricity was almost instantaneous because of its versatility, cleanliness, and economy; it rapidly replaced water wheels, steam engines, and other power sources. Thus the ultimate effect of the shift to electric power was the elimination of steam as an important energy source, but its initial impact was to increase the use of steam and the employment of steam engineers. Edison established the first central power plant in New York City in 1882, but it supplied lights only for homes on fifty blocks of lower Manhattan. Electric power for stationary motors and for the lights of commercial buildings was generated by steam-driven isolated generating plants in the basement of each of those buildings. Heat was supplied almost entirely from steam. Then, as centrally generated electrical power became more readily available and economical a decade or so into the new century, elevators, refrigeration and air conditioning plants, and other equipment, though no longer steam driven, made retention of a building engineer necessary. As a result, the number of stationary engineers operating such equipment grew rapidly from 23,000 in 1870 to

152,000 at the turn of the century, to 231,000 by 1910, and to a peak of 256,000 by 1930.

The stationary engineers did not consider themselves to be ordinary workmen. The craft required a high degree of technical competence acquired through study as well as experience. The engineers were isolated in their daily work from workmen of other crafts and often from those of their own craft; the responsibility was considerable in terms of economy, continuity, and safety of operations. Theirs was largely a standby job regulating the combination of fuel, air, and water for the greatest efficiency and economy, watching and recording gauge readings, recognizing trouble before it happened, and maintaining and repairing the machinery. The stationary engineer might work entirely alone or with an assistant engineer or a fireman. The power developed by the steam engine was essential to the operations it served. Carelessness could lead to a serious explosion. The building owner ordinarily knew little of the intricacies of engine operation, and the engineer enjoyed a high degree of autonomy, though he did not always get the respect, or the pay, he thought he deserved.

The steam engineers first organized around their professional interests in the National Association of Stationary Engineers (NASE) in 1882. Its dual purpose was to improve both the status and the financial rewards of the engineers by increasing their knowledge and ability and, thus, their value to employers, and to protect them from the competition of lesser-skilled handymen by promoting city and state engineer's license laws. A trade union of stationary engineers came into being only after this learn-more/earn-more doctrine had proved disillusioning. Hours of work remained at twelve or more per day, seven days a week, with the pay at $12 to $15 per week until the turn of the century. Collective bargaining, as well as knowledge and licensure, would be necessary if pay and working conditions were going to improve. Local unions of stationary engineers began to emerge around the country during the 1880s and early 1890s, some affiliating with the Knights of Labor and some as federal locals in the AFL. Delegates from six of those local unions—hailing from Boston, Chicago, Denver, Detroit, Kansas City, and St. Louis—met in Chicago on December 7, 1896, to found the National Union Of Steam Engineers, traveling to Cincinnati a week later to seek a charter from the 1896 AFL convention, which was granted on May 7, 1897. It was later in the latter year that the new union's name was changed to the International Union of Steam Engineers.

Hoisting and Portable Engineers

Meanwhile, steam engines were appearing on construction jobs and with them, steam engineers. Pumps to evacuate water from excavations had early been steam-driven; steam power was applied to air-driven rock drills as early as 1866 and to pile drivers a decade later. Building height was limited to the number of floors a ladder-climbing hod carrier could carry materials until the development of the structural steel framework and the elevator. The first skyscrapers built in Chicago after the great fire of 1871 required a practical hoisting engine to boost building materials to the work sites; it was first developed in 1875, and, of course, its motive power was the steam engine. Steam-powered concrete mixers appeared around 1900. The steam shovel was standard equipment on railroad construction after the Civil War, on the Chicago Drainage Canal in the 1890s and at the Panama Canal from 1903 to 1914. But these were cumbersome and largely limited to rail trackage. It was not until 1911 that a light revolving shovel became a practical excavator for building projects. The number of steam engineers employed in building sites was not large, but they too gradually began to organize. Only the Boston local among the original six was what came to be known as a hoisting and portable local—"portable" referring to the mobile equipment such as power shovels, road rollers, graders, and paving mixers that would soon begin to emerge as the automobile demanded streets, roads, and highways.

Sources of Bargaining Power

The working environment of stationary engineers had both advantages and disadvantages for collective bargaining. The high degree of skill, the essentiality of engineer services, and the small proportion of total costs that their wages represented indicated a powerful bargaining position. However, the isolated nature of the work made the engineers difficult to organize and left them without the support of other crafts. The NASE was a ready source of licensed engineers as replacements, and the more-or-less permanent attachment to single employers made stationary engineers reluctant to strike.

Hoisting engineers were in a singularly powerful position in contrast. All building materials had to be moved by their hoists, and the presence of other building tradesmen unwilling to cross a picket line made them irreplaceable on a union job. Since the willingness or un-willingness to hoist building materials could make or break a strike for the other crafts, hoisting engineers had considerable reciprocal support. The 1907 AFL convention gave the IUSE jurisdiction over "the motive power of all derricks, cement mixers, hodhoists, pumps, and other machines used on construction work." "Other machines" meant little in 1907 but had great significance for the future.

Career Leadership

The first few years of the union's history can be viewed as an attempt by the local unions to gain the advantages of a national organization while giving up a minimum of the prerogatives of local autonomy. From its beginning until 1905, the International Union of Steam Engineers was little more than a loose association of a few strong and many weak autonomous local unions. The conventions were cautious in delegating powers to the general president and executive board, but the most important restrictions on the power of the international were financial in nature. A strong, dynamic organization could not be administered by part-time officers. Full-time leadership had to await sufficient union income to pay adequate salaries; that did not occur until 1905. Nine general presidents and eight general secretary-treasurers had served part-time and with little compensation before Matt Comerford and Robert A. McKee came to serve full-time and for long enough terms to be considered professional labor leaders.

Constant internal political maneuvering marked all of the conventions until 1912; they struggled to achieve a workable constitutional balance between the powers of large and small locals and between the autonomy of the local unions and the gradually increasing discretionary powers of the national officers. Those constitutional issues were largely resolved, but never until 1940 were the general officers freed from the financial shackles that handicapped organizing and other international efforts. The per capita tax on the locals rose from 4 cents initially to 8 cents in 1900, 10 cents in 1901, 15 cents in 1903, and 20 cents in 1908. Receipts reached $23,585 by 1905 but were overspent by $5,000, as they continued to be until 1910, when $62,179 in expenses was for the first time comfortably exceeded by an income of $79,956. Membership experienced a rapid growth rate from 1896 until 1904, after which it essentially stagnated for the rest of the period at about 17,000.

Internal Policy Issues

The lack of membership growth was, in part, the result of craft-exclusiveness. The union admitted only fully qualified engineers working at the trade. Even stationary firemen, who looked forward to attaining the status of engineers, had their own craft union but were for the most part unorganized. There was no provision for trainees or apprentices of any kind. Foresighted leaders argued for admission of all those who might have sufficient knowledge to provide low-wage replacements, but without avail. The 1905 convention did agree to accept as members licensed engineers who were working as firemen while awaiting engineer positions, but it was not until 1912 that firemen and oilers were accepted as "apprentice engineers," though no actual apprentice training programs were undertaken. Even then, they were not accepted into the pristine engineer locals but into subordinate "branch locals."

Much of the opposition to apprenticeship came from the hoisting members, who were able to use their stronger bargaining power to require employers to hire full-fledged engineers to fire their boilers. However, operators of street-paving equipment did not enjoy the same bargaining power. Rather than allow into full membership those working at the less desirable and lower-paying road jobs, many of the hoisting locals relegated the "street pavers" to branch locals as well.

The stationary engineers tended to be stationary in their life-styles as well as in the equipment they operated, but not so the hoisting and portable engineers. Therefore, the traveling-member issue arose early with respect to the latter but not the former. Debates arose between national and local officers at conventions, the former advocating universal transfer among local jurisdictions and the latter insisting upon limiting the rights of members of other locals who might compete for jobs within their jurisdictions. The issue was vigorously debated but not settled at the 1912 convention. Some stated that they did not allow others to work in their jurisdictions; others limited time periods that nonlocal members could work, and some charged for the privilege.

Particularly bitter debates erupted concerning the international union's right to enforce local adherence to constitutional provisions. The only weapon at the time was expulsion of individuals or revocation of local charters—either of which left skilled workers or a dual local organization outside the union's control, available to whipsaw employers and destructive of union pay scales and work rules.

But most troublesome of all were internal jurisdictional disputes: among stationary locals in the same city; between stationary and hoisting and portable locals; and among hoisting and portable locals in adjacent cities. The first two were accommodated as the International grew stronger vis-à-vis the locals and could enforce jurisdictional lines. The last proved the most difficult because it involved the employer. Until construction became heavily mechanized, contractors did not need to be highly mobile. If no contracts were available in their localities, they could simply lay off all of their help and await better times, perhaps working as building tradesmen themselves during the interim. As they invested in equipment, they had continuing loan payments to meet and were under pressure to keep their equipment operating. If no contracts were available at home, they looked elsewhere and began to expand the geographical scope of their operations. Then, as roads and highways became a major source of contracts and employment, the geographical scope widened even more. As the operators of the equipment, the engineers were uniquely affected. If the new contract took the contractor into the jurisdiction of another local, who were to get the jobs? The contractor preferred the known quantity of his existing employees, who, of course, wanted the jobs but faced the vigorous opposition of those into whose jurisdictions they were trespassing. Though the issue arose during the Steam Engineers' period, a solution was not found until the 1930s.

But all of these were continuing struggles that had little to do with the 1912 name change. The motivating factor was the replacement of the steam engine by centrally generated electricity and by diesel and gasoline, especially among the hoisting and portable locals, which, though still a substantial minority, were the most rapidly growing source of the union's membership. The argument was that employers were refusing to recognize the union's jurisdiction if the motive power of their operations was not steam. The compromise solution was to change the union's title to the International Union of Steam and Operating Engineers.

Steam and Operating Engineers, 1912–27

Three general presidents served the union during the IUSOE years: Matt Comerford, 1905–16; Milton Snellings, 1916–21; and Arthur M. Huddell, 1921–31.

Charter Revocation and Supervision

Matt Comerford was born in Ireland, emigrating to the United States at the age of nineteen and ultimately settling in St. Paul. He was a popular president in the early part of his administration but created trouble for himself by revoking the charters of local unions that departed too drastically from International policies; he chartered new locals as replacements. Charter revocation had been used twice as a disciplinary measure by previous administrations, but Comerford revoked at least ten charters between 1909 and 1916. Each of these left a residue of animosity that became personal in nature and finally coalesced around Arthur M. Huddell, who served as vice president to Comerford from 1905 to 1910, then broke openly with the general president when Comerford revoked the charter of Huddell's home Local 3 in Boston.

Opposition to Comerford's charter revocation policies resulted in physical violence in 1914. Until 1912, the national union office was wherever the general president happened to reside. The general secretary-treasurer also maintained his home residence, thus causing considerable communication difficulties. The 1912 convention authorized the purchase of a former residence in Chicago to become the international union's first permanent home. However, although the acquisition of a headquarters building was a definite asset, its location in Chicago involved national officers in the often turbulent affairs of the Chicago locals.

International policy, but not constitutional law, required hoisting engineers to insist upon placing a stationary engineer in charge of the permanent equipment as soon as it was installed in a building under construction. This required the sacrifice of a few weeks of work for the hoisting and portable engineers, who might have operated the plant until building completion, but assured the permanent placement of union engineers in positions that might otherwise go to nonmembers. In 1914, a new business agent of Chicago Local 69 began forcing the members of stationary Local 401 off the permanent jobs in uncompleted buildings and refused to place them as new opportunities arose. By doing so, he retained the temporary jobs for his own members but lost many of the permanent ones. The business agent also refused to follow the past practice of allowing members of stationary locals to work, by permit, on building jobs when the hoisting and portable local could not supply the needed workers. When the local rejected International protest and supported its business agent, the local's charter was revoked.

That same evening, General President Comerford was ambushed a few blocks from his home, severely beaten and hospitalized. The Chicago Federation of Labor supported the expelled local and refused to recognize the newly chartered replacement, Local 569, despite the intervention of the parent AFL.

Except for the attack on Comerford, the issues and events were typical of the revocation process and response. Opposition generated by the Chicago incident and three other revocations during the same year strengthened the opposition to Matt Comerford, which he survived until 1916, when he was defeated by compromise candidate Milton Snellings. However, the new administration still faced the same issue. Snellings, a Washington, D.C. stationary engineer, was a popular man but never a strong president. He was overshadowed by Boston stationary engineer and General Secretary-Treasurer Herman M. Comerford, and Boston hoisting and portable engineer and First Vice President Arthur M. Huddell, who, in turn, were strong opponents of each other.

Inability of the international union to control its fractious locals during the high-demand era of the First World War brought further revocations with similar results. A long and complex series of disputes among Boston locals was rife when Snellings died while at the 1921 AFL Building and Construction Trades Department Convention in Denver, automatically elevating Huddell to the presidency. Huddell was then able to use Herman Comerford's continuing support of an expelled Boston stationary local, among other charges, to remove his enemy from office and reconstruct a general executive board of his own supporters. All future general presidents would be hoisting and portable engineers—each of whom either died in office or resigned between conventions. Their successors were appointed by general executive board action.

But Huddell still faced the same set of divisive internal issues. For instance, revocation of the charter of a rebellious Rochester local in 1920 resulted in its being granted an International Brotherhood of Electrical Workers charter and continued recognition by the Rochester Building Trades Council, in preference to the replacement IUSOE local. The answer was discovered in Cleveland and Pittsburgh in

1923. When the charter of Cleveland Local 293 was revoked and the local [itself] replaced by Local 874, the entire local membership was welcomed into the new local except for the three leaders of the opposition. However, the new local was placed under the personal supervision of General Vice President, Cleveland resident, and future General President John Possehl, and administration was not left to squabbling locally elected officials. Similarly, when Local 66 in Pittsburgh defeated and suspended its president for disobeying Huddell's order to cease using work permits, the local's charter was revoked and a new number, Local 889, was issued; but the new local was placed under the supervision of an International representative. The deposed factions sued, but the courts upheld the International's right to revoke charters and appoint supervisors. Then, when the squabbles disrupted work on Pittsburgh construction projects, the contractors intervened, forcing a compromise between the warring engineer factions, but leaving the new local and its Internationally appointed supervisor in place. From that time on, the national union simply exercised its supervisory power without going through the intermediate step of charter revocation. To facilitate that policy, the constitution was amended in 1926, adding to the clause "[the general president] shall have the direction and supervision of all local unions, with power to suspend either individual members or officers for incompetency, negligence or failure in successfully carrying out their duties," the words "and he shall designate the persons to fill the places of officers or members thus suspended who shall conduct the affairs of the local under his direction."

International Role in Collective Bargaining

Collective bargaining in the IUSE and IUSOE periods was strictly a local affair. Yet the lack of sophisticated leadership in many locals led the general officers to seek the authority to examine and approve local agreements before their consummation and to issue and refuse strike permission. The purpose was to prevent overly confident locals from making extreme demands (thus damaging long-term employer relationships in order to exploit short-term advantages) or calling strikes they could not win, and to avoid local agreements that might undercut or harm neighboring locals. An International strike fund established in 1904 gave the national officers some leverage, but its size was never sufficient to be very influential.

The necessity of waiting upon International strike permission was no hardship to the stationary locals, which rarely struck and then only in the context of contract negotiations and with ample lead time. In the building trades, on the other hand, negotiation strikes were a minority. Most of the work stoppages in construction were occasioned by employer violations of existing work rules or by jurisdictional disputes. The hoisting and portable engineers had to be ready to stop work immediately to enforce their own work rules, to protect their jurisdiction, or in support of other crafts. The time necessary to contact the general president for strike permission might be too long for effective action. Therefore, as the construction locals increased in number and influence, the issue became hotter.

The issue was brought to the floor of the 1914 convention by a number of locals that had been denied strike funds for failure to obtain International permission for their stoppages, all of which they felt had been for justifiable reasons. The predominance of stationary locals kept the hoisting and portable faction from prevailing. During the same year, General President Comerford reached an "offensive and defensive alliance" with the bricklayers, a strong and highly disciplined union at the time, to support each other's strikes and jurisdictions, but only if the joint actions followed national approval by both unions. The bricklayers threatened to withdraw from the agreement if the engineers could not enforce that provision. The International's limited control was further weakened by the anti-Comerford 1916 convention, which limited the advance approval requirements for strikes, for fund access, and for actions involving the bricklayers. Though Huddell led the opposition to national strike approval in 1916, he changed his position after succeeding to the union's highest office and won convention agreement in 1922 for a resolution that required local unions to submit collective bargaining agreements, as well as strike calls, for the approval of the general president.

The following two years brought another innovation that was ultimately to prove an extremely important element in the union's increasing bargaining power. Agreements were signed between the International office and the heads of three firms doing interstate business, which promised to hire union members wherever they went, to pay local scales, and to adhere to local work rules in return for promises of labor peace.

The Consequences of Increasing Mobility

The International agreement was another manifestation of the increasing mobility of the construction industry on both labor and management sides. The traveling-member problem, which had first become a convention issue in 1912, continued to accelerate. Since the employee-employer relationship in the building trades was a casual one and industrial activity fluctuated widely, many of the hoisting and portable engineers tended to follow the building booms from city to city. Power shovels were becoming a substantial employment source, and the IUSOE was trying to win back the jurisdiction it had lost by default to the International Brotherhood of Steam Shovel and Dredgemen. Shovel work was highly mobile and often rural, and the shovelmen were accustomed to universal transfer rights, which allowed them to work anywhere in the world without extra fees by virtue of their membership in a truly international brotherhood. The necessity of gaining acceptance of a clearance card before going to work every time a geographically restricted local boundary was crossed was an obstacle to enlisting shovel operators in the IUSOE.

The dislocations of war increased the urgency of the issue as construction work was closed down completely in some areas and boomed elsewhere in response to the needs of the war effort. The fortunate locals with employment opportunities within their jurisdictions were charging permit fees ranging from as little as a dollar a week to as much as a dollar a day. Since the duration of any particular job was short, the building tradesmen were constantly reentering the labor market. Any newcomer was a potential competitor. Most of the local unions were reluctant to accept a clearance card that introduced a member of another local as long as present members were unemployed. Since a labor shortage could turn into a labor surplus almost overnight, the locals were reluctant to accept new members even in prosperous times. Yet any skilled engineer outside the union was a temptation to employers and a threat to union control. Issuance of a work permit for expansion purposes allowed the local members to place the burden of unemployment on the transient members and non-members in slack times without inviting an influx of nonunion labor in boom times. Work permits could have been issued without cost, but this would have given transients the advantage of business-agent services and all of the past efforts that local members had expended in establishing favorable wages and conditions—a gratuity local members were usually unwilling to extend. Some enterprising business agents chose to issue work permits to nonmembers and pocket the money, a practice that was much less likely to succeed when more knowledgeable traveling members were involved.

The traveling members and those locals that were net exporters of engineers were advocates of mandatory acceptance of clearance cards or the right to work in any jurisdiction without transferring membership or payment of a permit fee. The International officers held for freedom of transfer in order to attract shovelmen, to win the favor of mobile employers who preferred to take their key employees with them into new territory, to minimize the temptations to corruption, and to keep all potential competitors within the organization. The issue was fought over at every convention throughout the IUSOE period without resolution.

The widespread use of the permit fee was just one symptom of a growing fever of exclusion that permeated hoisting and portable locals during the 1920s. Technologically, the future was promising. Construction work that had been traditionally performed by human or horse labor was becoming increasingly mechanized. The revolving power shovel and the trenching machine had taken over excavation work. Road rollers, cement mixers, and paving machines constructed city streets. Highways were spreading across the country, and new methods of earth moving were being developed. But paper jurisdiction was not enough. The union had to be able to furnish skilled operators for every piece of new equipment developed or see control of its jurisdiction slip from its grasp. International officers were in a position to see that the decline of steam was inevitable and that excavating and road construction offered many more jobs in the long run than hoisting. They were quick to claim jurisdiction over new machines and to encourage the membership to prepare for change.

Yet the long-run welfare of the organization was not necessarily consistent with the immediate benefits of the individual member. The hoisting and portable engineers had been aggressive organizers of the operators of steam-driven construction equipment that posed a direct threat to their wages and conditions on city building jobs. They had been less aggressive where street paving was concerned. They were notably reluctant to adapt to new machinery and to move out to open construction in rural areas. They still saw new members as competitors for their jobs. Many of the new machines were not replacing steam engines in the cities but horses and mules outside the metropolitan areas. Out of sight, out of mind. To control rural work, both increased travel and lower pay had to be accepted. The local member usually preferred to build a tight fence around the remaining steam and hoisting jobs, refusing to operate nonsteam machinery where they had the power, rather than to venture out technologically and geographically.

It was obvious to the International officers that the union must organize or die. To follow a policy of exclusion would be suicide. Not only would the existence of nonunion engineers in the same labor market always be a threat to wage scales, but soon the only operators capable of handling the new machinery would be outside the organization. Time after time during the 1920s, the general officers found it necessary to chastise local unions for refusal to organize their jurisdictions and for continued use of the permit fee for transferees and nonmembers. Finally, at the end of the period, Huddell began placing some of the more reluctant locals under international supervision, replacing the elected officers with his own appointees with orders to organize.

Meanwhile, with the increased mobility of the contractors and the emergence of state highway departments letting contracts on a statewide basis, clashes between neighboring locals multiplied. Each local wanted to reserve its own work, yet follow its employers when they moved into other jurisdictions. The employers wanted to pay the lower of whatever wage scales were involved, while those employees moving from high-wage areas wanted to maintain their scales and those in the lower-wage areas wanted to move up. In small cities with too few stationary and hoisting engineers to form separate locals, mixed locals existed, usually dominated by stationary engineers with pay scales more attuned to their year-round employment conditions. Contractors moving into those locations would want to pay the local scales, while any employees they brought with them would demand the metropolitan scales they had left behind, especially with additional costs of traveling and being away from home. Meanwhile, the branch-local issue was heating up—both where hoisting engineers were still resisting equal status for those working at excavation and street and highway construction and where both were denying full membership rights to firemen and oilers. Minority membership was still a nonissue, but clearly, pressures for reform were building.

Amalgamation

Viewed over the long run, the most important single event of the IUSOE period, and the one which marked its close, was the amalgamation with the International Brotherhood of Steam Shovel and Dredgemen in 1927. The Brotherhood had its birth on the Chicago drainage canal in 1896, coincident with the birth of the National Union of Steam Engineers. It grew with the "Soo" locks and the Welland and Panama canals, but its most important source of employment had been railroad construction and then the strip mining of copper and coal. The shovel engineer was the real "boomer" of the day, drifting from one project to another throughout the United States and Canada and abroad in a union that claimed the world as its jurisdiction. The Brotherhood might never have existed had the steam engineers' union been interested, but the city-dwelling stationary and hoisting engineers were not. However, strife grew between the two organizations as the IUSOE began to follow its contractor employers into rural areas. The Brotherhood's membership was too small to be viable, and neither union was strong enough to afford battle. Amalgamation made sense. Only 7,000 members were added to the IUSOE's numbers, but the merger sealed the union's future as a predominately construction union with a growing earth-moving emphasis. A name change, removing any reference to steam, marked the end of an era of transition. The 1927 International Union of Operating Engineers had a total membership of 32,000—a level it had reached in 1920 before falling off to 25,000 before the onslaught of the open shop movement of the time, the "American Plan." It could claim annual receipts of $189,387 in 1927, generated by a 60-cent per capita tax, but offset by expenses of $193,463.

The Depression Years, 1929–1940

The third period of the union's history began at the peak of one building boom and ended at the beginning of another, but the determining force was the dreary decade of depression between. It appeared briefly that Huddell had found a solution to the internal jurisdictional disputes and the restrictive "more members-less jobs" philosophy of the hoisting engineers in his supervisory policies, but because building trades employment plunged 80 percent between 1929 and 1933, the leverage of success disappeared. Throughout the entire history of the union, no other years were as full of internal turmoil as the last three years of the administration and life of Arthur M. Huddell. During the remainder of the period, 1931 through 1940, the union was led by John Possehl, an intelligent and farsighted man, but only in his final year did conditions give scope to his abilities.

Supervision and Consolidation

The process of supervision having been developed to replace revocation, thirteen locals were under supervision at the time of the 1928 convention. In each case, the international supervisors moved aggressively to organize the full jurisdiction, sometimes in the face of violent opposition. Going beyond the supervisory policy, Huddell began ordering the amalgamation of competing locals into marketwide units— for instance, combining twelve locals into two in Chicago, one each for stationary and hoisting and portable engineers. Some seceded rather than combine, and others took the International to court. One International supervisor was assassinated and another's home was bombed. But with the cooperation of the employers, who preferred the International's more orderly policies and procedures, the rebel locals died out and the members returned to the fold. Similar events occurred throughout the country during 1927–31 before a recess set in, probably because the deepening depression removed any motive for further organizing efforts.

The opposition generated may have caused Huddell's death, however. The union's headquarters had been moved to an office in the Carpenters' building in Washington, D.C., in 1929. On May 22, 1931, Huddell, General Secretary-Treasurer John Possehl, and Assistant Secretary Frank Langdon were sitting in a lunch room across the street when another diner pulled out two pistols and began shooting. Langdon lost an eye, but a bullet to Huddell's heart was absorbed by a leather-bound notebook in his pocket. Possehl was not injured. Huddell continued to perform his duties apparently uninjured but collapsed a few days later and died of a cerebral hemorrhage and pneumonia on June 1, 1931. In addition to the turmoil over supervision and amalgamation of locals, Possehl had just replaced the previous general secretary-treasurer, who had been found guilty of embezzlement and was suspected by some as the originator of the assassination attempt. The following year, Washington, D.C., police arrested four men and a woman for plotting to assassinate Charles Haury, supervisor of a Washington, D.C., local and then indicted one of the four for the 1931 attempt on Huddell. However, the alleged gunman died in prison while awaiting trial without ever admitting the crime or naming his employer. The automatic ascension of a first vice president having been removed from the constitution during the intervening years, Possehl, who had been a marine engineer and pile-driver operator in Georgia before becoming an IUSOE organizer and International supervisor of a number of Ohio locals, was elected to replace Huddell.

Depression Era Policies

Conditions of Possehl's administration were not propitious. A diabetic and workaholic, hard work and high living caught up with him in September 1940, just as industrial recovery was offering a test of his policies. Nevertheless, he had divided the IUOE into districts administered by district representatives, had promoted a revival of the stationary jurisdiction that had been neglected by Huddell, had begun organization of oil refineries, had rewritten the union's constitution for referendum approval in a period when no conventions were held for twelve years because of financial stringencies, and had won an increase in the per capita tax and a percentage of the permit and initiation fees. Membership of 33,628 in 1928 fell to 21,502 in 1933, then rose to 32,398 by 1936 and 53,969 by 1939. None of the growth resulted directly from NLRB elections. Moreover, construction relief projects were not performed under union conditions. On the other hand, Public Works Administration projects, increased federal highway expenditures, and massive reclamation projects provided employment opportunities for hoisting and portable locals, while the 1931 Davis-Bacon prevailing wage law tended to support union wage rates on federally sponsored construction. The added stationary membership came from sheer aggressive organizing by a newly appointed staff of International representatives assigned by industry to civil service, refrigeration, hotels, newspapers, theaters, office buildings, hospitals, and department stores.

Recovery Measures

A minor upswing began in 1937, followed by a milder downturn, and then recovery with the beginning of war in Europe in 1940. Possehl reached an accord with the Associated General Contractors (AGC) in 1939 that would be important as recovery accelerated. Recovery was spotty, with consequent increased mobility by both employers and union members. With large-scale projects—first reclamation and then defense—an influx might overwhelm a small, isolated local. With no further reluctance of the locals to organize, the permit fee, or "dobie," was accepted and regularized by the International. Anticipating an influx of unskilled union members that never occurred because the CIO industrial unions came into existence to absorb it, the IUOE had adapted the branch local system with "A" branches for the traditional fireman/oiler apprentice and junior engineers and "B" branches for organizing the unskilled. The latter proved useful for organizing construction-related activities such as sand and gravel pits and quarries, which the hoisting and portable locals were still reluctant to organize as a potential source of partially skilled, low-wage competition. Each of these were legitimized in the new 1938 constitution.

Most important was a return to amalgamation, but at a much different level. The 1927–31 amalgamation had been limited to multiple locals within the same city. In the interim, with the intensification of statewide highway construction and, primarily in the west, even multistate reclamation projects, as well as prospects for defense construction, accompanied by a wider geographical scope of contractor operations, some device was necessary to control mass movements of employers and workmen over vast distances. With the enthusiastic endorsement of the Associated General Contractors, announcement was made in 1939 that all hoisting and portable locals in Wisconsin, Ohio, and Colorado would consolidate into statewide locals. Pennsylvania was divided into eastern and western locals—with the eastern local covering Delaware as well. Northern California, all but two counties of Nevada, and all of Utah and Hawaii became Local 3, accommodating wide-ranging San Francisco-based contractors, while the rest of California and Nevada emerged as Local 12. Again there was opposition, but the approval of the employers, the more sophisticated structure of district and International representatives, the acceleration of employment opportunities, and the trend toward litigation rather than physical violence for the resolution of disputes, eased the process.

The stage was set for war and postwar growth, but also for public criticism yet to come.

The Growth Years, 1940–60

At the 1940 convention of the IUOE, General President John Possehl expressed pride in the major accomplishments of his administration—a net worth of $325,728 and a membership of 58,240 that was maintained and accumulated during the difficult depression years. Eighteen years later, retiring General President William E. Maloney passed on to his successor, Joseph J. Delaney, a new $3 million office building, a net worth of over $18 million, over $11 million of it in cash and government bonds, and an organization of 294,190 members. The major contributor to this growth had been the prosperous times of two wars, the cold war, and general economic growth. But wise policies and aggressive action were necessary to take advantage of the opportunities.

Maloney had been a hoisting engineer and business agent of Local 569 in Chicago during the difficult days of attempted gangster infiltration during the 1920s and became an International representative, supervisor of Chicago locals, and vice president of the international in the early thirties. He ascended to the presidency in the very year that the World War II defense program began and moved with that growth. IUOE members were soon involved in the construction of hundreds of military reception centers, training facilities, air fields, harbor and waterfront facilities, factories for war materiel, and other projects—not only in the United States but also abroad, where hundreds of operating engineers were killed or captured in the Pacific. To the oil refinery jurisdiction pursued in the 1930s was added synthetic rubber plants and the petrochemical industry generally. The 1,600 mile Alcan Highway project of 1942–43 used 11,000 pieces of road-building equipment, all operated by IUOE members. The 1,475 mile "Big Inch" pipeline was an inroad into a new industry, brought from a status of almost totally nonunion to over 90 percent organized by 1952, bringing 25,000 new members into the union. Atomic energy plants rounded out the war experience. After the war, there was an immense backlog of civilian construction to be completed, including housing projects, the interstate highway program, further reclamation projects, and the space program.

As noted, Possehl had reached an accord with Associated General Contractors in the last year of his life, and a few areawide and statewide heavy and highway agreements had been signed. But the real success of the campaign came during and after World War II, culminating in the creation of the National Joint Heavy and Highway Construction Committee, a joint organizing campaign of the engineers, carpenters, teamsters, and laborers under primary engineer leadership. In previously unorganized locations, Maloney institutionalized a policy he had practiced in his Chicago days—setting initially a lower rate that would allow union contractors to bid successfully with nonunion competition, then raising the rates as union control was attained. In that regard, the Davis-Bacon Act was an important tool since, once the union scale became the prevailing rate, no lower pay was allowed on federally financed projects.

To facilitate the widened scope of contractor operations, the Maloney administration continued and accelerated the amalgamation into marketwide, including statewide and broader local jurisdictions begun by Possehl. By 1958, only New York City and Washington, D.C., had construction locals limited to the city, and there was sufficient continuing building work in both those locations to justify the narrower scope. There were now 275,000 hoisting members in seventy-five locals and 80,000 stationary engineers in 276 locals. Nonconstruction membership had increased fourfold but was only 27 percent of the total.

With construction becoming increasingly mechanized and the engineers having primary jurisdiction over construction machinery, the IUOE inevitably became a key union in the Building Trades Department, with the others looking to it for leadership and support. Since the machines IUOE members operated were the bulk of any contractor's investment, their skills and availability were a critical consideration in the planning and conduct of any project. Huddell had pioneered the International agreement during the 1920s, but it had largely atrophied during the depression. Now it became a major tool of the Maloney administration. The building of highways and pipelines might require a contractor to move with his work through the jurisdiction of several locals, even after consolidation. The IUOE was one of the basic trades employed by the general contractor. The increasing size of construction projects led to the creation of larger contracting firms for which no one area was likely to produce enough construction to provide continuous operation. These general contractors had to be able and willing to pursue jobs over a broad area, often throughout the nation and beyond. In advance of bidding, they had to be certain of labor costs and their ability to perform. Into unfamiliar labor markets, they had to be able to bring a few of their key personnel but also to have instant access to skilled new hires who were trustworthy with expensive equipment and capable of immediate skilled performance.

For the contractor, the advantages of the international agreement were a ready source of skilled operators in an unfamiliar location, prior knowledge of wages and work rules in a prospective job area, the position of pattern-follower rather than pattern-setter, International mediation of threatened disputes, and International control of obstreperous local unions. For the union, the advantage was primarily organizational. Contractors who once employed union labor where the union was strong, and nonunion labor where the union was weak, now called for union engineers wherever they went. In case of a strike in the local area, the International contractor went on working, providing income for local members and promising retroactive payment resulting from the local negotiations. An added bonus for the international was employer support in case of an International-local dispute.

Nevertheless, International agreements were at times sources of conflict between the general officers and local unions. Their successful use presupposed a willingness to make concessions to a union contractor in localities where it was necessary to bid against competitors whose employees were not organized. Many locals feared that concessions to highway contractors, for instance, would endanger their superior wages and working conditions on building work, and they opposed the International organizing policy of meeting the competition. It was not unusual for a local union to enforce certain portions of a contract against an out-of-state contractor but not against a favored local contractor. At times, local unions also wrote contract clauses that were discriminatory against the national contractor. Since the International agreement required the contractor to comply with local wage rates and work rules, the International was obligated to protect the signatories against discrimination. Attempts to restrain local unions in these matters sometimes led to clashes between International and local policies.

Maloney was no less impatient than his predecessors with what he considered to be short-sighted local leaders who failed to see the superior advantages of International policy, but he was more reluctant to resort to International supervision. But once it was under supervision, he rarely took the initiative to release the local union back to autonomy, and since his eighteen years was the longest presidency in the union's history, the number of supervised locals accumulated, the high point being reached in 1953 when twenty-four local unions containing nearly one-fifth of the total membership were under International supervision.

Supervision cases during the Maloney administration fit into four general categories: (1) supervision to facilitate amalgamation, (2) weak locals dependent upon the International for leadership and subsidy, (3) locals characterized by weak and inexperienced leadership, dissipation of funds, and/or highly fluctuating membership, and (4) locals guilty of gross violations of International policy, usually in regard to relations with employers. Supervision was often requested in the first three categories. It was in cases of the last type that strong local leaders typically carried the International through long series of legal actions for the return of local autonomy and the primacy of local policy. International representatives responsible for the geographical areas were normally appointed as supervisors, with assistant supervisors administering the local's affairs on a day-by-day basis under their direction. Elected officers might or might not remain in office under the watchful eye of the supervisors, depending upon the reason for supervision. Member complaints would bring a request for explanation by the supervisor, and too many complaints often brought a change of supervisors, but otherwise supervision ended when the supervisor informed the International that the local had solved its problems and was ready for autonomy. The supervised locals were generally the most efficiently run and were preferred by the employers, but to outsiders, the practice smacked of dictatorship. In a day of investigative reporting and congressional inquiry, unions increasingly operated in a goldfish bowl. Thus the IUOE was praised for its efforts to prevent work stoppages during the Second World War and the Korean conflict, but the same actions got it star billing in the McClellan committee hearings of the late 1950s.

Among the criticized practices was the charging of permit fees to traveling members. The consolidation of hoisting and portable locals into statewide units largely eliminated the problem for highway work but not for heavy construction and major defense, reclamation, and atomic energy projects. For instance, the Savannah River atomic energy project was dropped suddenly upon a small town in South Carolina. A local of 100 to 200 members was inundated by over 1,000 newcomers, then fell back to its original size four years later. The local did not want the outsiders as members, since they had no continuing interest in its affairs; they would be a burdensome responsibility when the inevitable shrinkage of employment came. On the other hand, the local could not service the job and its employees without the income to employ the necessary staff. Yet politicians and the public often perceived the permit fees as the equivalent of a kickback. The

International's response was to allow but regularize and limit the fee to a maximum of $2.50 per week.

Related, and often confused in the public mind, was the problem posed by the Taft-Hartley Act's outlawing of the closed shop. The traditional hiring hall provided the out-of-the-area employer with a ready source of skilled labor and the union a means of rationing scarce job opportunities by rotation among its membership, as well as a device to limit job access by nonunion members. Taft-Hartley made it illegal to discriminate in employment on the basis of union membership or nonmembership, but hiring hall services still entailed substantial administrative costs. After considerable legal entanglements, a solution was found by referring to the permit fee as "travel service dues" where traveling members were involved and "applicants service dues" for nonmembers, making both pay the customary $2.50 per week for hiring hall and other services rendered.

The Goldfish Bowl

Despite its obvious successes, the Maloney administration ended with internal bitterness and external criticism. The 1956 convention was the scene of a near revolt by some supervised locals and by West Coast locals resentful of international pipeline and other agreements within their jurisdiction that were sparked by local and regional leaders with International political ambitions. Racketeering and corruption within labor unions had become a favored target of investigative reporting, and newspapers were charging some IUOE local and national officers with such practices.

Like any other segment of society, labor unions had known their share of impropriety—embezzlement of funds, mishandling of health and welfare benefits, acceptance of kickbacks from workers and bribes from employers, and discrimination against and physical abuse of political opponents. Typically these occurrences were at the local level, out of the glaring spotlight of the media and government investigators, and were typical of unions operating in small-scale and highly competitive industries where an employer might find it worthwhile to bribe a business agent for nonenforcement of a contract clause in search of an edge over competitors. In the building trades, the most common occurrence historically had been to "sell strike insurance"—that is, to threaten to call workmen off the job at a critical point when a job was behind schedule and monetary penalties for delay were looming. Operating engineers had been no less entrepreneurial than others, and a few local leaders over the years had gone to prison for just such activities.

All of the above were familiar characteristics of industrial relations in the construction industry, but they were neither familiar nor acceptable to the public at large. Between 1956 and 1959, the McClellan committee set out in pursuit of union wrongdoing, culminating in the Labor-Management Reporting and Disclosure Act of 1959—the Landrum-Griffin Act. Only the International Brotherhood of Teamsters seemed to raise the ire of the committee to a more intense level than the IUOE. The number of locals under international supervision and the number of members in branch locals were evidence of the absence of democracy. Permit fees were viewed as extortion. International and pipeline agreements were perceived as "sweetheart contracts." Simultaneous investment by both William E. Maloney and a major contractor in an oil well venture and the part ownership of a construction firm by a local union business manager were identified as unsavory relationships. Deposed local leaders exaggerated estimates of the size of their locals' treasuries. When taken under International supervision, they were accepted at face value as evidence of international looting. Convictions of a few local business managers over the years for extortion were generalized and treated as the norm. Incidents of intraunion and picket-line violence were spotlighted. Expense accounts and living styles of some union officials, including General President Maloney's, were criticized as excessively lavish.

That was the status of the International Union of Operating Engineers as General President Joseph J. Delaney gaveled the 1960 convention to a close—growing rapidly in membership, well organized within its jurisdiction, internally united, financially wealthy, respected by its organized employers, and valued within the labor movement, but nevertheless suffering from an image problem caused by an antiunion crusader from Arkansas. He managed to give the entire labor movement a black eye and saddle it with restrictive legislation that, in the long run, would have only a limited effect on its organizing and bargaining powers. Thirty-three years later, another politician from Arkansas would ascend to the presidency with the full support of organized labor and, it was hoped, would reverse the conservative and antiunion atmosphere that had existed for the twelve years prior to his election.

Chapter 3

THE ACCOMPLISHMENTS AND CONSEQUENCES OF COLLECTIVE BARGAINING, 1960–1975

Over the long run, the McClellan committee charges and their legislative aftermath would have little impact on the IUOE. Whatever its public image, the primary test of the effectiveness of a labor organization is its ability, through its relations with employers, to enhance the economic well-being of its members. By wise responses to favorable economic conditions, the union had been eminently successful in that regard during the 1940–60 period. Circumstances remained propitious until the early 1970s, but the collective bargaining successes of 1960–75 would come back to haunt the engineers during the late seventies and eighties, at least on the hoisting and portable side. Local building and construction trades unions were at the peak of their bargaining power, and they used that power to attain wage and fringe increases well above the rate of inflation, as well as work rules that were anathema to some contractors. The economic comeuppance would be the open shop movement described in chapter 6, followed by the IUOE counterattack detailed in chapter 7. The stationary membership would continue in a steadier state, confronted by legal and technological obstacles, which they too would learn to overcome.

Hoisting and Portable

The building trades unions, including hoisting and portable engineers, operate in a casual labor market; that is, their primary attachment is to the industry and to their crafts, generally with only job-by-job temporary attachments to individual employers.

Work Life in a Casual Labor Market

Billy Hurt is an example of a typical operating engineer working at his trade in a construction setting. Hurt became a member of Baltimore's Local 37 in 1950, and later transferred into Washington, D.C.'s, Local 77. He retired in January 1993, after working as an operator for forty-three years. During that time, Hurt worked for well over 100 different employers. "During one slow year," Hurt says, "when there were few long-term jobs in the Baltimore area, I worked for twenty-eight different employers on a short-term basis." When asked how he would have answered the question, "Who do you work for?" his response was immediate: "I would have said that I work for the International Union of Operating Engineers."[1]

Hurt's attachment was to his craft and his union, not to any one employer. He was not recruited and selected by contractors but referred to jobs by his union. Moreover, his union did not deal with one employer but with many. His job opportunities depended on his union's ability to sign contractors to agreements requiring them to place orders for needed help with the union hiring hall, though they might be given a limited right to request individual workers by name. His health and welfare insurance and pension plan were based on his union's ability to negotiate an agreement with all of the individual employers for whom he might work over time to pay a specified amount per hour into a multiemployer plan. Only a few construction workers might be considered key employees by their employers and kept on a year-round basis. (Lou Previti is an example.) For the rest, the vagaries of construction demand and the weather determined their employment stability on a project-by-project basis. Billy Hurt worked on Baltimore's Harbor Tunnel for over two years, but when the job was finished, he was back at the union hiring hall looking for another referral. In between jobs or during seasonal lulls, he accepted other temporary work, often outside construction, to tide him over until the next big job began.

As a consequence of these casual employment relationships, the role of a labor union in construction is quite different from its counterpart in a more stable industry. Craft unions in the construction industry not only represent their members in the negotiation and administration of collective bargaining agreements but also take on the responsibility of providing contractors with skilled craft workers on demand. That means that they must be involved in the processes by which those workers attain their skills, either through apprenticeship or work experience. The bargaining process itself is also more complicated in that multiple employers are involved, usually through employer associations.

Perhaps most important, however, is that organizing in the construction industry is traditionally a "top-down" proposition; that is, the goal is to persuade contractors to hire only union members in return for the use of the union hiring hall as a source of a guaranteed supply of skilled labor. The advantage to employers is that the union takes over a major personnel responsibility that otherwise contractors would have to provide at their own expense. Between jobs, the employing contractor can lay off unneeded personnel with the full assurance that skilled and experienced replacements can be obtained as needed simply by calling the union hiring hall for referrals. The process is disadvantageous only to those employers who could obtain from alternative sources equally productive workers at a lower wage or whose competitors can do so—in other words, when the union fails in its traditional objective of taking wages and other labor costs out of competition.

Thus a casual labor market is characterized by temporary employment. All employees are constantly engaged in working themselves and their fellows out of a job in terms of completing the project. Construction workers move from contractor to contractor as jobs begin and are completed, and they remain unemployed or seek work outside construction when construction activity is low. Unemployment compensation helps to bridge the income gap during off-seasons. In the organized sector of the industry, it is the union, not the contractor, that is responsible for providing the bulk of the labor for construction projects. That is the primary reason why Billy Hurt and his fellow hoisters consider their local unions as their "employers."

Economic Expansion

The union's growth during the 1960s was due mainly to expansion in the construction industry, especially new construction. Although construction's share of the gross national product has remained pretty much the same since the 1940s (14 percent), new construction climbed from about two-thirds of the total in 1947 to three-fourths in the 1960s. Expansion in highway, defense, space, utilities, and pipeline construction resulted in a steady decline in construction unemployment rates from a high of 13.5 percent in 1960 to 6 percent in 1969—the lowest rate since the World War II/Korea era. At the same time, construction wage settlement increases were between 4.1 and 5.2 percent, well above the relatively low inflation rates of the early 1960s (never above 1.9 percent between 1960 and 1965). In the late 1960s, however, the situation changed dramatically. Inflation began increasing at a rate of six percent per year and construction wage settlement increases soared from 7.8 percent in 1967 and 1968 to 13.7 percent in 1969, leading to the Nixon economic stabilization program of 1970. It was a period of great unrest in the construction industry; many of the wage increases were the result of bitter and costly strikes.

The upshot for the IUOE was a steady increase in membership and resources that continued into the seventies, based on a continuous expansion of those sectors of the construction industry in which the union and its members had the greatest interest and involvement. The industry is divided, for most analytical purposes, into residential, commercial, industrial, and heavy and highway construction. There is little employment for operating engineers in residential construction, except for site preparation. Commercial construction—office buildings, retail establishments, schools, and so forth—employ relatively few operating engineers. But some of those so employed—and particularly hoist and crane operators, as previously noted—have considerable bargaining power as long as they are supported by the other building trades. The hoisters' bargaining power was, in the past, sufficient to carry along the operators of pumps, compressors, and incidental equipment as well. Industrial construction such as oil refineries, power plants, and factories generally involve more site preparation and earth moving as well as cranes and hoists and have been important sources of operating engineer employment. Heavy construction—dams and other reclamation projects, airports, etc.—and highways involve primarily earth moving and are at the heart of employment of the hoisting and portable engineers.

Industrial and heavy construction had boomed during World War II and continued during the postwar expansion. The interstate highway program, defense, and nuclear and other energy projects continued the demand for operating engineers. The projects were of such size that firms that could handle them as general contractors were too large to find continuing work in any one locality. New contracting firms were formed, and familiar ones expanded to become national and international in scope. The prewar emergence of statewide and more extensive local union jurisdictions had placed the IUOE in a favorable position to take advantage of those developments.

Local contractors who were familiar with a particular labor supply might know personally most of the skilled-crafts workers in a locality. However, during the period of high construction demand, local union hiring halls were the only source of adequately skilled labor for those contractors who operated beyond narrow geographical confines. The Davis-Bacon Act put a floor under wages in the heavy and highway sectors, so, insofar as the union scale was the base for wage determination, any bidder was guaranteed against being underbid on wage costs. As long as skilled operators were not available from a nonunion source, each bidder in the construction sectors also bid on the assumption of paying union scale. As long as no competitor could obtain skilled labor for less, the level of the wage and its accompanying employee benefits were of limited relevance to the bidding contractors. Wage levels also were not of great concern to the government agencies responsible for public projects. Within reason, the engineers, like the other skilled construction craftsmen and craftswomen, could demand and get what they asked. As a result, construction wages and other costs spiralled sharply upward. For Billy Hurt, it was the best period of his career; his unemployment was primarily seasonal in nature, and his wages and benefits more than doubled.

Wage Settlement

Wage-setting for the engineers was a local process—though the geographical coverage of the hoisting and portable jurisdictions was extraordinarily wide in comparison with stationary locals and with other building and construction trades. Commercial rates were established by bargaining between IUOE locals and metropolitan associations of building contractors. Heavy and highway rates were set through negotiations with statewide chapters of the Associated General Contractors of America (AGC). Major industrial contractors were organized nationwide into the National Constructors' Association (NCA).

In a few localities, the basic trades (carpenters, laborers, cement masons, teamsters, operating engineers, and, occasionally, ironworkers), whose members were employed by general contractors, bargained jointly with those associations. More often, each trade bargained individually, mainly because of the differing jurisdictions and interests of the various unions. Carpenters and laborers, for instance, could usually find enough work close to home to keep them busy during a construction season and therefore tended to organize local unions within daily commuting range. The remainder ranged over entire states or even wider areas to find sufficient work and therefore structured their local union jurisdictions to conform with contractors who also operated over wide geographic areas. Specialty trades employed by subcontractors bargained with separate associations representing electrical, plumbing, painting, and other specialty contractors, usually in a more constrained geographical scope.

In dealing with the IUOE and other building trades that were party to national agreements, contractors from outside the local union jurisdiction initially had no objection to paying the rates bargained between local unions and local contractors, as long as the rates were known to them in advance of bidding and were extended to all competitors. They welcomed access to the IUOE hiring hall referral service as a source of skilled labor in an unfamiliar labor market. These outside contractors had two concerns about dealing with the local unions: (1) they did not want to become embroiled in local strikes when they could not be continuing parties to whatever agreements emerged; and (2) they resented the occasional discrimination when a local tried to "gouge" the outside contractor for benefits not sought from local contractors with which they had continuing relations. The national agreements discussed in chapter 2 took care of those two problems.

Pipeline contractors had the additional problem of possibly traversing the territory of several local unions in the course of a contracted project and being forced to change crews and compensation or work rules in midproject. By 1960, as noted previously, over 90 percent of pipeline work was organized, with original crews and conditions continuing to the completion of each spread. A committee of International representatives—initially Paul Askew, Paul Larsen, and Richard Nolan, replaced by others as time passed—negotiated national pipeline agreements. Another international representative, Forrest Burgher, headquartered in Kentucky and provided with a small airplane to reach isolated sites, monitored the contracts and served the pipeline membership.

Most large-scale commercial construction in urban areas throughout the country was organized, even in the South. Industrial construction of substantial size was organized almost everywhere. Highway work was well organized in twenty-eight states (the peak, as it turned out), partially organized in seven, and totally unorganized in thirteen, mostly in the South. Practically all public heavy construction was being done under union agreements.

National Agreements

As noted in chapter 2, national agreements, whether between the International and individual contractors or an association of contractors, were first introduced in the 1920s by then General President Arthur Huddell. However, it was William Maloney who expanded their use and made them a key factor in the union's organizing program. National agreements provide that the signatories work union and respect local wage rates and other conditions of employment. In turn, they provide that there be no work stoppages and that differences between the parties be resolved in an orderly manner.

The pipeline agreement was already in effect when Delaney became general president in 1958, but both he and Wharton expanded its use considerably. When industrial contractors engaged in the construction of oil refineries, power plants, and the like began contracting for the maintenance of those facilities, using crews that moved from one facility to another in rotation, national maintenance agreements were signed between the International and the industrial contractors. Wage agreements separate from construction were negotiated, compensating for the fact that the jobs were nonseasonal, of long duration, and with preferred working conditions. Time-and-one-half for overtime around the clock and throughout the work week, in contrast to the double time often included in building agreements, and elimination of the travel and subsistence benefits of heavy and highway agreements were other concessions.

Often, unionized maintenance was being performed in facilities where the operating personnel were totally nonunion. Because the agreements involved other building trades unions and bypassed local construction agreements, and to differentiate them from other maintenance agreements later negotiated, they were called the General Presidents' Project Maintenance Agreement by Contract or, more familiarly, the General Presidents' Maintenance Agreement. Forty-one such contracts covering 103 locations in the United States and Canada were reported to the 1968 convention, rising to fifty-seven contractors and 117 projects by 1976.[2] Similar agreements were concluded with commercial and industrial maintenance contractors, onshore and off-shore oil drillers, and railroad maintenance and construction contractors. Later, under succeeding administrations, national agreements relating to nuclear power, bridge, and stack and chimney construction were signed.

Although national agreements were instrumental in increasing job opportunities for union workers, the old problem of local union refusal to abide by their terms sometimes resulted in work stoppages, thus making the International liable to lawsuits. Local union violations of its national agreement with the IUOE led the National Constructors' Association to sue the International for damages in 1972 and resulted in the collapse of that long-standing agreement. Conflict with the Associated General Contractors relating to heavy and highway construction during the same period ended national contracts in that segment of the industry, although the International continued to execute national agreements with individual contractors. The large wage increases carried over from construction were also threatening contract maintenance agreements that were executed with individual contractors rather than with associations. By 1980, however, as the open shop challenge grew, local union resistance subsided, and national agreements provided a means of responding to that challenge.

The Central Pension Fund

Although not the result of an International agreement, a major contribution of the international union to the collective bargaining successes of its locals and the economic well-being of their members was the development of the Central Pension Fund during the 1960s. The larger and stronger local unions had begun in the 1950s to negotiate health insurance and pension provisions, while the International had launched two internal pension plans—one for international officers and staff and another for officers and staffs of local unions. But that left out the smaller locals that lacked the critical mass of membership to sponsor a pension plan, even if they were able to win employer agreement. As Peter Babin, Jr., of Local 406 (New Orleans) put it:

> The only pension we had at the time was a hat we would pass around
> when retirees would come to the union hall to get something to do
> because they had no money. I hated to see a good and respectable aged
> man who did not have any income after he retired. In those days the
> equipment was different and the operator had to be strong to handle it.
> You had to have strong shoulders and knees, and after 30 years of work
> the machinery would wear you down.[3]

The logical answer was a multilocal pension plan to which all of the
employers of the members of several locals could contribute. Since the
stationary locals tended to be the smallest, theirs was the greatest need.
A catalyst was Local 501 of Los Angeles. Though it was one of the
few stationary locals large enough to launch its own pension plan, Ray
Tucker, business manager of Local 501, persuaded his members to
become the base for a central pension fund into which other locals
could join. By good fortune, Lane Kirkland came over from the AFL-
CIO Social Security Department to serve as Research and Education
Director of the IUOE, lending expertise at a crucial point in the delib-
erations. Soon after the plan was approved by the 1960 convention,
Kirkland returned to the AFL-CIO to become an assistant to President
George Meany and eventually his successor, leaving to his replacement, Reese Hammond, the task of selling the concept to other local
unions. By 1972, with $84 million in assets, 65,000 members, and
3,500 pensioners, a ten-year vesting provision could be added, with
early retirement offered at sixty years of age. As of 1992, the plan's
assets totaled $3 billion dollars, and close to $140 million was being
paid in annual benefits to 35,000 beneficiaries.[4]

The Construction Industry Joint Conference (CIJC)

The Construction Industry Joint Conference (CIJC) was launched in
1959 by the Labor Joint Administrative Committee of the Building and
Construction Trades Department and the Associated General Contractors of America (AGC). John T. Dunlop of Harvard University, whose
idea it basically was, became its impartial chairman, with the president
of each building and construction union and the head of each national
contractors association as members. Its purposes were to resolve mu-
tual problems of contractors and unions, preserve and promote the
contract method in construction, and promote the welfare of the building

and construction industry in the public interest. It lasted until 1972, when AGC contractors began to create doublebreasted organizations and the AGC itself became more responsive to the open shop movement. At about the same time, the AGC withdrew from the Impartial Jurisdiction Disputes Board and other joint labor-management initiatives discussed in later chapters.

Perhaps the CIJC's greatest contribution was in obtaining agreements at Cape Kennedy, the Missile Test Center on the Gulf coast of Mississippi, and other missile sites. Daily liaison with NASA, the Secretary of Labor, the Missile Sites Commission, and the Air Force and the Defense Department, among other agencies, was maintained. Prior to the CIJC's efforts, nonunion contractors had been awarded a great deal of the work at missile sites. The CIJC's "project agreements" reversed that trend.

The National Joint Heavy and Highway Construction Committee (NJHHCC)

As also noted in chapter 2, the NJHHCC was formed in 1954 by the general presidents of the basic trades, chiefly as an organizing tool in heavy and highway construction. It was dissolved in 1958, when the Teamsters Union was expelled from the AFL-CIO, much to the consternation of the rest of the building trades unions, which were, of necessity, allied with the Teamsters on construction jobs. The committee was reactivated in 1964 with the Operating Engineers, Carpenters, Cement Masons, Brick Masons, and Laborers as members, but with a policy of full cooperation with the Teamsters. National, area, and state committees were established. The NJHHCC sponsored negotiations for a number of state-wide and project agreements. The principal activity was in areas where the work was, for the most part, unorganized in the past.

One of the committee's most notable successes occurred in Alabama and Mississippi—two notoriously nonunion states—and involved the operating engineers in a highly innovative organizing initiative. In late 1973, the Guy James Construction Company, a non-union contractor, was awarded the first contract let in what would eventually be a billion-dollar series of projects connecting the Tennessee River with the Gulf of Mexico. Known as the Tennessee Tombigbee Waterway Project (Tenn-Tom, for short), the project was under the supervision of the Corps of Engineers.

Tenn-Tom was a project of tremendous magnitude—the construction of a 253-mile water route that would accommodate barge traffic between the port of Mobile and the Tennessee River. For example, one component of particular interest to operating engineers—the "divide cut"—involved a contract to move 147 million yards of dirt. The project ran through the western part of Alabama and the northeastern part of Mississippi—an area commonly known as the Black Belt. Historically, this had been open shop country, and, accordingly, the Department of Labor set the predetermined wages at such a low level that it would have been impossible for union contractors to compete under the bidding process. However, IUOE Local Unions 312 and 624 (Alabama and Mississippi, respectively) formed a coalition with community action groups to protest the low predetermined wages.

As a result of this citizens-labor coalition, a new wage survey was conducted that resulted in sharply increased predetermined wage rates, and union contractors were the successful bidders on three of the four major contracts that were let through 1975. As part of the coalition's activities, the two locals sponsored training programs to prepare minority residents of the Tenn-Tom area with entry-level skills as heavy-equipment operators and mechanics. Over 200 residents were trained in eastern Mississippi and northern Alabama; most of them became part of the Tenn-Tom work force. Thus the IUOE, which became the target of civil rights activists during the 1960s in other locations, was able (in cooperation with the NJHHCC) to use the civil rights issue as an organizing tool against open shop contractors in a notoriously non-union area.

Economic Stabilization

By the close of the 1960s, many unions were facing slow growth or even loss of membership, but the building and construction trades, including the operating engineers, were still riding high. But the end of the growth era was near at hand. The cause of its demise would be the emergence of an aggressive open shop movement that was fueled by construction wage increases during the Vietnam military involvement. The intervening instrument, which, if successful, might have avoided both events, was the Nixon administration's attempts to curb Vietnam era inflation through the Economic Stabilization Acts of 1970 and 1971.

The inflationary spiral began when the Johnson administration chose to fight an undeclared war in Vietnam without the tax increases and wage and price controls that would have been politically available only with a formal declaration of war. With the conflict still raging at the beginning of the 1970s, the Nixon administration attempted, for the first time since the Korean "police action" (another undeclared war but one susceptible to wartime controls because of its denomination as a United Nations exercise), to impose wage and price controls during "peacetime." Rapidly escalating construction costs were among the key forces that led the administration to undertake a stabilization policy. But there was much more at issue for the construction industry and its unions, the explanation of which requires some historical background.

The fragmentation and decentralization of the construction industry had proved troublesome in both World War II and the Korean "police action." The demand for construction services was high during both periods. Skilled construction labor was scarce. The industrial and heavy construction components of the industry—the components most affected by defense demands—were generally well organized, and neither the contractors nor the contracting agencies had strong incentives to restrain costs. Although building and construction trades general presidents and national contractor association officials were responsive to government pressures, they had no control over their local counterparts and no role in decentralized collective bargaining.

During the Second World War, the wage- and price-stabilization needs of the construction industry were met by a Wage Adjustment Board, an adjunct to the War Labor Board and the National Wage Stabilization Board. In fact, the construction industry wage-stabilization problem was perceived as sufficiently crucial that wage controls came to the industry five months earlier and lasted one year longer than controls on the rest of the economy.[5] Less than four years passed before a tripartite Construction Industry Stabilization Commission was instituted for the same purpose under the Korean-era Wage Stabilization Board.[6] These governmental organizations did not survive the military conflicts that brought them into existence, but the experience demonstrated to national, union, management, and public-member participants the value of some centralizing influence for the industry. And no less important, they produced a cadre of people in government and out who were experienced in their administration.

The Taft-Hartley Act of 1947 had also forced some centralizing experiences on the radically decentralized industry. Among them, Section 10(K), which outlawed jurisdictional disputes, had provided an incentive to unions and management to establish their own private jurisdictional-disputes settlement machinery as an alternative to having the NLRB decide work-assignment issues. The resulting National Joint Board for the Settlement of Jurisdictional Disputes established in 1948 was another experience in centralized review of local decisions. There followed, in the early 1960s, the tripartite Missile Sites Labor Commission to mediate disputes among government agencies, local unions, and contractors who were engaged in that high-priority defense effort. A key participant in all of these industry joint efforts had been Professor Dunlop. He resigned as neutral umpire of the jurisdictional disputes board for a 1957–58 academic sabbatical at the International Labor Organization in Geneva, Switzerland. Upon his return, Dunlop was asked by labor and management leaders to chair the CIJC discussed above.

In effect, a national planning system encompassing one of the economy's most decentralized industries was in the process of development. IUOE General Presidents Maloney, Delaney, and Wharton had all been strong supporters of those centralized policy efforts. In fact, because of the size and strength of some of their locals, their need for a mechanism to win local adherence to national policies was even greater than that of some of the other building trades with smaller and weaker locals. All that experience was available as a base in both the industry and the union when the issue of construction wage and cost acceleration arose in the late 1960s.

The Nixon administration took office in January 1969 during the fourth year of heavy Vietnam military involvement and in the midst of accelerating inflation, construction being only the leading edge of a general problem. Median first-year wage increases in construction labor agreements, which had ranged from 4.1 percent to 5.2 percent between 1961 and 1966, had jumped to an annual rate of 7.8 percent in 1967 and 1968, and in 1969 recorded first-year increase of 13.7 percent (see Figure 3.1).

Nixon's first Secretary of Labor, George Shultz of the University of Chicago, turned to his long-time academic colleague Dunlop for assistance and asked him to create a Construction Industry Collective Bargaining Commission, which was established by executive order of the president on September 22, 1969. In effect, the bipartisan Construc-

Figure 3.1 **Construction Wage Trends: Union and Total Industry, 1960–1975**

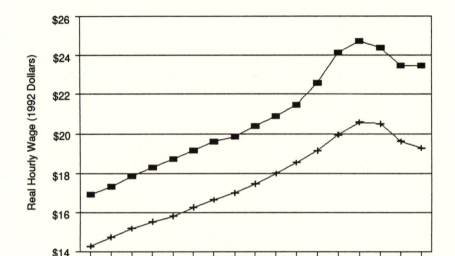

Sources: Union Construction Wages: 1907–1978, *Historical Statistics of the United States, Colonial Times to 1970,* p. 171; U.S. Department of Commerce, 1979–1992, *Statistical Abstract of the United States,* pages vary by year; Average Construction Wage: *Employment, Hours, and Earnings, United States, 1909–1990,* Volume I, U.S. Department of Labor, Bureau of Labor Statistics.

tion Industry Joint Conference had been transformed into a tripartite government-sponsored body with Hunter Wharton of the IUOE as one of four labor members. The assignments were to: (1) increase the quantity and quality of construction labor; (2) reduce the instability of demand for construction labor; (3) extend the average number of weeks of employment; (4) strengthen the role of national labor and contractor organizations in the collective bargaining and dispute settlement processes of the industry; and (5) adapt the structure of collective bargaining to the dictates of technological innovation and changing economic and political demands.

The immediate results were disappointing. More than one out of three construction negotiations in 1970 resulted in strikes, over 500 stoppages (many of them lengthy), and the first-year wage increases negotiated averaged 17 percent. Recognizing their inability to restrain their local bodies throughout the country under the prevailing economic circumstances, and mindful of the forthcoming round of preseason collective bargaining in the spring of 1971, the Collective Bargaining Commission foresaw the need for drastic action. Since Shultz had left the Labor Department to head the new Office of Management and Budget, Dunlop and his union and management colleagues proposed to Secretary of Labor James D. Hodgson in December 1970 that he advise the president to impose wage controls under the authority of the Economic Stabilization Act of 1970, using the commission as a knowledgeable instrument for their administration. Hodgson carried that request to the White House early in January 1971, only to be refused in favor of an executive order suspending both the federal Davis-Bacon Act and some thirty-seven state "little Davis-Bacon" prevailing-wage laws.

The result was chaos. Not only did a number of governors and their state attorneys-general go to court and challenge the president's authority to negate state law but contractors were left without knowledge of their prospective labor costs as they began bidding for projects in the coming construction season. Management officials were effective in convincing the White House of the ineffectiveness of its approach, resulting in the establishment of a Construction Industry Stabilization Committee (CISC) by a March 29, 1971, executive order. Dunlop, one of the four public members, chaired the committee. Wharton of the IUOE served as one of four labor members, with the heads of four major contractor associations representing management.

The CISC assignment was a challenging one, coming near the end of a construction boom with a wage structure already badly distorted by several years of inflation and chaotic bargaining and beginning late in a bargaining year with a substantial number of 1971 agreements already in place. The executive order establishing the committee gave it authority to review and approve or disapprove negotiated settlements —a process that required the review of some 1,500 agreements each year. To facilitate that task, seventeen Craft Dispute Boards were established, essentially one for each building- and construction-trades craft. Assistant to the President Frank Hanley cochaired with a management official the Operating Engineers Craft Board. For Hanley, the exposure to a broad range of government, management, and labor personalities, as well as to difficult negotiations, would be an important factor in his rise to the presidency and in his performance as president of the IUOE.

The criteria the CISC would apply had been worked out in advance by its participants and written into the executive order. It was not enough to merely restrain further construction wage increases. Hundreds of local unions of the eighteen building trades had, in effect, negotiated and were constantly negotiating some 4,500 separate agreements. Representatives of these local building trades in labor markets across the country, each trade bargaining individually and at different times but mindful of the status of the others, had been "playing leapfrog"—each trying to win higher wage and benefit increases than the others. Wage differentials among crafts, built up over the years from different forces of supply and demand, varying skill and training requirements, and changing technology, had become badly distorted, thus providing motivation for further catch-up or "leapfrog" strategies. Differing geographical jurisdictions of each agreement and overlap between urban and rural agreements had introduced distortions in traditional and accepted geographical wage relationships. These inequities, which had emerged from the chaotic years, had to be remedied so as not to motivate further conflict or distort future recruitment and training relationships. Therefore, two criteria had been written into the executive order:

> • productivity improvements and cost of living wage increases but not to exceed the average increases in wages and benefits prevailing between 1961 and 1968.
> • equity adjustments to restore traditional relationships among crafts in a single locality and within the same craft in surrounding localities.

The committee did not intervene in negotiations, except for a few cases of lengthy strikes, but reviewed agreements after the fact for either approval or rejection. The Craft Dispute Boards were advisory, telling the parties upon request what they thought the CISC was likely to accept and counseling them concerning resubmission after rejection. Negotiated agreements went first to the craft boards, which reviewed them and forwarded them to the committee with recommendations for approval or disapproval. Of course, both the union president members of the CISC and the union representatives on the craft boards were placed in the unenviable position of informing their local unions that they could not receive what they had already won through negotiations with their employers.

The CISC had no authority to revoke agreements reached and put into effect before its March 29, 1971 initiation, but it could, and did, revoke some 2,000 previously negotiated increases scheduled to take effect after that date. In addition to rejecting and referring agreements that exceeded its dual criteria, it also allowed increases, some of them quite large, which were necessary to adjust inequities and restore historical wage structure relationships. After first-year average increases of 17 percent in 1970 and 15.7 percent for the first quarter of 1971, second and third quarter increases were 12.0 percent and 11.4 percent, respectively. The average rate for 1972 was approximately 6.5 percent, followed by 5.5 percent for 1973.[7] Strikes in 1971 were one-third of the 1970 number, with working time lost through work stoppages cut by 60 percent. Of course, there is no way of knowing what would have happened in the absence of the CISC process, but judging from what occurred after controls were lifted, it appears that the CISC was the only successful mechanism of the entire economic stabilization program.

President Nixon imposed a general wage-price freeze on the whole economy in October 1971, accompanied by a tripartite Pay Board, chaired by Dunlop, to administer wage controls generally. However, the CISC, thereafter chaired by Dunlop's student and former secretary of the committee Daniel Quinn Mills, continued to function independently for the construction industry.

By the time the Economic Stabilization Act of 1970 expired on April 30, 1974, Dunlop had been appointed secretary of labor by President Gerald Ford. Prior to the April expiration, which ended the life of the CISC, the parties comprising it had sought legislation to continue some form of a continuing stabilization program for the construction industry. Their motivation was the reappearance of the pre-CISC conditions. After only 272 construction strikes in 1973, there were 437 in 1974. First-year increases in major construction settlements bounced back up to an average of 10.8 percent, while manufacturing increases were averaging only 8.8 percent. Some construction settlements were reaching 15 to 20 percent, reintroducing wage structure distortions.[8]

Unsuccessful at their efforts to preserve the CISC, exploratory meetings between labor and management continued and resulted in an April 1, 1975, executive order from President Ford that established a new Collective Bargaining Committee in Construction consisting of ten labor and management members, along with the director of the Federal Mediation and Conciliation Service, and chaired by the secretary of labor. The committee met productively throughout 1975, reaching a decision to seek legislative empowerment. However, the legislation introduced, in the late summer of that year, became entwined with separate labor-sponsored legislation to reverse the 1951 NLRB Denver Building Trades "common situs picketing" decision, later endorsed by the U.S. Supreme Court, which forbade picketing of a nonunion subcontractor on an otherwise union building project.

Local construction union leaders had never been happy about the involvement of their national leaders in centralized joint planning committees. In fact, Hunter Wharton and other construction union leaders had been careful to make no endorsements of the various presidential executive orders concerning construction wage stabilization, preferring to appear to be submitting to government fiat. But at the same time, the "common situs picketing" issue was more important at the local than the national level. Each secretary of labor since 1951 had agreed that the "common situs picketing" decision had been too far-reaching; even Senator Robert Taft, Sr., author of the Taft-Hartley Act, had favored an amendment to reverse the decision, but that had never been accomplished. Now with the two proposals welded together—a national interest in wage stabilization married to a local interest in greater picketing freedom— Secretary of Labor Dunlop won the commitment of President Ford to sign the combined Economic Rights of Labor in the Construction Industry Act of 1975.

But that reckoned without presidential politics. The act was passed by both houses of Congress in December 1975. However, President Ford's position as a vice president ascending to replace a resigning president had never been secure. Attacked by potential challenger Ronald Reagan for his endorsement of the situs picketing component, President Ford reneged and vetoed the entire bill on January 2, 1976. The labor members of the Collective Bargaining Committee in Construction immediately withdrew, and Secretary of Labor Dunlop, considering his credibility irretrievably damaged, resigned as well. Commented General President Wharton:

> The entire program, in the name of stabilizing the economy, was nothing more than a device to make the average worker and consumer both

the victim and the goat, while the banks and big business piled up mounting profits and interest rates soared.[9]

But those comments were meant primarily for local union consumption. Actually, Wharton was praised by John Dunlop as "very supportive of the CISC's attempts to protect the industry from excessive wage increases. . . . He not only cooperated with me and the contractors, but also became very persuasive with our clients in selling the rest of the Council on the program."[10] Had the proposed act passed, the building- and construction-trades unions, including the IUOE, would have had a legislatively guaranteed position in something approaching a national planning system for the construction industry. The wage restraints imposed at the national level, along with the requirement for International union approval of local strike calls, would likely have taken much of the steam out of the open-shop movement. Instead, a seven-year effort at joint labor-management-government cooperation in construction industry collective bargaining came to an abrupt end. Furthermore, since management interests were splintering over the growth of the open shop movement, and national labor officials had been weakened vis-à-vis their local counterparts by the "common situs picketing" failure, the private parties were never able to reorganize on a bipartisan basis. Therefore, the 1976 fiasco sounded the death knell of centralized planning in the construction industry.

Although the growth period ended on a sour note, the period as a whole had been a good one for the hoisting and portable engineers. Not only was there a sharp increase in membership, but the wages and benefits of the hoisters rose well above the rate of inflation, as well as above the increases enjoyed by most other unionized workers. There would be losses in the future, but the gains made during the years 1960–75 would provide a solid foundation for counterattack.

The Stationary Engineers

The very term "stationary" implies stability and absence of change. Hoisting and portable engineers once referred to their stationary counterparts as "nail cutters" because of the sedentary nature of their employment and their lack of mobility. Nevertheless, numerous technological and societal changes between 1960 and 1993 forced adjustments in the jurisdiction, organizing techniques, and collective bargaining patterns of stationary engineers. Those of 1960–75 are discussed here and the remainder in chapter 7.

In 1958, Garth Mangum defined stationary engineers as "all those members of the union who are not employed in the building and construction industry."[11] Today, however, even that definition is not sufficient to distinguish between "stationary" and "hoisting and portable" engineers, primarily because many hoisting and portable locals now have members who are not employed in construction. Art Viat, IUOE vice president and business manager of the largest stationary local (Local 39—northern California), often refers to his sister hoisting and portable local (Local 3) as "the other stationary local in northern California." Over 8,000 of Local 3's 35,000 members are not employed in construction.

Although the core of the stationary jurisdiction remains the operation and maintenance of power plants (with the emphasis on "maintenance"), its organizing base has broadened considerably. Several factors account for the change, including ever-advancing technology, the encroachment of industrial unions, employer resistance, the demands of organizing in the public sector, adverse NLRB decisions, and just plain economics. It costs as much to negotiate for a unit of a half-dozen people as it does for a much larger unit. Small stationary locals that cannot afford to hire staff are uneconomic and ineffective, with regard to both collective bargaining strength and organizing potential.

Having begun as a union of stationary engineers who predominated among the union's membership until the Second World War, stationary engineers comprised less than one-third of the IUOE membership by 1960. Until about 1940, the union adhered to strict craft lines. According to Mangum, "even a decision to admit firemen, who actually were apprentice [stationary] engineers, was the occasion for a bitter floor debate at the 1912 convention. Since 1940 and particularly in the postwar years, the IUOE has often departed far from its definition of a stationary engineer in its organizing efforts."[12] Since 1960, the trend away from "craft purity" has accelerated. Nevertheless, the basic jurisdiction still sought is that core group of workers who are responsible for the operation and maintenance of central heating, air conditioning, refrigeration, and electrical and electronic units in major buildings. Other building-maintenance workers must often be included in order to gain the core units, but the latter are the primary organizational targets.

Al Lake, special assistant to the general president for stationary engineers, in testimony before the NLRB, described the skills necessary to maintain today's modern equipment—and may have made Board members a trifle nervous in doing so. "[There are] over 4,344,760 pounds of explosive force . . . in the basement of 1717 Pennsylvania Ave [the NLRB building]," he said, "fortunately under the control of a group of skilled maintenance employees."[13] He then made a suggestion to board employees and members:

> And while I will be presenting you with evidence concerning the skills required to maintain modern physical plants, I would suggest that any employees of the National Labor Relations Board, including Board members, who truly desire empirical evidence, gather some first-hand by venturing down to the engine room of 1717 Pennsylvania Avenue. Observe what goes on there, ask some detailed questions of the chief engineer, ask him to explain why you have heat in the winter and air conditioning in the summer; why the lights go on when the switch is thrown and water comes out when the faucet is opened; ask how a boiler thermostat works, a refrigeration machine, the safety devices, or a power transformer; then ask what happens when they don't work properly. When you have absorbed all that—and are beginning to understand that maybe law school was not so tough after all—consider that the NLRB is a relatively small office building with systems not nearly as complex as those found in today's large health care institutions. I assure you that such a visit will be at least as enlightening as several pounds of transcript that will be produced in these hearings.[14]

Lake also questioned the proposition that today's systems are foolproof, or that skilled technicians are no longer necessary to operate and maintain today's automatic equipment, and that boiler explosions are a thing of the past. "The empirical evidence," said Lake, "is quite to the contrary." He pointed to a report issued by the National Board of Boiler and Pressure Vessel Inspectors which disclosed that, in 1987, there were 3,318 accidents involving boilers and other pressure vehicles that resulted in 259 injuries and 102 deaths in the United States. He also noted that deaths from such explosions had increased from fourteen in 1976 to 102 in 1986. "It is my personal view," Lake concluded, "that this alarming trend has resulted from insufficient resources being invested in the retention and training of qualified maintenance personnel and to a heavy reliance on so-called automatic safety devices."[15] Craft purity is no longer the *sine qua non* of stationary organizing efforts, but by no means has it been abandoned altogether.

A Matter of Priority

Not surprisingly, in an era when the hoisting and portable branch of the union was growing at a rapid rate, the problems of stationary locals were not given high priority. Maloney, Delaney, and Wharton were building tradesmen whose natural priority was the construction field. Moreover, stationary engineers were not at all affected by seasonal factors and only marginally affected by economic conditions and anti-union movements. Stationary engineer locals were constantly negotiating, not with associations of employers, but with a whole host of individual employers in a wide variety of industries. Although stationary growth was slow, the jobs won for the union were permanent full-time positions and resulted in permanent full-time union members. The turnover in the stationary branch was (and still is) much lower than in the hoisting and portable branch. Still, it was clear to many stationary business managers that unless their locals were allowed to organize outside the "blood lines" (i.e., the pure craft jurisdiction), they could not survive.

New Directions

Requests by stationary business managers to organize outside the traditional jurisdiction were turned down by Presidents Delaney and Wharton. The major reason was that such a policy would bring the IUOE into conflict with other AFL-CIO affiliates. The fact that jurisdictional disputes were endemic in the construction industry was the major reason for this policy; the International did not want to create any more problems than it already had. Articles XX and XXI of the AFL-CIO constitution, although protecting the stationary engineers where they had previous bargaining arrangements, restricted attempts to enroll their counterparts who worked under industrial union agreements or to engage in new organizing campaigns where other unions already had collective bargaining contracts. Article XX prevented raids by one AFL-CIO affiliate against another, and Article XXI outlawed organizing campaigns in industries where other affiliates already had collective bargaining status. Since so much of the stationary potential consisted of small units that otherwise might be absorbed into the facility-wide units of industrial unions, the only defense available to the IUOE stationary branch was an aggressive offense—that is, to be the first to organize, thereby gaining the protection of Articles XX and XXI rather than becoming subject to their restraints.

Despite his reluctance to declare open warfare with other AFL-CIO claimants to overlapping jurisdictions, Wharton did act to strengthen the stationary branch. He created a committee under the chairmanship of General Secretary-Treasurer Newell Carman, former business manager of the San Francisco stationary local, to study and review all matters pertaining to stationary engineers, and he appointed A. W. (Ray) Tucker of Los Angeles stationary Local 501 as a special assistant to the president for stationary engineers.

But to Art Viat in San Francisco, survival depended on organizing outside the "blood lines." "It was very obvious to me," Viat said, "that we couldn't survive. There is no way that you can survive when industries are being shut down . . . and everything is moving out of the area . . . because of San Francisco's high tax structure."[16] In 1960, most stationary engineers were employed in local breweries, bakeries, ice storage plants, and similar facilities—most of which would disappear within ten years. Moreover, technological change was altering the very nature of stationary employment. Not only did the stationary engineers have to branch out into new industries (while avoiding violations of Articles XX and XXI, if they could), the members also had to be trained for the high-tech jobs of the future. And, unlike the hoisting and portable locals that organized from the top down, the stationary locals had to do so from the bottom up, contacting employees individually with an appeal to sign authorization cards and then vote union in secret-ballot NLRB certification elections.

The fact that the stationary branch continued to grow despite the disappearance of many of the industries in which its members traditionally had been employed is a tribute to the organizing skills and training efforts of local stationary unions throughout the country. It wasn't until the later administrations of Turner, Dugan, and Hanley (especially the last) that the stationary branch would receive substantial help from the International. During the period 1960–75, it was the locals themselves that were primarily responsible for the slow but steady growth of the stationary branch.

New Fields to Conquer

Stationary engineer locals had moved in a small way into the organization of utility and petrochemical employees prior to 1960. Thereafter, these industries were given more attention. Recognizing additional potential from interaction between the construction membership building such facilities and stationary members seeking operating jobs, Wharton, in 1968, appointed specialists from both fields to coordinate such interaction. James T. Horaitus was appointed utilities coordinator and G.E. McCoy coordinator for the oil and chemical industry. Several developments, including a presidential executive order, an additional prevailing wage bill, and legislative action at the state level all served to focus IUOE attention on public-sector opportunities.

Utilities

During the post-World War II era, the rapid growth of the electric utilities industry, as well as the projected growth of nuclear plants, presented opportunities for stationary locals. In some areas of the country, the generating capacity of public utilities was being doubled every ten years or less, thus resulting in an increasing number of potential jobs for stationary engineers and, of course, a ripe area for organization.

The stationary engineers had been active in the utilities field for a good many years, generally employed in small operating and maintenance units within a single utility. Thus many small locals with only a handful of members entered into agreements with single utility companies. However, with the introduction of the "grid system," or "inter-ties," the bargaining position of the small locals was weakened to the point of ineffectiveness. If an IUOE local struck an individual power plant, the grid system continued to provide power to the area. A strike could be effective only if the striking local was able to convince sister unions to walk out in support of the strike (if, in fact, the other interconnected utilities had collective-bargaining agreements with other stationary locals, or if other unions were cooperative). The only real solution to the problem was amalgamation and merger to cover the entire grid system. That mutually reinforcing need plus the high administrative expenses of small locals were the major reasons for an International policy of merging and consolidating stationary locals, a policy that had been extremely effective for hoisting and portable locals two decades earlier.

For example, five midwest stationary locals, which had collective-bargaining agreements with three interconnected utilities, merged into one local union. After the merger, the union bargaining position was strengthened, better working conditions were negotiated, higher wages were obtained, and the combined membership was able to employ a full-time business manager. Many of the stationary mergers that occurred during the late seventies and the eighties were designed to strengthen local union effectiveness in the utilities field. Nevertheless, IUOE membership in utilities employment remains minor compared with that of the Electricians and the Utility Workers, except in the state of Wisconsin.

Nuclear Energy

When it appeared in the early seventies that there would be a swing toward nuclear plants, the IUOE sent nineteen local and International staff members to classes at Oak Ridge, Tennessee, to qualify as teachers of nuclear plant operation. The nineteen graduates of the Oak Ridge course would then train local stationary engineers. However, because of the problems experienced at Three Mile Island and the Chernobyl disaster, and because construction and operating costs turned out to be far higher than expected, the construction of nuclear plants came to a dead stop. If ever there is a revival of the use of nuclear power in the utilities industry, the expertise gained by IUOE trainers will be available to train nuclear stationary engineers.

Oil and Chemical

IUOE members are employed by oil and chemical industry employers in refineries, manufacturing plants, bulk stations, tank farms, drilling platforms, pipe lines, textile finishing, and oil fields. They are employed as licensed stationary engineers, operating personnel, maintenance workers, fire inspectors, gaugers, laboratory technicians, plumbers, roustabouts, and utility workers, among other occupations. Local 347 in Texas City launched an apprenticeship program for distillate operators in the 1960s, though the employment picture for stationary engineers in the oil and chemical field has been erratic.

The energy crisis of the 1970s helped in two ways. With swollen demand and profits, the IUOE successfully negotiated an average increase of over two dollars an hour for its members in the oil and chemical industries between 1972 and 1976. Outside that industry, the contributions of building engineers rose with energy costs. There, ability to save on the consumption of more expensive fuels was translated into both cost reduction for the owner and increased success in wage negotiation for the local unions.

At the time, the union predicted increased activity in the oil and chemical industries as an increasing number of refineries were either on the drawing board or under construction, particularly in the Gulf Coast area. Nevertheless, despite organizing efforts, the oil and chemical boom did not result in a membership increase. One of the problems was automation, but it was also acknowledged that organizing in the industry was becoming increasingly difficult, mainly because unorganized employers were matching union wages and fringe benefits. Apparently, employer concern was not the cost of these items but the money they saved by avoiding union work rules. Total flexibility in the deployment of their personnel was cited by oil and chemical employers as their primary motive for avoiding union organization. The IUOE sought stationary engineer units, while the Oil, Chemical, and Atomic Workers Union pursued facility-wide organization, but the employers preferred to avoid unionization under any auspices.

The Public Sector

Three developments helped spur public sector organization within the IUOE. The first was President Kennedy's 1962 executive order allowing union recognition and limited collective bargaining in federal agencies. The second was the passage in 1965 of the Service Contract Act, which set prevailing wages for the employees of contractors who provided various services or maintenance work to federal agencies. The third was the passage of state laws governing collective bargaining for public employees.

The Kennedy Order: In July 1962, President Kennedy issued Executive Order 10988, "Employee-Management Cooperation in the Federal Service." The order provided recognition of "*bona fide* organizations of federal employees which are free of practices denying membership because of race, creed, color or national origin; which are free of corrupt influences and do not assert the right to strike or advocate the overthrow of the Government of the United States."[17] Under the order, "exclusive recognition" would be given to any organization chosen by a majority of employees in an appropriate unit and would give that organization the right to bargain collectively with management on non-bread-and-butter issues.

Following the issuance of Executive Order 10988, the IUOE signed the first agreements ever negotiated for civil service employees of the Department of the Army at the Memphis, Tennessee; and Granite City, Illinois army depots. Naval shipyards locals, working with the AFL-CIO Metal Trades Council, won exclusive bargaining rights in ten of the nation's eleven shipyards. Another "first" was recorded when the union broke the navy's objection to craft units by winning recognition for powerhouse units in several naval installations in the San Francisco Bay Area. Finally, air force employees at the North Carolina Seymour Johnson Air Force Base picked the Operating Engineers as their collective bargaining representative.

Service Contract Act: Although the Service Contract Act of 1965 was not directed toward federal employees per se, because the beneficiaries of the act were employees of contractors providing services to federal agencies, it nevertheless was "in the public sector." The act required employers who provided services or maintenance work under contracts of $2,000 or more to pay blue-collar workers wages and fringe benefits (or the cash equivalents of the fringe benefits) that were at least equal to those paid for similar work in the locality, and that all federal contract workers be paid at least the minimum wage as specified under the Fair Labor Standards Act.

The act defined "service employees" as guards, watchmen, and all persons engaged in a recognized trade or craft or other skilled-mechanic craft or in skilled, unskilled, and semiskilled manual labor occupations; and other employees, including foremen or supervisors in a position having trade, craft, or laboring experience as the paramount requirement.[18] Administration of the act was assigned to the Department of Labor's Wage-Hour and Public Contracts Division.

The major benefit of the act to the IUOE was that it increased the likelihood of union contractors bidding successfully on federal service contracts. Recognition of union wage rates for stationary engineers and other skilled crafts as prevailing would eliminate the competitive advantage of nonunion contractors. For example, the IUOE was able to secure construction rates on exploratory drilling in many areas of the country. This type of work had been a problem, since it was not covered by the Davis-Bacon Act. By means of the Service Contract Act, union contractors were able to bid successfully on this work, but only if the union had been successful in organizing sufficiently that the union scale was the prevailing wage for the type of work in question. A prevailing union scale could be protected from being undercut but could not be created by the law. The latter remained the task of union organizers. Stationary engineers employed by employers contracting to manage government buildings was another group benefiting substantially from the act's prevailing wage requirements.

State Legislation: By 1993, thirty-seven states had enacted laws covering collective bargaining for public employees, and government employment was the fastest-growing employment sector in the nation. The organization of state and local workers, therefore, became a target for many labor organizations, including the IUOE. But the expanded organizing activities did bring the International and its stationary locals into conflict with other AFL-CIO affiliates and resulted in major internal AFL-CIO battles, as well as landmark NLRB cases. These later events are described in chapter 7.

Assessment

All in all, 1960–75 proved to be a good period for the Operating Engineers. The combination of favorable economic conditions, farsighted international policies, joint union-management, and interunion efforts resulted in membership growth and increased bargaining power for the hoisting and portable engineers. The growth of the stationary branch was slow but steady and, unlike the hoisting and portable branch, continued on into the eighties and nineties. Aggressive bottom-up organizing and an emphasis on training and retraining were primarily responsible for the success of the stationary branch throughout those years.

But the era was not without its problems. The union met challenges in the areas of apprenticeship training, civil rights, and public policy, all of which will be covered in the succeeding chapters of Part I.

Chapter 4

TRAINING: THE KEY TO CRAFT STATUS

Despite the highly skilled nature of the hoisting and portable and stationary engineer crafts and despite the union's desire to present itself as a ready source of skilled workers, the IUOE was notably reluctant to follow the lead of most craft unions in developing formal apprenticeship programs. A union functioning in an industry of stable employment could leave training to the employer, the individual, or to the community. Once the majority of an establishment's employees signified in an NLRB election their preference for a union as their collective bargaining representative, it really did not matter that there were other potential employees available who were as capable of doing the jobs as the incumbent employees (although that fact might encourage an employer to hire replacements during an economic strike). But in a high turnover situation like construction, an employer with access to skilled labor outside the union could soon dissipate a union majority and had little reason to accede to union demands. The IUOE was dependent on the skills of its members, but there were difficulties in the apprentice route and alternatives to it.

The concept of "craft" assumes the ability to perform a wide range of related functions without supervision. The apprentice approach assumes that the bulk of those skills cannot be learned in a classroom setting; they must be learned on the job under the tutelage of those who have already acquired the requisite skills. All of that is true for operating engineers, both hoisting and portable and stationary, but there are significant differences for each, even though they were equally slow in launching apprenticeship programs.

Hoisting and Portable Apprenticeship

On the construction side, there is an extraordinarily wide range of machines to be mastered. For instance, Davis-Bacon prevailing wage determinations on a major heavy or highway project might list ten or more separate rates for various machines, and they would not include the many forms of hoisting apparatus used on a building job. No single contractor has the necessary complete range of equipment, and few engineers ever learn to operate all of the machines used in construction. The tradition had been to become "apprentice" oilers on a machine, to depend upon the good will of operators to teach the apprentices how to operate it, and to eventually hire out as operators with other employers. Some might remain specialists on one machine, suffering the penalty of limited employability; others might follow the same "pick-up-the-trade" practice with several machines until reasonable income security was assured.

There was also the wide geographical expanse an operating engineer often had to cover in order to remain steadily employed. There was usually enough work in one community to keep an electrician or carpenter employed, but that was less likely for an operating engineer. A hoister might be working with earth-moving equipment on a highway job for several months, then move to a crane on building construction. And the job locations might be far apart, making apprenticeship coordination difficult. Carpenters and electricians can learn their skills in the shop, and the tools and equipment they need are not prohibitively expensive. Hoisters must learn their jobs in the field, working on extremely expensive equipment. Seasonality and weather conditions also had to be overcome in providing for the training of operating engineers.

As long as the union was small and industry growth was minimal, family contacts could be an adequate source for the sponsorship implied in the "pick-up-the-trade" process. With little need for related academic instruction at the time, such as the math an electrician or carpenter might require (though crane operators had to at least judge if not calculate the load factors that determined the angle and elevation at which a boom could be operated), most of what apprenticeship could do for the operating engineers was to formalize the process of transfer among employers and jobs until the desired range of machines and processes had been mastered. That was hardly worth the challenge of negotiating and administering apprentice programs, at least until there were stronger incentives to do so. Meanwhile, the informal process worked.

Jay Neeley of Local 3, for instance, learned to operate a bulldozer in the Civilian Conservation Corps during the 1930s, moved on to other Bureau of Reclamation irrigation projects, and then broadened and polished his skills in defense-plant construction during the labor-short war years.[1] Bill Snow and Nick Matoris of the same local began as truck drivers—Nick in Panama and Bill on the Deer Creek Dam in Utah. Both were able to persuade the operators who were loading their trucks to let them "kick the machines around a bit"; then Bill, on defense plant construction, and Nick, as a battalion bulldozer operator in Iceland and under combat conditions in Europe, went on to acquire the added experience upon which they based their operating careers.[2]

Billy Hurt of Local 77 followed the more traditional oiler route. He said:

> An oiler was not someone who ran around sticking a 3-in-1 oil can into holes in various machines. When I was an oiler, the engineer who sat up in the cab was God. He even wore a suit and tie to work. We not only lubricated and cleaned the machines under his direction, we learned everything there was to learn about how those machines worked and how to repair them. We didn't get up into the cab until we knew every inch of the machine we were working on and how to operate it. It may have taken a lot of years, but by the time we received our book, we were skilled mechanics and operators.[3]

According to Hurt, the day he received his book was one of the proudest moments of his life. "You didn't get an actual book. What you got was recognition by men you respected that you were their equal, that they considered you qualified to operate and maintain any machine a contractor may throw at you."[4] It didn't come easy. Hurt worked for five years for that recognition, during which time he was employed by a host of contractors and was trained on practically every construction machine available at the time.

Others followed the family route. When Budd Coutts was nine years old, he operated a bulldozer on a highway job in the Peace River country of Northern Alberta, Canada. Of course, his father was the superintendent on that job and Budd admits that maybe you couldn't call it "operating," but, well, he handled the machine. "In fact," Budd says, "my father once let me operate a bulldozer and I drove it right into a swamp!" For many years, Budd's father was a construction worker and supervisor in the Peace River country. Later, the family moved to Edmonton, when his father went to work for a contractor in a town near that city. Between the ages of fourteen and sixteen, Budd worked for his father during summer vacations. He left school when he was sixteen years old and hired out to operate equipment for various municipalities and small contractors. Later, he went to work for a firm called New West Construction and took one of their machines into the northern part of British Columbia. Before he left, his father told him that, if he got the chance, he should join Local 115 of the International Union of Operating Engineers. "No matter what the circumstances," the elder Coutts said, "you should join the union." Budd joined the union twice. When an "organizer" showed up on the job, Budd and several other operators turned over to him their $65 initiation fees. The organizer told them that their membership cards would be mailed to them. Three months later, when the membership card still hadn't arrived, Budd went to the union office in Dawson Creek and asked why he hadn't received his card. The business agent said that he had never heard of Budd or any of the operators who had signed up with him; he and his cosigners had been the victims of a scam. An additional $65 was accepted by the legitimate union representative and Budd Coutts became a member of the Operating Engineers. He continued to operate equipment until he became a business agent and later business manager of Local 955. Today, he is the general secretary-treasurer of the IUOE.[5]

Larry Dugan's father moved from Oklahoma to Arizona in a covered wagon, arriving in Alpine, high up in the White Mountains, in 1914. Later, they moved to Phoenix, where Larry was born in 1930. His father was a charter member of IUOE Local 428. When Larry was a boy, he and his family used to follow his father from job to job. "We had a car trailer. My dad would load the whole family in the car and all our supplies, including a tent, in the trailer. We would strike out; he was looking for work and we would live in a one-room tent. Naturally, I would watch him on the job and, sometimes, sit up in the cab with him." Larry joined the union in 1948, starting as an oiler on a truck crane and eventually becoming a bulldozer operator. In 1973, Larry became the business manager of Local 428 and, in 1985, ascended to the presidency of the International.[6]

Thus the route to craft status was informal, featuring training on the job and eventual recognition by skilled operators and mechanics enrolled in local unions. Entry into the local union itself was often dependent upon the sponsorship of relatives or friends or on being an employee of a contractor who signed an agreement with a local union. Lacking any of those entry routes, even after four years of military operating experience, Nick Matoris had to pay a permit fee and hang around the San Francisco hiring hall for months until he persuaded the dispatcher to refer him to a difficult but lengthy job no one wanted before he was admitted into the union.

Later this would change as the union began to organize surveying crews, as operators had to read and understand the marks on the surveyors' stakes to excavate to closer tolerances, as the shift from drum and cable to hydraulics for the control of blades and booms introduced a new science, and as the knowledge required of mechanics became more technical. All of this added to the need for related classroom instruction, which was best provided in a classroom setting. But before that, in the late 1950s and early 1960s, it was an NLRB decision that shook up the hoisting and portable branch of the IUOE and thrust the union into the business of apprenticeship.

Skilled Craft or Service Trade

In a 1959 ruling, the NLRB declared that the operation of construction machinery was a "service trade" rather than a "skilled craft" because of the absence of a federal apprenticeship program.[7] Many other industries had operators of complex equipment who were classified as semiskilled rather than skilled workers because their skills were deep rather than broad and performed under supervision rather than autonomously. What, for instance, made the operator of a continuous miner in the coal industry semiskilled and a bulldozer operator skilled? Unless the operating engineer had the skill to move from one machine to another over a broad range of skills without retraining each time, how could that operator claim skill status? And without a formal apprentice program, where was the evidence that breadth was the rule rather than the exception?

The factors enumerated earlier, along with reduction in the oilers (the traditional source of operators) because of the development of hardier, self-lubricating machines, an increased number of larger-sized projects, and an increase in the number and cost of machines (which made the union referral process even more complicated), would all have demanded apprenticeship eventually. But it was the NLRB ruling that advanced the timing and forced the union into the apprenticeship field. President Delaney declared in 1960:

> While we believe that these [NLRB] rulings are wrong, they are nevertheless effective as an obstacle to our progress. They stand in the way of our ability to carve out our proper bargaining units from larger bodies of employees and severely hinder our organizational activities. The only way to overcome this problem is through the development and promotion of recognized apprenticeship training programs.[8]

Delaney's involvement was fortuitous in that his New York Local 15 was one of the few that, under his direction as business manager, had begun to formalize apprenticeship, a fact of which he was justifiably proud. In cooperation with local contractors and employers in the equipment sales and rental field, the local inaugurated a program offering training in heavy equipment, light equipment, and welding. Local 15 members donated their time as instructors, and a training site for heavy equipment was made available by cooperating contractors and equipment dealers. Later a section of Idlewild Airport (now John F. Kennedy International Airport) was donated by the New York Port Authority for the heavy-equipment school.

The union-operated training site was to become an essential element in the IUOE approach to apprenticeship. In most other crafts, hands-on learning of skills occurred on the job, with production work being performed under the tutelage of a skilled journeyman. Classroom-related instruction consisted of the intellectual and theoretical content, such as shop math or electrical theory. However, for a hoisting and portable apprentice to learn all job skills in a production setting would require a skilled operator to ride each machine while providing instruction to the novice. Two workers to a machine was an expense few contractors were willing to accept. On the other hand, one instructor paid from negotiated apprenticeship funds could observe several apprentices as they operated loaned or donated equipment in a nonproduction setting. Later, when the apprentices had obtained some familiarity with the machines, a supervisor could take over the instructing role, but with less intense involvement required. Beginning with equipment loaned by cooperating contractors, the Operating Engineers later learned how to obtain federal excess property equipment for use in training centers where initial prejob operating experience could be obtained.

Others were moving in the same direction. The first formally negotiated operating engineer joint labor-management apprenticeship program was launched by Local 428, Arizona, in 1959. The local negotiated the establishment of a joint apprenticeship fund, financed by employer contributions, for the development and support of a federal apprenticeship program covering the trades of grading- and paving-equipment operator, heavy-duty mechanic and repairman, universal-equipment operator, and plant-equipment operator (the latter a stationary craft). Each course called for 6,000 hours of training.

The Arizona program, designed and promoted by Vice President and Local 428 Business Manager William Gray, and sponsored by the IUOE's Western Conference, was also the first to apply a set of recommended apprenticeship standards, including draft language for joint apprenticeship agreements; suggested practices for joint committee meetings; duties and functions of directors, officers, and committee members; rules governing apprentices on the job; and the duration of on-the-job training and related instruction. In 1961, a study was made of existing training programs, privately operated heavy equipment schools, U.S. Army Engineers, Navy Seabees, and in-service programs for employees of the Bureau of Yards and Docks. Course curricula were obtained, as well as on-site observation of the programs by union representatives. The result was a draft of National Apprenticeship Standards for Operating Engineers, put in motion by Delaney and presented to the General Executive Board in February, 1962. The approved draft was submitted to the Bureau of Apprenticeship and Training (BAT) and was approved by the U. S. Department of Labor.

Meanwhile, during 1961, Reese Hammond, a young New York local business agent with both operating and organization experience and with a Cornell University degree in labor relations, was brought to Washington and installed as the director of the department of research and organization with additional responsibility for education and training design.

When the union's agreement with the National Constructors' Association (NCA) was renegotiated in 1962, a new article was included:

> Article XIII. The Association and the Union hereby agree to establish a National Joint Apprenticeship Committee composed of three Association members and three Union members to consider and develop National Standards for Apprenticeship for the trade of Operating Engineer.[9]

At the initiative of the NCA, the Associated General Contractors were urged to join as well into a tripartite program. National apprenticeship standards were adopted at a March, 1963, meeting of the newly formed Joint Apprenticeship Committee, presented to BAT, and approved by the Federal Committee on Apprenticeship. The IUOE was now fully committed to the promotion of apprenticeship, and the civil rights legislation of the 1960s added an additional motivation to pursue apprenticeship as a means of entry into the union. As discussed more fully in the following chapter, the family, friendship/ personal sponsor approach to union membership reduced access by minorities and women. Formal apprenticeship provided a more impersonal and objective entry route.

Launching into apprenticeship with enthusiasm, Hammond, as IUOE education and training director, contacted and negotiated with responsive community and other colleges for dual enrollment of apprentices, allowing them to receive academic credit for their on-the-job experience as well as their related instruction.

In addition to the equipment operators and stationary engineers, during the 1960s some hoisting and portable locals began to organize the members of surveying crews who established the lines and grades that guided equipment operators in their earth-moving assignments. Although the surveyors were logical candidates for apprenticeship, their training required a more intensive classroom component than the operators, making dual enrollment attractive to them as well. At the 1976 convention, it was reported that about 3,000 apprentices were eligible to receive from one-third to one-half of the credit necessary to obtain a community college two-year associate degree.[10]

At the same time, the International developed or obtained from a variety of sources instructional materials for use in local programs. Simultaneously, the International began research to establish specific performance objectives for each major type of machine. For that, Hammond employed the services of industrial psychologist Dr. Sydney A. Fine, who had been responsible for developing the classification system for the *Dictionary of Occupational Titles* for the U.S. Department of Labor. A functional job analysis of the operations of twenty different construction machines was undertaken. From these analyses, training standards, curriculum materials, and standardized proficiency tests were developed for each operation. The purposes included not only assurance of the standardized quality of training and assurance of apprentice competency throughout the union but was also designed to encourage movement from traditional time-on-task criteria to demonstrated performance as the basis for apprenticeship progress and completion.

By 1968, hoisting and portable locals were collecting and disbursing apprenticeship and training funds at an annual rate of $5 million. Thirty-eight construction locals had active programs with approximately 2,100 indentured apprentices. By 1980, the number of registered apprentices in hoisting programs reached a peak of 7,327. From that point until 1985, however, because of a combination of adverse economic conditions and incursions by open shop contractors, the number of apprentices declined to 4,090 in 1986. Since 1986, the number has risen slightly to 4,671 enrolled in programs operated by seventy-five locals in 1992.

Stationary Training

The stationary progression was similar, though formal apprenticeship is still not as widespread as among hoisting and portable locals.

Al Lake lived with his grandparents in a small West Virginia village until he graduated from high school. "I had no formal training," Al says. "Steam had been in the family for a long time. My grandfather was a railroad engineer and, on short runs when he expected to get back late in the day, he would take me with him. And I would ride! I loved steam, I loved the smell, the feel of it, the whole thing." The main industry in the village was a sawmill. The sawmill had four steam engines, all under the care of a Mr. Johnson. Al and his friends would go over to the sawmill on Saturday mornings and would watch Johnson tear down the engines and put them back together again. "It is amazing," Al says, "what you learn when you're not really trying." He eventually went to work in a factory with a modern power plant; there were no steam engines, but in licensing examinations the State of Ohio still asked questions about steam. "The book would tell you how it worked, but I had the picture in my mind of what Mr. Johnson did and it made the whole process very clear to me." Al obtained both his boiler operator and engineer's licenses when he was only twenty-one years old. He retired in 1993 as assistant to the general president for stationary engineers.[11]

Just as the air force staffed the aviation industry after World War II, the navy and the merchant marines "dumped on the beach," especially on the West Coast, large numbers of men with almost the same training and experience needed by stationary engineers at the time. Art Viat was one of them. He learned a good deal about engines and power plants in the U.S. Navy and Merchant Marines. When he left the Merchant Marine, he went to work in the private sector as a junior engineer. On his own, he attended school at night and eventually obtained a job as a stationary engineer. He worked for more than ten years at the trade before he was elected business manager of Local 39 (northern California) in 1965. Art was self-motivated and self-educated, and today he is a firm believer in both training and retraining. Art is now an International vice president and business manager of the largest stationary local in the nation, his local spends more money per capita on training and retraining than any local in the country. Political and technological developments had convinced him that in the future the informal route would be the exception rather than the rule.[12]

The stationary engineers craft lends itself more to traditional apprenticeship training (that is, theoretical classroom instruction combined with on-the-job training) than does the hoisting and portable craft. However, because of the nature of stationary collective bargaining, it is far more difficult to negotiate joint programs with employers. Stationary engineers are employed in small units by employers in a host of different industries. Whereas hoisting and portable locals negotiate contracts with employer associations, making it possible to involve many contractors in a single apprenticeship program, stationary locals negotiate with hundreds of employers who are not necessarily related to each other in any meaningful way. As a result, most stationary programs are not joint labor-management programs; they are far more apt to be financed and administered by the local unions themselves. Some are registered state programs, and a few do receive funds from employers, but the vast majority are not registered with the Bureau of Apprenticeship and Training of the U.S. Department of Labor.

Whereas a paucity of written materials about the operation of construction equipment added to the need for formalized apprenticeship, the plethora of textbooks and other written matter covering every aspect of stationary engineering and the inclination of the stationary engineers to study it at their own initiative reduced the incentive for formal apprenticeship for them. Because of the necessity for theoretical classroom instruction, stationary training programs rely heavily on courses offered at local community colleges and adult education institutions. They also receive training and retraining grants from the Department of Labor and from vocational education. The changing nature of the stationary craft, because of the application of advanced technology to power systems, requires retraining for existing engineers as well as initial training for incoming engineers.

Many jurisdictions had always required licensure, necessitating considerable self-education. Elimination of steam as an energy source only changed the nature of the intellectual commitment involved, not its depth. Heating and air-conditioning equipment, and especially the jurisdiction won in hospitals as noted in chapter 7, persistently pushed the stationary engineer's assignment in a "high-tech" direction.

Dan Goodpaster of Local 501 in Los Angeles is typical of this trend. His stationary-engineer father had encouraged him to obtain all of the related experience possible during military service to prepare for a career in the same occupation. Dan first worked as a stationary engineer in 1971 at a Pepsi-Cola plant in southern California, servicing and maintaining the bottling equipment. The work was grueling—ten hours a day, six and seven days a week—and the $5.25 an hour was considerably less than the wages enjoyed by hoisting and portable engineers in the same area. But as energy costs accelerated during the 1970s, and as technology became more complex, employers began to recognize that a well-trained and competent corps of stationary engineers could save them substantial amounts of money.

Goodpaster credits Local 501 Business Manager Bob Fox (also incidentally a U.S. Merchant Marine veteran) with developing the training program that enabled him to take advantage of the new opportunities. Military training and other work experience had provided an adequate supply of qualified stationary engineers in the Los Angeles area, but by the time Fox became business manager in 1965, the technology was changing too rapidly to be learned on the job. Employers were bringing in specialists at considerable expense to perform operating and maintenance tasks beyond the capability of their regular employees. Convinced that a good stationary engineer ought to be able to do anything in a building, from fixing a broken toilet to trouble-shooting state-of-the-art electronic equipment, Fox began establishing commensurate training programs at the local and encouraging members to enroll at community colleges and technical institutes for skills and knowledge the local could not provide.

Dan Goodpaster says he has taken every course Local 501 offers and, in addition, is almost continuously enrolled in evening and week-end technical courses. Now chief stationary engineer with the defense contractor TRW he is responsible for all heating and air-conditioning in its Carson, California, facility—not just for the comfort of personnel but for the protection of delicate machinery—as well as the maintenance of all machinery in the plant. He reports that the most technical aspect of his job is running the Johnson Control Power Conditioner. The electrical power provided by the local public utility is not of the amperage required by the complex equipment used at the plant, so constant transformation is required. A computerized monitoring system watches the power conditioner and catches some 85 percent of its frequent problems, but the rest are totally dependent upon the judgmental diagnosis of the stationary engineer. For that judgment, and for being on call twenty-four hours a day, Dan enjoys a pay, wage, and fringe package of over thirty dollars an hour.[13]

IUOE Involvement in Federal Employment and Training Programs

The launching of a more centralized education and training policy in the early 1960s was coincident with the passage of the Area Redevelopment Act of 1961, the Manpower Development and Training Act of 1962, the Vocational Education Act of 1963, and the Economic Opportunity Act of 1964, all largely concerned with skill training for displaced workers and disadvantaged youth. Despite the early ambivalence of many building trades unions toward these programs, the IUOE's involvement became substantial in virtually all of the federal initiatives.

In a casual labor market, any time spent "on the bench" between jobs is evidence to craft workers and their unions of an excess supply of labor, whereas employers who do not perceive a constant flow of well-qualified applicants fear labor shortages. Although the unions loyally supported the passage of laws that offered training to the disadvantaged and displaced, they had grave reservations about their application and opposed any training for occupations in areas where labor-management apprenticeship programs existed. General President Hunter Wharton said in 1964:

> At the outset, building-trades unions, as well as some others, made clear their resistance to any effort under MDTA to infringe upon union ap-

prenticeship programs. Apprenticeships are labor-management programs and should be left as such.[14]

And about the Omnibus Vocational Education Act of 1963, Wharton said:

> Some of the provisions of this new legislation . . . we view with some alarm, and it will require constant vigilance on the part of our apprenticeship and training efforts to assure that our local unions maintain control of the manpower pool for our industry. If training is undertaken for which there are no real shortages, a pool of unemployed, semiskilled workers is created. Such a pool—when no job vacancies exist—presents a threat to incumbent employees and to their standards of wages and working conditions.[15]

But as a matter of fact, the Operating Engineers had few apprentice programs in place at the time. They were anxious to keep others from providing such training outside their control, thus creating a nonunion supply of skilled operating engineers. But at the same time, at least the International officers were eager to take advantage of whatever funds were available to support training as long as it presupposed union membership and as long as there were jobs for them as there were during the 1960s. On the other hand, many local unions were wary of the implied job competition. Locals preferred to see the federal funds used to upgrade the skills of their existing membership rather than develop new competitors for jobs. To them, it did not make sense to create new craft programs where such programs already existed and even less sense to glut the market with unneeded craft workers. The International agreed with the need for upgrading but assumed that if the unions did not control training, others would have incentive to do it anyway outside of union influence. Therefore, Hammond, on an almost full-time basis, under Wharton's direction, pursued every avenue possible to involve the IUOE in federally funded training programs. Later, the challenges of civil rights groups to the predominately white locals and their perceived protectionist policies would give the union an additional need for training involvement.

Between 1964 and 1968, the IUOE developed the concept of "continuous total training," including preapprenticeship, apprenticeship, skill improvement and upgrading courses, and dual enrollment. In addition, the union began participating in the Neighborhood Youth Corps

(NYC), Job Corps, and other antipoverty programs. For example, Local 545-D (Syracuse) trained sixty disadvantaged youths as surveyor aides under NYC. The enrollees who completed the course went to work as rodmen and became members of the local. MDTA money was used for retraining in Montana, Minnesota, California, Colorado, Ohio, Arizona, Idaho, Pennsylvania, Tennessee, and New York. Eventually, a National Training Program was developed, and the first union Job Corps program was launched by the Operating Engineers at Jacobs Creek, Tennessee, in 1966. These and other training initiatives during the Delaney-Wharton years are described below.

National Training Program

Between 1966 and 1982, the U.S. Department of Labor awarded over $16 million in government contracts to employment, training, and research initiatives of the Operating Engineers under what the union designated as its National Training Program. Beginning in 1966, under MDTA, the International assisted local unions in developing apprenticeship and training programs. Training standards and performance checklists were developed. The program was continued under the Comprehensive Employment and Training Act of 1973 (CETA), but the federal funds available to the IUOE were substantially reduced as budgets declined sharply under the Job Training and Partnership Act of 1982 (JTPA). However, the IUOE still receives a small amount of JTPA moneys for coordination as it continues its involvement with JTPA service delivery areas and national programs throughout the country.

Since JTPA, the IUOE has targeted the economically disadvantaged, minorities, and women for participation in local apprenticeship programs. In April, 1992, 200 individuals were enrolled in apprenticeship programs through this initiative. Other components of the National Training Program included technical assistance to local unions in obtaining federal funds for training purposes, labor market research to identify the needs of the construction industry, and assistance to local unions in acquiring excess government property for use in training programs.

The last is of particular note. In 1973, the National Training Program received a $1.5 million CETA grant to train disadvantaged and displaced workers as heavy equipment operators. Since the training was for federal purposes, the contract provided for the use of $50 million worth of excess government equipment. Local unions conducted training at the entry (basic skills), preapprenticeship, and journeymen/journeywomen levels. The National Training Program staff was responsible for researching the need for training; designing appropriate programs to meet the need; negotiating subcontracts with local unions or Joint Apprenticeship Committees; conducting instructor training prior to each program; and record keeping, participant selection, and monitoring.

Excess Property Program

That experience opened the door to obtaining excess federal equipment for the broader apprenticeship and training efforts of the union. As noted, few contractors have all the equipment necessary for training well-rounded operating engineers. Without some supplement to available on-the-job training, IUOE apprentices are likely to be too narrowly specialized. Joblike experience in off-the-job settings is essential to breadth. As noted, employers and sales and rental firms had loaned Local 15 equipment and even a training site for its introductory effort—later moved to Idlewild (John F. Kennedy International) Airport. But few contractors elsewhere were willing or able to follow that precedent. By having access to surplus federal equipment, other locals could establish similar training centers where apprentices could gain practical experience, even during off-seasons and other periods when no employment opportunities were available.

The excess property program grew steadily from 1968, when the first piece of equipment was ordered by Local 37 (Maryland), until the present. Local 3 was able to buy a vast tract of land at Rancho Murieta near Sacramento and, using federal surplus equipment operated by apprentices for learning purposes, and journeymen and journeywomen for skill upgrading, created a huge housing development and retirement community, complete with golf courses and a shopping center. By 1988, seventy local unions were participating in the excess property program with less ambitious projects. Since February 1982, when the cost of administering the program was assumed by the National Joint Apprenticeship and Training Committee for Operating Engineers, the user's fee, ranging from $800 to $16,000 annually, depending upon amount and value of equipment and always accompanied by substantial amounts of expendable supplies, has remained the same over the intervening years. Participant locals were not only able to acquire hands-on training equipment such as bulldozers and cranes, and such support equipment as trucks and trailers, but also building and welding materials, tools, oil, and more.

Orlando Sanchez was an early participant at Rancho Murieta. As an apprentice in Utah where most open construction ceases during the winter, he came to California for a few weeks during each of three winters in the early 1970s to perfect his skills on equipment not available from his summer employment. Late in his apprenticeship experience, a master mechanic took him under his wing for training as a mechanic, a position that provided him with close to year-round employment, keeping equipment running during the construction season, then reconditioning the equipment during the slack season.[16]

The high cost of construction equipment, as well as concern for damage suits, has made employers more reluctant to allow inexperienced apprentices to operate their machines. At the same time, much modern equipment is self-lubricating, limiting the oiler approach to learning the trade. All of these influences have increased the need for preemployment operating experience. Steve Brown, who completed his apprenticeship in 1976 and is now an apprentice instructor, describes how the excess property program transformed Local 77's program:

> When I first started in the early 1970s, one of the major problems we faced was a lack of equipment. The classroom instruction was good, but without training equipment we had to depend on training on-the-job, and that depended on whether a contractor would let an apprentice practice on his or a rental company's machines. With more contractors being sued for damages, the cost of liability insurance was rising as fast as medical malpractice insurance, so contractors were extremely reluctant. Now we have a wide range of equipment [excess government equipment] right on the training site. When apprentices go out on a job, the contractor knows that they have already had operating experience.[17]

Special Projects

The training program to provide entry-level training for minorities and women in connection with the Tennessee-Tombigbee Waterway (discussed in chapter 3) was one of the initiatives launched under the

National Training Program. Opposition from open shop contractors and some politicians had to be overcome before the Army Corps of Engineers was convinced that it should support IUOE training programs.

Another special project involved heavy construction on the Navajo Reservation in the Four Corners area of Colorado, New Mexico, Arizona, and Utah. Since the 1950s, operating engineers locals have been involved in heavy construction on the reservation, including the construction of two dams, a power plant, and a coal strip-mine operation. During this period, Navajos were trained both informally on the job and through a more formal training program designed to produce well-rounded operators, mechanics, and welders. A special effort was made to make Navajos aware of the opportunities available to them by holding special registration for Navajos only on the reservation.

In 1976, the union reported that more than 500 Navajos had been trained as heavy equipment operators capable of holding down jobs for any contractor. Their income had risen from $3,000 to $5,000 a year to $11,000 to $22,000 thousand per year.[18] That program has continued as further employment opportunities have become available.

Job Corps

Among federally financed employment and training programs, none has faced more controversy and emerged with higher marks of approval than Job Corps. A high-cost program involving full-time residency as well as training, the program is the only one with a positive record for rehabilitating severely disadvantaged youth. The largest enrollments have been in urban centers specializing in classroom training. In those, the IUOE has had no involvement. But the union has been deeply involved in the so-called conservation centers, modeled on the 1930s Civilian Conservation Corps, where the learning methods are hands-on in work settings. Sargent Shriver, brother-in-law of President Kennedy and first director of the Office of Economic Opportunity, was extremely proud of persuading major industrial firms to become contractors for operation of Job Corps urban centers. But he was not attracted to the notion of union involvement in any of the Job Corps activities. It was a major selling effort on the part of the IUOE, lobbying directly with Shriver as well as other members of the administration and Congress, to win a major role for itself and other building-trades unions in the training functions of the civilian conservation centers operated by the Forest Service. Once begun, however, the Office of Economic Opportunity awarded the operating engineers a Job Corps gold medal in 1967, and its involvement with the Job Corps was singled out for particular praise in a 1980 research report:

> Even more spectacular were the outcomes for union programs. Two out of three Job Corps enrollees enrolled in union-related programs completed their courses. Of these, 66 percent were placed in jobs. . . . Nine out of ten were placed by the various participating unions, including the Operating Engineers . . . .[19]

The union success can be attributed to the realism of union programs and a network of hundreds of local unions throughout the country ready and willing to absorb Job Corps graduates as apprentices. Job Corps men and women enrolled in the IUOE programs were taught by skilled union members and received hands-on training on excess government equipment. Individual case histories reveal that Job Corps graduates became local union business agents and contractors as well as apprentices and, eventually, skilled journeymen and journeywomen.

Jeanita Martin, a Navajo woman in Page, Arizona, took typing and shorthand courses in high school, thinking she might try court reporting, but she found the courses boring. What she really liked was the one year of auto mechanics she took, but she didn't see much to attract her in the automotive jobs held by tribal members in Page, a town dominated by tourism connected with Lake Powell, power generation from the Glen Canyon Dam, and a coal-fired plant. It was the last that led to her becoming a Job Corps alumna and operating engineer. Her father was a construction laborer, so she was no stranger to that industry, but an older brother was sent through the CETA program to be trained in Illinois open-pit coal mines and returned to the reservation as a dragline operator at Peabody Coal's Black Mesa Mine near Kayenta, Arizona. When she saw his paycheck, she exclaimed, "Good God, what do you do to earn that kind of money?"

Jeanita contacted her high school counselor to ask how to obtain similar training. The response was, "Oh, you don't want to do that. Those are men's jobs." But a tribal official was more encouraging, telling her about a Job Corps recruiting office in nearby Tuba City (on the reservation, anywhere within 100 miles is nearby). She applied, and after high school graduation found herself at the Weber Basin Job Corps Center in Utah. The Mine Workers were not involved in that program, but the Operating Engineers were. She was enrolled for six months in training as a painter while waiting for an opening and then eighteen months in the operating engineer program. There she did some classroom work, but mostly it was hands-on training, burying trash with earth-moving equipment at the county landfill and learning about surveying and other related subjects at the center.

At the end of her two Job Corps years, Martin took an examination and was admitted to IUOE apprenticeship. She was given no time credit for her Job Corps experience, but because she had the equivalent and more of what was initially taught Local 3 apprentices in the familiarization phase at the local's training sites, she went directly to paid employment as a first-year apprentice with a Utah contractor and obtained further training at a union training site in Spanish Fork, Utah, during the off-season. After experience with several in-state and out-of-state contractors working in the Utah district of Local 3, she finished her apprenticeship with W.W. Clyde Company, one of Utah's two largest union highway contractors, which now requests her referral at the beginning of each construction season. Recognized as a skilled operator of every type of highway construction equipment, she is steadily employed eight or nine months each year, averaging, with overtime, between $30,000 and $40,000 a year, and spends the winters back on the reservation at Page. Now nearing ten-year vesting under Local 3's pension plan, she entertains the possibility of transferring to Arizona Local 428 thereafter to work nearer home. Despite the loneliness of motel living during the construction season, she still considers her employment exciting and rewarding—employment that would be unavailable to a Native American woman without the marriage between Job Corps and the union.[20]

The first *union* Job Corps program was initiated by Local 917 at the Jacobs Creek Job Corps Center in Bristol, Tennessee, in 1966. The program eventually expanded to thirteen centers, but after a Job Corps reorganization, the program was cut back to nine centers, enrolling 375 Job Corps men and women (two out of three participants in one center are women). Of the 198 men and women who graduated from the nine programs between July 1, 1989, and June 30, 1990, all were either employed (181), in school (10), or in the armed forces (7) in 1992. Approximately 40 percent of those employed were working in training-related occupations, and thirty-six (20 percent) were earning $10 an hour or more.[21]

Following the trail blazed by the Operating Engineers, seven other labor organizations initiated Job Corps programs: Carpenters, Bricklayers, Plasterers, Cement Masons, Marine Cooks and Stewards, United Auto Workers, and the AFL-CIO Appalachian Council.

Nuclear Energy Training

The outlook for job opportunities in the nuclear energy field appeared to be good in the 1960s. The industrial application of nuclear energy was promising for stationary engineers, and various radiation methods used to determine both the moisture and density content of soils and for quality control of poured concrete and asphalt paving appeared promising for hoisting and portable engineers.

A study by the Stanford Research Institute (SRI) indicated that radiation measurement and control devices were in widespread use in industry and growing rapidly. The Atomic Energy Commission (AEC) contracted with SRI to develop training outlines in this field. SRI, in turn, asked the IUOE to cooperate in this effort by conducting pilot training programs in accordance with the SRI outline. The materials developed during this time by IUOE instructors became a combination text-work book entitled *Radiation Safety and Radioisotope Industrial Applications.*

SRI conducted a training seminar in San Francisco under the auspices of the Western Conference of Operating Engineers in 1961. Because the course required actual practice in the handling of radioactive material and the measuring instruments, the union applied for and received a license to possess and use these materials from the AEC.

Following the seminar, the instructors returned to their home locals and trained hundreds of members in the advanced course. A third Instructors Training Course was held in Oak Ridge, Tennessee. Eventually, however, cost considerations, accompanied by the ecology and antinuclear campaigns, negatively affected job opportunities in the nuclear energy field. The expected explosion of job opportunities never occurred, but the union had demonstrated its willingness and ability to respond to projected training and employment needs.

Staff Training

During the same period that the IUOE increased its involvement in the career preparation of its members, it also increased its attention to the training of International and local staff. Two of the most outstanding of the International programs are the hazmat and organizing programs described in chapter 7. Local programs are conducted in such fields as safety and health leadership, the introduction and use of training materials for apprenticeship, and other training programs.

International representatives have attended instructor courses at the University of Michigan and courses on current collective bargaining at the University of Wisconsin and Harvard University. The IUOE has been a major supporter of the Harvard University Trade Union Program. By special agreement with Antioch College, the George Meany Center for Labor Studies in Silver Spring, Maryland, offers a college degree program to trade union staff and officers. Students spend one week in residence at the center each six months to plan their courses of study. They do their studying at home or at local colleges, conferring with center mentors by mail and phone. More Operating Engineers staff have received B.A. degrees from this program than the staff members of any other trade union.

A Training Union

The NLRB decision that forced the Operating Engineers into the apprenticeship field was a blessing in disguise. A union that depends for its survival on its ability to supply skilled workers to contractors and to the employers of stationary engineers must take an active part in the training of those workers. The union's apprenticeship programs provided an orderly means for producing skilled hoisting and portable and stationary engineers. But the NLRB decision also had the effect of expanding the union's training activities in areas other than apprenticeship. After a period of skepticism regarding federally funded employment and training programs, the union embraced a national training program, became a trailblazer for the Job Corps, and improved its staff training considerably. A package of ten amendments to the 1964 International convention recognized and sealed its new commitment by establishing a special membership category of registered apprentice and by protecting that status.

As viewed from the end of the growth period in 1975, it was not yet clear the extent to which training would continue to be an IUOE priority in the future. New programs would be undertaken in the fields of pipeline construction and hazardous materials, and staff would be trained in the latest methods of organization. The theme of the 1993 convention was "training for the future," recognizing training as a key factor in combating the open shop and assuring future growth. Thus from a reluctant beginning, training became a major undertaking and lasting commitment of the International Union of Operating Engineers.

1. Frank Hanley,
   General President (1990-).

2. Larry Dugan, Jr., General President
   (1985-1990).

3. J. C. Turner, General President
   (1976-1985).

4. Hunter P. Wharton, General President
   (1962-1975).

5. Joseph J. Delaney, General President
   (1958-1962).

6. IUOE General Executive Board (1993). Seated from left to right: Lionel J. Gindorf, General Secretary-Treasurer, N. Budd Coutts, General President, Frank Hanley, William C. Waggoner. Standing from left to right: Thomas J. Stapleton, Fred P. Dereschuk, Joseph E. Beasley, Vincent J. Giblin, William E. Dugan, Vergil L. Belfi, Patrick E. Campbell, Art Viat, Peter Babin, III.

7. IUOE Trustees (1993). From left to right: Jan Pelroy, James R. DeJuliis, Gerald Ellis, Gary W. Kroeker, Sam T. Hart.

8. IUOE General President Hunter P. Wharton greets IUOE General Counsel Albert Woll (1969).

9. Expansion of the Toyota manufacturing plant in Georgetown, Kentucky (1992).

10. Split hull hopper dredge operating off-shore of Ocean City, Maryland (1988).

11. Woman apprentice operating D4 dozer at Local 18 training site in Logan, Ohio.

12. Pipeline spread in western Canada (1991).

13. View of the Chicago skyline from the seat of tower crane operator John Rickert of Local 150.

14. General President Hanley with staff and local union hazmat instructors at MSHA Academy in Beckley, West Virginia (1992).

15. General President Hanley addressing delegates at the IUOE General Convention in Chicago, Illinois (1993).

16. IUOE Job Corps Director Howard Brown displays model bulldozer to Lane Kirkland, AFL-CIO President, and Ann McLaughlin, US Secretary of Labor (1988).

17. Hazmat trainees going through decontamination line during field exercises (1992).

18. Excavator operator extracting a barrel during "hands-on" training exercise for hazmat training in Beckley, West Virginia (1992).

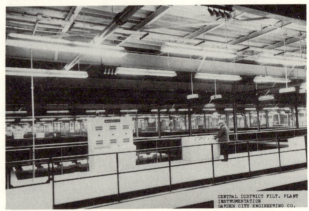

19. IUOE Local 399 stationary engineer at the controls at Central District Filtration Plant, Chicago, Illinois (1965).

20. IUOE Local 917 operators at Watts Bar Nuclear Power Plant (TVA) (1974).

21. Excavation and construction of New York State Government Center in Albany, New York (1970).

23. Woman apprentice training at IUOE Local 18 training program in Richland, Ohio (1992).

22. Erection of the St. Louis Gateway Arch by members of Local 513.

24. Apprentice being evaluated by IUOE local union training instructor under the Training Standards Project.

25. Newly organized members of Local 501 celebrate organizing
victory at Bakersfield (California) Memorial Hospital (1991).

26. IUOE training provided to Navajo apprentices in New Mexico.

27. Local 15 training instructors and trainees at newly opened
facility in Queens, New York.

28. Construction of the second span of the Chesapeake
Bay Bridge in Maryland.

29. Engineer repairing a Cleaver
Brooks' boiler.

30. Engineer operating an energy management
computerized system.

31. Engineer testing and
    calibrating a pneumatic
    control of an HVAC system.

32. Engineer repairing a personal computer.

33. Engineer checking the operation of the facilities'
    boilers.

34. Engineer repairing a facility's escalator.

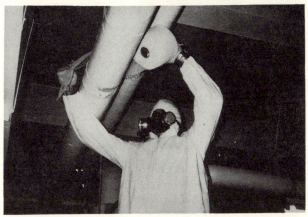

35. Engineer repairing asbestos pipe cover.

36. Local 99 apprenticeship instructor Ed Murphy explaining refrigeration system trainer to his top students.

37. Console operator at Catalytic Cracking Unit,
    Citgo Refinery, Lake Charles, Louisiana (Local 407 member).

38. Operators at Alkylation Unit, Citgo Refinery,
    Lake Charles Louisiana (Local 407 members).

39. Operator at Reformer Unit,
    Citgo Refinery, Lake Charles,
    Louisiana (Local 407 member).

40. Console operator at Unicracker
 Unit, Citgo Refinery,
 Lake Charles, Louisiana
 (Local 407 member).

41. General President Hunter P. Wharton and other
 IUOE and federal Office of Economic Opportunity
 officials signing documents concerning IUOE
 responsibility for Job Corps operation, 1966.

42. IUOE Research and Education Director Reese
 Hammond (center right) and Office of Economic
 Opportunity Deputy Director Hyman Bookbinder
 (center left) with two unidentified instructors at
 Jacob's Creek, Tennessee Job Corps Center (1967).

43. San Francisco Local 39 stationary engineer at work.

44. San Francisco Local 39 stationary engineer at work.

45. San Francisco Local 39 stationary engineer at work.

Photographs supplied by the International Union of Operating Engineers.

Chapter 5

LEGISLATION AND PUBLIC POLICY

During the growth years, the operating engineers union felt strong enough to reach beyond its own immediate institutional concerns and pursue legislation designed to improve the lot of the less-advantaged members of society. The union threw its support behind progressive amendments to the Fair Labor Standards Act, extended unemployment insurance benefits, Medicare and other enhancements to Social Security, the Area Redevelopment Act of 1961, the Manpower Development and Training Act of 1962, the Economic Opportunity Act and the Civil Rights Act of 1964, the Voting Rights Act of 1966, and more than eighty bills designed to improve conditions for federal civil servants. At the same time, the union supported legislation that would help create jobs for its members, including economic development, continuation of the interstate highway program, mass transit, construction of facilities for the mentally retarded, housing for the elderly, and environmental protection facilities.

But the most serious public policy activities of the union were defensive, adapting to the legislation of the forties and fifties, beating off state efforts to enact so called "right-to-work" laws, parrying federal attacks on the Davis-Bacon Act and other prevailing wage legislation, and, finally, reacting to the civil rights movement which challenged some cherished IUOE policies.

Living with Landrum-Griffin

The primary legislative product of the McClellan committee investigations was the Labor-Management Reporting and Disclosure Act of

1959, better known after its authors as the Landrum-Griffin Act. Considering the rhetoric at its passage, it is ironic to note that thirty-three years later the general consensus among both national and local labor leaders is that the act no longer poses serious difficulties for labor unions. There are complaints, of course, of uneven administration of the act and excessive record-keeping requirements, but on the whole the unions have learned how to "live with Landrum-Griffin."

Back in 1960, however, General President Delaney called Landrum-Griffin "a vicious law aimed at the very existence of organizations such as ours."[1] Though not a basic challenge, the law forced substantial changes in the IUOE constitution as well as in the constitutions of many of its local unions. In addition, the International was named in lawsuits brought by dissident members against local unions and the International, made possible by Landrum-Griffin's "Membership Bill of Rights." In most of the latter cases, charges against the International were dismissed because the International had no prior knowledge of the actions taken by the local unions. However, a Florida State Supreme Court decision in the late 1970s held that the International was liable for a local union's action, whether or not the International had prior knowledge. The result was several judgments against the International, forcing the union to impose much tighter control on Florida locals. No other state has chosen to follow Florida's lead.

The Landrum-Griffin Act required fifty-two changes in the International's constitution, as well as changes in the by-laws of local unions. The major revisions involved the rights of members of "branch" locals, rules regarding the placing of local unions under International supervision, the election of convention delegates, and appeals from general executive board decisions.

Branch locals originally were formed to accommodate lesser-skilled and lower-paid engineers. The purposes were to control entry into the union and to protect the wages and jobs of the higher-paid engineers. Prior to the passage of Landrum-Griffin, the members of branch locals were not allowed to vote for local officers or to be candidates for local office. The act required that branch members be allowed to nominate candidates, vote for candidates, and be candidates themselves. (Actually, the last was not made clear in the legislation, but a subsequent court decision mandated that branch members be allowed to run for office.)

The requirements regarding international supervision were the result of the McClellan committee's allegations of lack of justification for placing local unions under supervision and keeping them under supervision for too long a period of time, thus (according to the committee) usurping the democratic rights of local union members. The International's constitution was changed to modify the rules for placing local unions under supervision and specify the reasons for which supervision could be imposed, to require hearings before the general president to determine the necessity for taking such action, and to require annual review of the need to continue supervision.

The high point of International supervision had already occurred in 1953, when twenty-four locals with a combined membership of 41,416 (19 percent of the total membership) were put under international supervision. Since the Delaney administration, not more than five unions at any one time have been placed under supervision, and the majority were so placed at their own request.

Delaney noted to the 1960 convention that twelve locals were under supervision when he assumed the presidency in 1958. By 1960, only four were left—three in the process of returning to local autonomy and one held up by a court suit. One of Delaney's major policies was the ending of International supervision except in the most extreme circumstances. "I am unalterably opposed to depriving any segment of the international union of its autonomous state," he declared. "Fairness and justice are preferred to perfection."[2]

Other significant constitutional changes made as a result of Landrum-Griffin related to the selection of delegates to general conventions, the terms of local officers, and internal-appeals procedures. Prior to 1960, the constitution was silent on the selection of convention delegates. Some locals elected their delegates, and the delegates were appointed by the business manager or the local executive board in others. Landrum-Griffin required the election of convention delegates by secret ballot. The act also mandated a reduction in the terms of local officers from four years to three. Finally, prior to 1960, members found guilty of union violations were not able to appeal to the courts until all internal-appeals procedures had been exhausted, regardless of how long such procedures took. Landrum-Griffin limited that requirement to those portions of the appeals procedures that could be completed within four months.

Union financial practices had also been Landrum-Griffin targets, but the IUOE always had been markedly conservative in the handling of its funds. There had been occasional local peccadillos, but the International had restricted its investments to federal government securities, preferring low return to any risk of loss or misuse. Not until 1972 did the General Executive Board approve investment of a part of the union's treasury in top-grade corporate bonds, thereby improving its interest rate by an additional two percent—a tripling of actual return.

All in all, although the constitutional changes made necessary by Landrum-Griffin were numerous, their long-term impact on the union's governance was minor—a mere blip in the overall history of the union.

Right-to-Work Laws

To achieve their classic objective of taking wages out of competition, craft unions had traditionally sought to persuade employers to hire none but union members, a practice known as the "closed shop." This was especially true in industries such as construction, where the relationship between the employee and the employer was casual and temporary. Workers were attached permanently to their trades and the industry, but they moved frequently among employers. In more stable employment situations, including those existing for most stationary engineers, a union could organize the employees one by one and establish a continuing bargaining unit. In an industry of casual employment, such "bottom-up" organizing would require continual pursuit of a rapidly changing body of new employees. Stability in labor-management relations could be accomplished only by "top-down" organizing— persuading the employer to hire only union members.

However, the Taft-Hartley Act of 1947 had outlawed the closed shop, allowing only the compromise "union shop" approach in which the employer hired anyone, regardless of union membership. But if the majority of employees voted for union representation and the union could persuade the employer to agree, a union-shop clause could be introduced into the labor agreement requiring the newly hired worker to join the union within thirty days. But thirty days was forever in many construction industry situations. Job tenure was often too short to make the thirty-day requirement practical. After the courts had struggled for twelve years with the issue, the Landrum-Griffin Act of 1959 provided a workable compromise. A building trades union and a construction employer—or more realistically, a multiemployer association of contractors—could negotiate an enforceable agreement to require union membership after the seventh day of employment. Included also was the alternative for a successful bidder to enter a prehire agreement with a union to obtain all of the needed workers through the union hiring hall but with the union required to refer union and nonunion workers without discrimination. Once it was established that the majority of the employees engaged in the project were union members or preferred union representation, the union could be certified. But that did not change the referral requirement.

However, Taft-Hartley went even further than the closed shop abolition in weakening union security. The standard legal rule is that federal law preempts state law in areas of legitimate federal power. But in this case, Congress authorized the states to pass more restrictive union security laws. The result was the so-called right-to-work movement, in which state legislatures forbade the union shop as well as the closed shop. Of course, no "right to work" was guaranteed, only the right to avoid union membership.

Prior to 1960, nineteen states had enacted right-to-work laws, only one of which, Nevada, had a strong union sector.[3] But in the late 1950s, four heavily unionized states—California, Washington, Ohio, and Colorado—as well as Idaho and Kansas were considering the passage of right-to-work laws through either referenda or state legislation. The Operating Engineers, together with other trade unions, launched a major drive to defeat their enactment in the six states. The union forces prevailed in all but one of the six states; only in Kansas did the right-to-work forces win. Commented President Delaney:

> Destroying a building is not the wisest way of plugging a leaking pipe. Removal of our freedom does not . . . justify the extreme measures encompassed by "right-to-work" laws and similar legislation. Those who are sponsoring "right-to-work" laws . . . are doing a disservice to themselves, management and the country as a whole.[4]

Though the issue has been a subject of legislation or referenda in several other states since, only one of them, Louisiana, has enacted a right-to-work law.

Davis-Bacon

The Davis-Bacon prevailing-wage act for construction was introduced during the early years of the Great Depression to protect local wage rates against the incursions of outside contractors. In 1927, Congressman Bacon of New York became disturbed when a southern contractor was the low bidder on a New York veterans' hospital. The contractor brought in a large number of nonunion employees, housed them on the site behind guards, and paid them at a rate far below that which prevailed in the area. When the job was finished, the workers were left to shift for themselves. The Davis-Bacon Act, passed in 1931, requires that workers in specific job categories employed by contractors performing federal public works costing $2,000 or more must receive wages and fringe benefits no less than those predetermined by the Department of Labor as "prevailing" for similar types of construction in a particular locality. The concept was sufficiently attractive that forty-two states and the District of Columbia soon passed "little Davis-Bacon Acts" governing state-funded construction projects. Nine of the state acts have subsequently been repealed, and one has been declared unconstitutional (Arizona). Over the years, approximately one-fifth of construction activity has been performed under prevailing-wage laws, but that one-fifth includes most heavy and highway construction so important to the Operating Engineers.

However, as the years have passed, the primary objective of the construction prevailing-wage law has been turned on its head. Whereas the initial intent had been to protect local contractors and their employees from outside invasion, thus minimizing the geographical scope of competition for government-financed construction projects, the operative result became the opposite. The primary effect of Davis-Bacon was the announcement of wage rates below which no competing contractor would be allowed to pay. Therefore, a contractor based far from the site of planned publicly financed construction could bid using the declared prevailing rates to estimate labor costs, secure in the fact that no local contractor familiar with the local labor supply would be able to obtain labor for less. This was a dual advantage for the construction unions. Not only was there a strong likelihood that the union scale might be determined as prevailing, as noted below, but if the outside contractor was a successful bidder, where was he more likely to be assured of access to a skilled local labor supply than through the local union referral mechanism? Hence, unless the successful outside bidder was prepared to bring his work force with him, reliance on the union hiring hall was the most likely result.

Until 1983, the regulations adopted by Frances Perkins, Roosevelt's secretary of labor and the nation's first woman cabinet member, were used by the Department of Labor in determining prevailing wages. Perkins adopted the survey as the method for identifying wage rates, using the county as the geographic boundary within which to identify wage rates paid to various classes of workers. She then adopted a three-step procedure for identifying the prevailing rates: (1) If of the rates identified by the survey, any one rate was paid to the majority of workers, that rate was taken as prevailing; but (2) if there were no such rates, then any rate paid to at least 30 percent of the workers was adopted as prevailing; and (3) if there were no such rates, then the average of all such rates found in the survey was adopted. This method has been commonly called the 30-percent rule. In areas of substantial organization, the application of the "majority" and "average" standards have been rare; the 30-percent rule has been the standard most commonly used.

The construction unions prospered under the 30-percent rule. If there was a single rate (identical to the penny) paid to that many workers in a specific occupation, it was almost certain to be the union scale. Therefore, effective top-down organizing of associations of contractors in the heavy and highway construction fields almost ensured that the union wage would become the prevailing wage. The contractors, in turn, once they were organized, became allies of the unions in organizing others to eliminate their wage advantage.

Critics of Davis-Bacon maintained that the act had the effect of establishing collective bargaining rates as prevailing because the Department of Labor historically had used union contracts rather than actual surveys to establish prevailing wages. The fact that 40,000 to 70,000 wage predeterminations had to be made each year during the 1960s an era of little antiunion protest, made that practice, if it occurred, less than surprising. Lacking resources, the states were even more likely to rely on union rates in establishing prevailing wages. Union influence was adequate during the 1960s to defend and even add to the scope of prevailing wage laws. For instance, in 1959, the unions had protested 4,213 of the Department of Labor 's predeterminations, resulting in the modification of 3,012 in the direction favored by the union. But clouds were gathering, with a storm to arise twenty years later. Meanwhile, in 1964, one concerted attack on the administration of Davis-Bacon was defeated, and one extremely important victory was won.

A legislative proposal of that year by the U. S. Chamber of Commerce, the National Association of Manufacturers, and the Associated General Contractors of America would have subjected Davis-Bacon prevailing-wage predeterminations to judicial review. The building and construction trades unions foresaw chaos in the proposal that would render the Davis-Bacon Act inoperable. Each of more than 60,000 annual predeterminations issued by the Department of Labor could have been challenged in the federal courts, and the unions would have had to employ an army of lawyers and spend a prohibitive amount of money in fighting such actions. In the meantime, new determinations of prevailing wages in many areas of the country would have had to await judicial review—a lengthy process that would, in the last analysis, render the Davis-Bacon Act impotent. It would have become impossible to complete a determination in advance of bidding so that a nonlocal employer could know what rates would have to be paid. Only local contractors and those who intended to bring their work forces with them would be able to accurately estimate their labor costs. Actually, the proposal for judicial review was a classic piece of union-busting legislation. Not only would it have destroyed the administrative viability of Davis-Bacon, but it would also have struck deep into the pocketbooks of the construction-trades unions. At the same time, it would have once again narrowed the geographical scope of product market competition in the construction industry. The net result of these downward and upward pressures on construction costs would be difficult to predict.

Johnson's secretary of labor, W. Willard Wirtz, aware of the serious consequences of judicial review, established a Davis-Bacon Wage Appeals Board composed of three members recommended by organized labor, government, and contractor associations and appointed by the secretary of labor. Contractors could appeal what they believed were erroneous predeterminations to the Wage Appeals Board. However, according to Northrup, less than fifteen cases per year reached the board. The reason was that the appellant had to demonstrate that the original determinations were in error. To do so required a private survey of local wages, demanding substantial investigative resources. Since the appellant had no guarantee of winning a contract even if he won his case, few appeals were heard by the board.[5] However, private surveys would also be required under judicial review. The difference was that the Wage Appeals Board was an administrative adjunct of the

Davis-Bacon Act enforcement process, staffed by experts and able to move expeditiously, whereas judicial review had the effect of removing prevailing wage decisions from the Department of Labor to the courts, with consequent delay followed by generalist decision making. The antiunion forces proved to be more interested in the delay than in the review process and largely ignored the Wirtz compromise.

On the more positive side from the union point of view, on July 2, 1964, Public Law 88–349 was passed, which included the following as "wages":

> . . . the rate of costs to the contractor or subcontractor which may be reasonably anticipated in providing benefits . . . for medical or hospital care, pensions on retirement or death, compensation for injuries or illness . . . , unemployment insurance, disability and sickness insurance, or accident insurance, for vacation and holiday pay, for defraying costs of apprenticeship or other similar programs, or for other bona fide fringe benefits . . . [6]

This was an important victory for the construction trades unions and union contractors. Whenever the unions were successful in extending their collective bargaining agreements to enough employers for their wages and fringes to be declared prevailing, nonunion contractors could no longer gain a bidding advantage by paying the union scale but avoiding the payment of benefits. Of course, where unionization was not widespread and the prevailing rates involved no or fewer fringe benefits, the union employer was still at a disadvantage in bidding on federally supported construction projects.

Taft-Hartley

As already mentioned, the Taft-Hartley Act outlawed the closed shop but permitted the thirty-day union shop (later amended to a seven-day union shop for construction). Under the closed shop, which prevailed in the construction industry prior to the 1947 Taft-Hartley Act, the union hiring hall was the major source of labor for most of the skilled crafts. The workers were attached to their crafts and, in organized segments of the industry, to their unions. They moved fluidly among employers as jobs became available. The union shop election procedures under Taft-Hartley presumed, as they had under the Wagner Act, a continuous employment relationship in which a certification election could be held among employees who were going to continue with the same employer. But in the construction industry, wages, benefits, and conditions of work, as well as the means of gaining access to the available work force, were all agreed upon in advance of hiring. Under Taft-Hartley, could an employer negotiate with a union for employees not yet hired? Could a union-operated hiring hall be used without denying to employees their right to choose their own collective bargaining representative? Could and should a union hiring hall be expected to refer those who had not chosen to be members?

Brown-Olds/Mountain Pacific

The Operating Engineers were among the first victims of the Taft-Hartley Act's union security provisions.[7] The Guy F. Atkinson Company, a contractor on the Hanford (Washington) atomic energy installation, signed a closed shop contract with fifteen building trades unions in 1947 after the law was passed but before it became effective. Later, a member of the machinists' union applied for work and was referred to the Operating Engineers local, which issued him a work permit. In February 1948, he was discharged at the union's request "for failure to keep himself in good financial standing with the union," the only responsibility of membership enforceable under the law. The NLRB awarded the machinist back pay and ordered the company to cease recognizing the Operating Engineers as the representative of any of its employees until the union had been certified by the board.

In the 1956 Brown-Olds case, the Board required a plumbers' union and an employer to reimburse employees covered by an illegal hiring agreement for all fees, dues, and other assessments that they had paid into the union within the prior six months.[8] Then, because of the drastic nature of the decision, a moratorium was decreed until November 1, 1958, to give the unions an opportunity to bring their agreements and practices into compliance.

Finally, in 1958, the board issued its Mountain Pacific decision that found the language of a hiring clause violative, apart from evidence of discrimination to encourage union membership, because it made the union involved the sole agency for recruitment and referral of employees.[9] The board made it plain that the union hiring hall was not under attack, but the possibility of its use to encourage membership was, in effect, a violation of the law. Therefore, the Board laid down guidelines that had to be followed for an agreement to be considered non-discriminatory: (1) Selection of the applicants for referral to jobs shall be on a nondiscriminatory basis and shall not be based on or in any way affected by union membership, bylaws, rules, regulations, constitutional provisions, or any other aspect or obligation of union membership, politics, or requirements; (2) The employer retains the right to reject any job applicant referred by the union; (3) The parties to the agreement shall post, in places where notices to employees and applicants for employment are customarily posted, all provisions relating to the functioning of the hiring arrangement, including the safeguards deemed essential in the legality of an exclusive hiring agreement.[10]

All of this had occurred and was treated in the earlier history, but not the final conclusion. The Brown-Olds and Mountain Pacific decisions created a good deal of work for IUOE General Counsel J. Albert Woll and House Counsel Gerard Treanor. Local unions constantly sought the services of counsel in drafting hiring-hall clauses to meet the standards demanded by the NLRB in the Mountain Pacific decision and the Brown-Olds remedy. In general, years of employment in the industry in the geographical area (the equivalent of seniority with a specific employer in more stable employment situations), rather than union membership, became the criterion for priority among applicants. If the area had been well organized in the past, the change had little practical impact. But, given the continuing hassle, it was with noticeable pleasure that Woll announced to the membership in 1961 that the Mountain Pacific case had been reversed by the Supreme Court and that the Brown-Olds remedy had been overturned. The Supreme Court found that the NLRB had exceeded its authority in the Mountain Pacific case and termed the Brown-Olds remedy punitive rather than remedial. Referral arrangements and hiring halls still had to be conducted on a nondiscriminatory basis, but the NLRB could no longer base its finding of a violation on the absence of one or more of the three specified guidelines.

Occupational Safety and Health

Construction has the highest injury rate of any of the nation's industries (14.6 injuries per hundred workers in 1988).[11] Yet IUOE hoisting and portable locals had not placed a high priority on safety issues until the advent of Hunter Wharton to national office. Stationary engineers, on the other hand, had long been strong advocates of safety, not only because of the dire consequences of a boiler explosion, but because safety was a frequent justification for the licensing of stationary engineers, which, in turn, had the effect of limiting the labor supply and assisting organization. The union's activities in the safety and health field can be usefully divided into two periods: pre-Occupational Safety and Health Act (OSHA) and post-OSHA.

Pre-OSHA

During the pre-OSHA period, the union developed its own internal safety and health programs and interacted with the AFL-CIO, National Safety Council, and other concerned organizations. In 1959, the AFL-CIO called a National Safety Conference (NSC) and established a permanent safety committee. At about the same time, the National Safety Council established a Labor Division, and IUOE representatives served on both the labor and construction sections of the NSC.

Safety received its biggest boost during the administration of Hunter Wharton. He created a Department of Safety with responsibility for the development, coordination, implementation, promotion, guidance, and review of all safety activities. Among the Safety Department's assignments were development of safety standards, preferably jointly with employer organizations, coordinating local union safety efforts and acting as a clearinghouse for safety developments. Each local was urged to establish a Safety and Health Committee with thirteen specific functions, and Regional Safety Committees were established to develop safety reports for use in developing agendas for regional safety conferences.

The IUOE was awarded a Public Service Award by the NSC for its safety campaign carried out in the union's journal, *The Operating Engineer*, in 1961. In the following year, the union won the council's Exceptional Service to Safety award. Later in the same year, Wharton was appointed chairman of the Building and Construction Trades safety committee. In 1965, Wharton received a plaque at the Labor Conference of the National Safety Council for his distinguished service. Robert Farrell, a member of Chicago Local 150, received an individual award, and honors also went to Local 150 and

Locals 143 and 143-D. In a separate presentation, the Operating Engineers were honored for their safety record in the construction of the Barclay Dam at Paducah, Kentucky.

Prior to 1966, management refused to bargain on safety issues on the grounds that safety was a management responsibility. In 1966, however, in a case involving the International Brotherhood of Electrical Workers (IBEW) and the Gulf Power Company, the NLRB ruled that the company's refusal to discuss with the union a contract proposal providing for a joint negotiation of safety rules was a violation of the bargaining requirements of the National Labor Relations Act.[12] The board found that the term "safety" was covered under the phrase "other conditions of employment" contained in the act. Thereafter, collective bargaining on safety issues became routine in the unionized sector of the industry.

The Operating Engineers union has been active in promoting licensing regulations throughout its history. However, management and manufacturer opposition to licensing laws has been generally effective, particularly because of the absence of comprehensive statistical data regarding industrial accidents and the natural disinclination of anyone involved in such accidents to provide information, especially when there is injury or loss of life. Insurance companies (which could benefit from licensing laws) are reluctant to release information because of their client relationship with management and manufacturers, and boiler inspectors are wary of the consequences if they speak too freely of specific accidents.

Al Lake cites the following as an example of such industrial stonewalling:

> In October 1974, a Sunday School in Merit, Ohio, was severely damaged by a boiler explosion which caused the death of six children and substantial injury to eight others. . . . The governor of Ohio formed a task force to study that disaster and I was on the task force. . . . There was so much pressure brought to bear against the task force! For example, the state fire marshall went to the scene and took some pictures. We could not find the pictures. We tried to subpoena them, but we could not get them. The state representative from Merit, Ohio, refused to testify before the task force. There was pressure coming down from every point—you know, "we don't need any more regulations, we don't need qualified operators." We tried to get a law passed, but we were not successful, not even after a disaster that killed or injured 15 children.[13]

The IUOE claimed in 1964 that, despite the arguments of manufacturers that modern equipment with its automatic controls and safety devices is safe enough to be operated by untrained personnel, over 3,000 boiler explosions occur per year, not counting refrigeration, compressed air, and other gas system accidents. The International, therefore, asked local unions to report all such accidents and established liaison with the National Board of Boiler and Pressure Vessel Inspectors. Nevertheless, only five states, some counties and about fifty cities require some sort of operator certification.

Post-OSHA

The trade union push for occupational safety and health legislation reached its zenith during the period 1968–72. In 1969, President Nixon signed the Construction Safety Act, which covered workers employed on federal or federally assisted construction projects and for which Wharton had lobbied intensively. The passage of this act provided the momentum for broader safety coverage. The Construction Safety Act was joined by the Mine Safety and Health Act during the same year, covering the next most accident-prone industry. Building on those bases, the building-trades (Wharton again playing a major role) and mining unions were joined by other unions in a drive to provide comprehensive occupational safety and health coverage to the majority of men and women working in America in virtually all industries.

The Occupational Safety and Health Act was passed in 1970 with widespread bipartisan support and the praise of the White House. Key features of the law provided for establishment of safety standards, a system of inspection priorities with employee representatives accompanying the inspectors, establishment of a National Institute of Occupational Safety and Health (NIOSH) to conduct hazard evaluation surveys, and an Occupational Safety and Health Review Committee before which both employers and employees can contest actions of the Department of Labor.

The Department of Labor was given the responsibility for the development and adoption of safety standards and regulations as well as their enforcement. Penalties for violations of the act could involve fines of up to $20,000 and a year in jail for a single violation. Alan Burch, the IUOE's Director of the Department of Safety and Accident Prevention, was appointed to the three-person OSHA Review Commission. In addition, Operating Engineers' representatives served on a number of safety standards committees and worked with OSHA's Office of Standards Development and its mine safety counterpart on their internally developed standards. Operating Engineers' personnel also served on subcommittees of the American Society of Mechanical Engineers Boiler and Pressure Vessel Code, as well as on technical committees of the Society of Automotive Engineers, which promulgate safety standards for the operation of mobile hoisting equipment.

In 1974, the Building and Construction Trades Department Safety Committee, with Hunter Wharton as chairman, obtained an OSHA contract to train 100 building tradesmen in construction safety. The contract was for $225,000 and provided for four weeks of residential training and sixteen weeks of field assignments. Nine operating engineers completed the training. A new contract was negotiated in 1975, this time for joint training of 100 building trades workers and 100 management safety representatives. The classes were subdivided into groups of twenty with equal labor and management members in each class. In 1975, the joint labor-management program was funded by OSHA in the amount of $1.5 million for five additional years.

Perhaps the most important aspect of the IUOE's safety program was the protection of individual members on the job. Billy Hurt, for example, believes that he owes his life to the union's safety program.[14] But Hurt also points out that the union protected him from overly strict safety regulations as well. Hurt suffered the loss of an eye when helping a fellow worker cut cable. He was a young man when it happened, at the top of his career, and he was afraid that the injury would end his career. However, tests proved that the loss of an eye did not affect his ability to operate machinery. He tells the story of J. C. Turner, then business manager of Hurt's local, later IUOE general president, who argued against a proposed Department of Labor regulation that would prohibit men like Hurt from operating cranes. Turner, who suffered an eye injury himself while boxing at Catholic University, took an OSHA representative out to a project where four cranes were in operation, one operated by Hurt. "Which one," Turner asked the official, "is being operated by a one-eyed man?" The respondent was not able to answer the question; thus Billy Hurt went on operating cranes until he retired in January 1993.[15]

However, Hurt would agree that the union's willingness to back up its members on safety issues, to intercede with employers if necessary, and to make the members themselves safety conscious were important contributions to the elimination of hazardous conditions on the job.

The Civil Rights Challenge

The experience of minorities in the American labor movement, especially black Americans, has been subject to the same racism that tainted most other American institutions. As late as the 1950s, blacks were either barred from many craft unions or were segregated in black-only locals. Segregationist policies began to crumble with the rise of industrial unionism in the 1930s, but as late as 1962, when President Kennedy issued Executive Order 10988 recognizing federal unions, it was still necessary to specify that recognition be extended only to unions "which are free of practices denying membership because of race, creed, color, or national origin. . . ."[16]

During the 1960s most of the construction trades, including the Operating Engineers, were challenged by civil rights groups because of the low number of minorities enrolled in union apprenticeship programs and as members in the construction trades unions. There are several reason why the building trades were singled out for attention by civil rights groups. First and perhaps most important, wages and fringe benefits in construction were among the highest of all blue-collar occupations. Second, entrance into the building trades did not require a great deal of education. (Most crafts workers had no more than a high school education, and many had less.) Third, with the exception of the "trowel trades" in some areas of the country (bricklayers, plasterers, cement finishers, etc.), the building-trades unions were primarily white, a prima facie indication of racial discrimination.

But the causation was not that simple. The building trades unions were organized by men of the white working class, and because of the casual nature of the construction labor force as well as seasonal fluctuations in employment, entrance into the unions often was determined by family ties and/or personal connections with local union officers, members, and contractors. Thus minorities (as well as white males without "connections") were excluded from building trades unions, not by overt discrimination alone, but because they were, so to speak, "out of the loop." That is not to say that discrimination or negative racial attitudes did not exist within the unions, but the exclusion of minorities and many whites was based more on what might be termed a white, working-class "old boy network" than by racial discrimination. In some areas of the country, notably the South, whites and blacks were in open competition with each other; that did lead to discrimination in some instances, but in most areas of the country, minority membership was not an issue—i.e., there was no policy barring minorities, but few minorities entered the union because they were outside the traditional entry route.

The major reason why civil rights groups focused on the building trades was because the educational requirements were low and the wages were high, not because there was more discrimination in construction than in most other segments of the American economy. Minorities were underrepresented in the retail and banking industries, for example, but there was no concerted effort to open up these industries to minorities, primarily because of the high turnover, low-wage characteristics of most entry-level retail and banking jobs. And those academicians who decried the so-called racism of "redneck construction workers" had only to look around their own campuses to realize that minorities were vastly underrepresented in the halls of academe, where, of course, because of the educational requirements, the white male academic elite faced little competition from minorities—or women. The blue-collar craft unions provided a more "appropriate" or "convenient" target. But those expectations of quick success were based on a lack of understanding of the access routes into unionized construction employment. As craft unions, entry was possible only after obtaining craft skills or through programs designed to teach those skills. For operating engineers, with a declining use of oilers as an informal route to acquiring skill, it was necessary to acquire a journeyman/woman level of skill before applying for union membership, to become employed by a contractor subsequently organized by the union, or to apply and be admitted to an apprenticeship program—the last an avenue never open to more than a few thousand of all races each year in the entire international union.

The question of a color bar in the membership requirement of the operating engineers union arose at only one convention. The issue was debated in 1910, when a southern local advocated a "whites only" clause. The clause was rejected, not for altruistic reasons but on pragmatic grounds. "The union was then essentially a stationary engineer's organization with no control of the labor supply. The Negro engineers could not be excluded from employment. Therefore, it was considered preferable to include them in order to control them. . . ."[17] The organization rejected the color bar but also refrained from articulating any policy regarding racial issues until 1961. The matter was left in the hands of local unions, and as the hoisting and portable branch of the union grew, minority membership declined and the operating engineers became a ripe target for civil rights activists.

In May 1961, a few years before the issue grew hot, the IUOE published a "Statement on Civil Rights":

> Since it was chartered in 1896, the International Union of Operating Engineers has been dedicated to the proposition that all men are created equal. Our history clearly demonstrates that color, religion or national origin has never been a bar to the full enjoyment of membership. At the present time we number among our ranks many representatives of minority racial and religious groups.
>
> While we take justifiable pride in the advances made to improve the wages, hours and working conditions of our membership, we have never lost sight of our consistent policy to aid and encourage all workers within our craft, without regard to race, creed, color, national origin, or ancestry, to share equally, in the full benefits of membership in this International Union. Deviation from this policy, no matter how slight, has always been opposed by this International Union.
>
> The International Union of Operating Engineers will affirmatively cooperate, within the limits of its local and contractual authority, in the implementation of the policy and provisions of the Executive Order establishing the President's Committee on Equal Employment Opportunity, issued by the President of the United States on March 6, 1961.[18]

As noted, the IUOE supported the successful campaigns to obtain passage of the Civil Rights Act of 1964 and the Voting Rights Act of 1966, as well as the Manpower Development and Training Act of 1962, the Vocational Education Act of 1963, and the Economic Opportunity Act of 1964. Nevertheless, the building and construction industry unions, including the Operating Engineers, were confronted with charges of discrimination. In 1968, the Department of Labor's Office of Federal Contract Compliance began withholding funds from federally financed projects in several locations and imposing a quota system of hiring minority workers in the skilled trades.[19] The latter was applied to projects in counties surrounding Philadelphia and came to be known as the Philadelphia Plan.

The Operating Engineers opposing the imposition of quotas, considered training to be the key to solving the minority access problem. General President Wharton, in his report to the 29th convention, said:

> Aside from our belief that any system requiring racial quotas is wrong, neither the old Philadelphia Plan nor the so-called "new" Philadelphia Plan included any provisions for training new minority workers. Without the training provisions, the Philadelphia Plan was doomed to failure and now, after three years of effort, controversy, litigation, and extraordinary expense, those persons who supported the Philadelphia Plan realize there are no shortcuts to equal employment. The hard fact remains that there has been no significant increase in minority membership in the local unions covered by the Philadelphia Plan. Simplistic formulas are no substitute for trained mechanics and an equitable dispatching system.[20]

In August 1968, Wharton appointed James H. Gary to the International staff with the primary responsibility of assisting the International union and its locals in resolving civil rights problems. Gary, together with the representatives of other construction trades unions, entered into meetings with the Office of Federal Contract Compliance to discuss alternative ways (other than quotas) of achieving compliance. The result was the development of an areawide Affirmative Action Plan for IUOE locals having jurisdiction in Pennsylvania and Ohio. The plan, which called for a substantial increase in the number of minority apprentices, resulted in the exemption of IUOE Local 542 (Philadelphia) from the Philadelphia Plan, thus providing federal recognition of Wharton's idea of increasing minority representation through training rather than quotas.

Additional affirmative-action plans, coupled with specially designed training programs, became operational in Pittsburgh; Los Angeles; New York City; Indianapolis; Atlanta; the states of Ohio and Michigan; Chicago; Birmingham; and Hamden, Connecticut. On the other hand, suits were filed against IUOE locals in California, Oregon, Pennsylvania, Ohio, Kentucky, and other areas. The U. S. Justice Department obtained a consent decree from Local 3 (Northern California, Utah, Hawaii, and part of Nevada) that ended the alleged practices of assigning blacks and Mexican-Americans to the least desirable jobs, failing to give them credit for past experience, and limiting their entrance into apprenticeship programs. A similar consent decree was obtained from Local 18 (Ohio and parts of Kentucky) and the Ohio Operating Engineers Apprenticeship Fund.

But all of that was focused on racial and ethnic minorities. Women as construction workers and even as stationary engineers were not an issue until after the abolition of sex discrimination had been written into the Civil Rights Act, Title VII, as a floor amendment by its enemies; they hoped to defeat the bill or, failing that, to make it unenforceable. However, they underestimated the tenaciousness of both its beneficiaries and its early enforcers.

The Operating Engineers responded to the consent decrees with an apprenticeship outreach effort that was successful in enrolling both minorities and women in local apprenticeship programs. Since the late 1960s minorities have composed between 30 percent and 36 percent of all IUOE registered apprentices; the figure for women has been between 10 percent and 17 percent.[21] But unfortunately, these groups are less likely than the majority to have the resources and family support to carry them over the substantial periods of unemployment that often generate apprenticeship dropouts.

Women face additional challenges in heavy and highway construction. Jeanita Martin, whom we met in chapter 4, realizes that her situation would be impossible if she could not leave her two children, aged six and three, with her parents on the Navajo Reservation during her eight or nine months of ten-hour days and motel living each year, along with occasional visits to their remarried carpenter father. She cites one woman operator who meets child-care responsibilities through year-round employment in a copper mine within commuting distance of home while her husband is away during the week as a construction foreman; another who, with her operating engineer husband and their children, follows the jobs in a trailer but who says others of her acquaintance are either childless, have raised their children, or limit themselves to nearby building and construction jobs.

The IUOE's Job Corps and National Training Programs have resulted in additional minority and women entrants into the union. The Tennessee-Tombigbee and Navajo Projects described in chapters 3 and 4 were directed toward the same purpose. Today, minorities compose approximately 40 percent of the Baltimore and Washington, D.C., locals.

William Harris of Local 77 is typical of this membership. Born and reared in Charleston, South Carolina, and having moved to Washington, D.C., with his family as a young man in 1959, he held only unskilled and semiskilled jobs until he was drafted into the army in 1966. He was assigned there to the combat engineers and taught to operate heavy equipment. Upon returning to civilian life in 1968, he went to work for the National Park Service. However, he soon became aware that his earnings were below those of construction equipment operators, yet he experienced the same seasonal layoffs. He first found employment with a nonunion contractor, but he became an IUOE member when that contractor was organized by Local 77. That was just in time to be employed "off and on for the next twenty years" on construction of the Washington, D.C., Metro system, along with major road jobs and operating a power crane on the repair of the Washington Cathedral.

Harris describes unionized construction employment as "the best part-time work a man can have. You work eight or nine months a year, and the pay and benefits are good." Along the way, he upgraded his skills through union-management–sponsored training programs. But for those who try to enter the industry through apprenticeship, the sporadic nature of the employment contributes to a high dropout rate. If it were not for the union scale and benefits, Harris reports that, in all probability, he would have left construction employment years ago. He has seen the Washington, D.C., construction industry go from 70 percent union-employed to 30 percent, but at fifty-four years of age, he still considers the future to be bright. "Our contractors are bidding on all of the big jobs coming up, and the concessions granted by the building trades unions have kept them competitive. We'll do all right."

The Baltimore/Washington minority membership ratios are similar for many other big-city locals throughout the country, though statistics for the union as a whole have never been collected. Independent surveys indicate that the percentages of minorities and women in IUOE locals throughout the country are increasing. The Federal Highway Commission, for example, collects detailed data on employment by race and sex on all highway projects for which federal funds are allocated. Operating engineers are the major craftspersons on highway construction, accounting for 53.4 percent of total federal highway employment in 1990. Table 5.1 shows these data for the years 1981 and 1990 for seven occupations and on-the-job training (OJT) trainees. The percentage of minority operating engineers was 20 percent in 1990, an increase of 5 percent since 1981.

Table 5.1

Minorities Employed on Federal-Aid Highway Projects, 1974–1990

Craft	Number Employed 1981	% Minority	Number Employed 1990	% Minority	Difference 1981–90
Operating Engineers	32,612	15	32,922	20	+5%
Ironworkers	3,569	23	4,649	26	+3%
Carpenters	9,355	19	10,238	23	+4%
Masons	4,374	52	5,299	49	–3%
Electricians	1,342	14	2,210	14	—
Plumbers	341	31	383	43	+11%
Painters	509	16	1,549	17	+1%
Apprentices	1,931	38	2,180	22	–16%
On-the-Job Trainees	2,824	54	2,275	56	+2%
Total	56,857	22	61,705	25	+3%

An additional data source is the United States Equal Employment Opportunity Commission, which requires union referral bargaining units of 100 or more to report membership by race, sex, and occupational group. Table 5.2 shows minority and female employment for four construction crafts and laborers for 1988, the latest date for which the data are available.

Close to 13 percent of the members of the forty-nine Operating Engineer locals were minorities, and 3.5 percent were women. (Why more locals were not included is not apparent.) Three factors indicate that the civil rights problems experienced by the Operating Engineers have been minimized. The first is that challenges by civil rights groups have all but disappeared since the 1960s. Second, the entry route into the union has been opened by actively recruiting minority and women apprentices. Finally, the increase in public sector workers in the IUOE has resulted in a corresponding increase in minority and female entrants into the union. In other words, the "loop" that was previously closed to minorities and women has been substantially widened.

On July 1, 1977, General President Turner created a Department of Civil Rights and appointed Louis J. Brady of Local 3, San Francisco, as director. Later, under the presidency of Frank Hanley, the Department of Civil Rights was combined with the Office of Organization, thus targeting minorities as a priority for the union's organizing activities. Further increases in minority and female membership depend to a great extent on whether the union itself continues to grow. If growth contin-

Table 5.2

Membership in Four Construction Crafts and Laborers by Race and Sex, 1988

Craft	Number of Unions	All Members	% Black	% Hispanic	% Other	% Female	% Min
Operating Engineers	49	131,985	5.2	3.6	4.1	3.5	12.9
Electricians	272	153,531	4.3	4.2	1.7	1.9	10.2
Carpenters	279	160,167	4.6	7.7	1.3	1.2	13.6
Plumbers	266	162,539	3.1	3.5	1.4	0.9	8.0
Laborers	275	172,457	20.3	16.2	1.2	3.5	37.7

Source: Membership in Referral Unions, by International and by Race/Ethnic Group/Sex 1988, Nationwide Summary (EEO–3)

ues during the remainder of the twentieth century, it is virtually certain that the percentages of minority and female membership will also grow. If not, the very fact that the older members are white and predominately male will, by itself, generate some inevitable proportional change.

A Score Card

All in all, the Operating Engineers won some notable victories in the fields of public policy and legislation during the period 1960–75. Among the most important were the extension of fringe benefits as wages under Davis-Bacon and the passage of OSHA, both of which would come under intense attack during the Reagan-Bush years. The building trades were also successful in reversing the onerous Brown-Olds and Mountain Pacific decisions and in helping to defeat right-to-work law initiatives throughout the country. Finally, the union was able to put its house in order under Landrum-Griffin and was a significant force in the movement to improve conditions for low-wage workers, the unemployed, and the elderly.

But clouds were gathering on the horizon during the mid-1970s. Poor economic conditions, a growing open shop movement, and, beginning in 1981, a twelve-year period of conservative national leadership would once again put the IUOE and its sister unions on the defensive and eventually call for a union counterattack. The conditions that brought about the open shop incursion and the union's response are the primary subjects of Part II.

PART II

CHALLENGE AND RESPONSE, 1976-1993

Chapter 6

A TIME OF TROUBLES

When Hunter Wharton stepped down from the presidency in 1976, he was succeeded by General Secretary-Treasurer J. C. Turner, former business manager of Local 77, Washington, D.C., and a leading figure in local and national Democratic Party circles. Turner was the subject of a cover story in the February 26, 1976, issue of the *Engineering News-Record.* Noting that the IUOE was one of only a handful of unions that had increased its membership by over 100,000 between 1962 and 1972, Turner predicted that the union's membership would increase by another 100,000 in six years, spurred by an increase in the stationary segment of the union—a prediction that was destined to fall far short of the mark.[1] The open shop, aided by economic recession, was making its move.

Proof that the open shop had taken root was evidenced by a spate of articles that appeared in the *Engineering News-Record* in the mid-1970s. The first was the announcement of the formation of a National Construction Industry Council by the top elected officers and staff of thirty-one major trade and professional organizations. "Representatives of labor organizations," the article read, "were not invited to participate, a decision two council members called the most constructive step the council has taken."[2] That was followed by an article about the president of the Associated Builders and Contractors (ABC), Philip Abrams, who gloated that "the current economic slump is selling the concept of open shop construction to users and contractors throughout the country."[3] An article about a Tennessee "merit shop" contractor appeared in August 1975 and, in September of the following year, the magazine featured a story about an open shop contractor who "crosses picket lines for profit." According to the article, the contractor "used a special bus with iron grating on the windows and puncture-proof tires to drive open shop workers through lines of angry union pickets."[4] No such articles had ever appeared in the construction industry's trade journal before. They were a sign of the growing influence of open shop contractors.

"The answer," Turner said, "is a stepped-up emphasis on organization." A former organizer with forty-two years of union experience, Turner believed strongly that unions "have too much to offer and the advantages of union membership are too valuable for thinking workers to ignore. Those workers outside our organization are the losers."[5] Turner hoped to use his considerable skills and experience as a lobbyist to enhance the union's position. He was a delegate from the District of Columbia and national committeeman at Democratic national conventions in the 1950s and 1960s, and a member of the Washington, D.C., City Council in 1967. His official union lobbying efforts began in 1972, when he was named assistant to the general president for legislation. Later, as the union's general secretary-treasurer, he headed the Engineers' Political Education Committee, which channels voluntary membership contributions into federal election campaigns. But Turner assumed these assignments at a time when the political powers of organized labor were already waning, consequent to its representation of a rapidly declining proportion of the nation's labor force. The union movement's priority legislative objectives were lost by presidential veto under Gerald Ford and by senatorial filibuster during the Carter administration. Thereafter, Turner's considerable lobbying skills would be neutralized by the election of Ronald Reagan in 1980 and a subsequent twelve-year period of conservative administration at the national level.

However, the major setback for the IUOE was the economic consequences of the internal politics of the Ford administration, which ended the promise of wage stabilization. Following Ford's veto of the Economic Rights of Labor legislation and John Dunlop's resignation as secretary of labor, construction labor costs rose until there were incentives and opportunities for a successful open shop incursion into the organized sectors of the construction industry that caused substantial membership declines in the 1970s and 1980s. Between 1975 and 1988, the union suffered a loss of 54,108 members. However, Turner was right about the direction for the stationary engineers; during that same period, stationary membership increased from slightly over 90,000 to close to 100,000.

The Open Shop Movement

There were three essential ingredients for a successful open shop movement: (1) competent contracting organizations willing or anxious to work outside the collective bargaining structure; (2) cost relationships that allowed insurgent contractors to underbid; and (3) the availability of a skilled nonunion work force to enable them to get the work done. A revolt by the purchasers of construction services provided motivation for the first; the building and construction trades themselves had created the second as a consequence of their short-term bargaining successes; and deep economic recessions in the mid-1970s and early 1980s, accompanied by a two-decade slack economy after 1972, provided the final ingredient.

Concentrating on the labor market alone, a successful building trades union had only to be able to provide upon request workers as competent as any available and to guarantee that no competing bidder could obtain equally productive workers at lower wages. In bidding for work, the contractor/employer had little reason for concern about the level of labor costs, as long as the prospective labor costs of competing bidders were not lower. In general, the larger and more mobile the contractor, the greater the advantage of using union referral systems as sources of skilled labor. Only small and localized contractors were likely to know personally and to be able to obtain competent people on short notice or to be able to provide steady work to permanent employees. Such local contractors were not serious competitors in bidding on the major jobs of interest to the larger contractors.

The product market was another matter. The political decision makers administering public construction might not be cost sensitive, but not so the private purchasers of construction services. After a decade of rising prices and accelerating energy costs, it was the latter who rebelled. Nationwide manufacturing and retailing firms which were frequent purchasers of construction services for the building of factories, oil refineries, office buildings, retail facilities, and warehouses joined together in 1969 to form the Construction Users Anti-Inflation Round-table under the initial chairmanship of Roger Blough of U.S.

Steel. That organization, in turn, merged with others in 1972 as the Business Roundtable, an association of the chief executive officers of some 200 major business firms.[6]

The construction users' group agreed to rely primarily on nonunion contractors and put pressure on other owners to select open shop contractors wherever possible, thus assisting in the organization of the Associated Builders and Contractors of America (ABC) as a trade association for such contractors. Faced with competitive pressures, construction-industry trade associations such as the Associated General Contractors, previously representing primarily union contractors, splintered and became mixed or primarily nonunion. Noting these developments in his 1980 report to the Operating Engineers' 31st Convention, Turner said:

> The growth in the influence of the Business Roundtable has added fuel to the fire created by inflation. The Roundtable is the organization of the largest industrial construction users in the country. These giants are using contractors and their associations as soldiers in the anti-union battle. The Roundtable has been the prime force in the open shop construction movement in this country.[7]

It was not that simple, of course. There were three potential areas of open shop competitive advantage. One was work rules. For instance, there were still some local unions within the IUOE that insisted on the manning of automatic equipment or on restricting the number of pumps and other small machines one individual could service. The open-shop contractor had a free hand in all such decisions. A second was skill organization. The building trades commitment was to craft organization with fully skilled personnel performing all operations, assisted by a few apprentices. The open shop contractor was free to subdivide tasks and to use a small number of skilled workers to direct larger numbers of unskilled workers, if the task lent itself to that deployment. Third, employee benefits such as health insurance, pensions, holidays, and other time off with pay could be avoided by the open shop contractor. Building agreements often called for double time for overtime, whereas the open shop contractor only had to meet the legal time-and-one-half requirement. Heavy and highway agreements had travel and show-up time provisions that could be avoided by nonunion contractors if alternative employment opportunities were not available.

Nonunion contractors could work four 10-hour days per week without overtime, a schedule forbidden by most collective-bargaining agreements.

The Obstacle and Challenge

Related to these areas of competitive advantage, there were six major reasons for the growth of the open shop movement: (1) union-won wage and fringe-benefit increases far above the inflation rate; (2) movement of construction to the suburbs and exurbs; (3) the reluctance of local unions to make appropriate concessions; (4) conservative administration of labor laws; (5) the admittance of open shop contractors into associations that once operated solely union; and (6) a switch in contractor policies regarding doublebreasting. These merit comment.

Wages and Fringe Benefits

Between 1970 and 1980, according to the Bureau of Labor Statistics, construction union wage rates rose from an average of $6.18 an hour to an average of $12.21 an hour. Although a near doubling in nominal terms, the increase did not even hold its own in real terms. However, on the average, the real wages of the majority of nonconstruction workers were falling even faster. Employer benefit payments advanced from 80 cents an hour to $2.83 an hour, an increase of more than 300 percent. According to the Construction Labor Research Council, the average increase in wages and fringe benefits from 1974 to 1984 was close to 125 percent, bringing the combined wage-fringe hourly rate to $19.35 per hour.[8] Moreover, despite the lowest wage increases in ten years in 1983, wages and fringe benefits in union construction had risen 47.5 percent in the five years prior to 1984.

Although these wages and benefit increases helped protect union workers from the ravages of inflation and were a proof that the unions were doing what they had been established to do, in the long run, IUOE locals were setting themselves up for a fall. The wage expansion was supportable only as long as there were no alternative sources of cheaper, adequately skilled labor. The purchasers of commercial and industrial construction services were becoming restless. A firm that had only one building or other facility constructed during its corporate life might not bridle at its costs, but nationwide department stores; oil, electrical, and other energy companies; and other frequent purchasers of construction services began exploring for alternatives.

As the interstate highway program neared completion, the Vietnam involvement ended, and the Organization of Petroleum Exporting Countries (OPEC) recognized and exercised its bargaining power, their opportunity came. OPEC flexed its muscles in the winter of 1972–73 with an embargo and the tripling of oil prices, simultaneous with the Vietnam withdrawal. The resulting 1974–75 recession was the deepest since the depression of the thirties. It was an economic era described as "stagflation." Normally, inflation occurred during periods of high demand for goods and services and, therefore, for labor. But now, inflation emerged from the pervasiveness of higher energy costs, while funds allocated to the purchase of foreign oil at swollen prices reduced the purchasing power available to buy U.S. goods and construction services. Recovery from the 1974–75 recession was never complete before another tripling in oil prices in 1979 sparked another downturn. Attempts to stifle the primarily energy-caused double-digit inflation rates of the 1970s brought an even deeper recession starting in 1981. Although the energy crisis sparked the construction of the Alaska pipeline, creating thousands of jobs for operating engineers, employment opportunities elsewhere were drastically reduced.

The downturn in construction demand left an abundance of skilled and experienced construction labor unemployed and vulnerable to employment offers from open shop contractors. Construction unemployment reached 20 percent in 1982 and fell only slightly to 18.4 percent in 1983, resulting in depression conditions for building trades workers. Private sector purchasers of construction services were able to demand and enforce departures from union scales and conditions. IUOE membership plunged, and many who retained union membership worked nonunion when no other employment was available, thereby shattering union bargaining power. This, combined with the continued reluctance of many local unions to welcome into membership all competent operators, placed union contractors at a competitive disadvantage.

The costs imposed on society by the declining provision of health insurance and pensions was a side issue but one of public importance. Because of the number of injured construction workers who began to report to hospital emergency rooms without insurance, Dade County, Florida, required as a bid qualification evidence that health insurance would be provided to all project workers.

Movement to the Suburbs and Exurbs

The post-World War II movement of commercial construction away from the cities (which were traditional union strongholds) favored open shop contractors. Starting with relatively small jobs, such as the construction of gas stations, individual stores, small warehouses, or professional buildings, open shop contractors gradually gained the expertise to challenge union contractors. The movement away from the union strongholds in or near metropolitan areas made union organizing and policing activities more difficult.

International and Local Union Policies

As early as 1972, the International began to realize the extent of the open shop threat, and by 1976, when J.C. Turner assumed the presidency, membership began a decline that would continue until 1988. Perhaps no other statement better described union concern than a 1972 communication by a local leader of the Sheet Metal Workers International Association. It was entitled: "The Honeymoon is Over." New York State Building and Construction Trades Council leader Henry Landau said:

> In Syracuse they started with a $4.5 million shopping center. The Building Trades took them on and made a full-scale effort to get the job switched to Union. The Trades put pickets on the project for nine months. When injunctions were issued another Trade would proceed to picket. Unfortunately the Building Trades did not remain strong and eventually even some unions went in there to work. Needless to say, the project was completed without going too far beyond the anticipated completion date. As a matter of fact, the job went so well ABC went to other side of Syracuse and built a $6.5 million shopping center, and this job went that much easier. They use each completed project as advertisement and leverage to gain the next. They are presently involved in a Student Housing Project on one of the universities in the Syracuse area. The final estimate of this project will exceed $30 million. You can see where it would be relatively easy for them to convince an owner to have his construction done by them, especially when they have built up such an impressive track record.[9]

The above is a statement by a *local* union leader, but it was generally the national leaders who were the first to recognize and respond to the open shop threat. Most local leaders were late in recognizing "the end of the honeymoon" and resisted International pressure to make concessions that would improve the competitive position of union contractors. Where national contracts were negotiated between the International and contractors' associations, local unions often rebelled against the lower wage rates and modified work rules contained in the national agreements, sometimes leading to lawsuits against the International.

Excessive wage increases and jurisdictional disputes were not the only factors affecting the union position. Even contractors who were traditionally signatories to union contracts resented work rules that they claimed encouraged featherbedding, inefficiency, and higher production costs. Requiring supervisors to be union members and the employment of shop stewards who spent most of their time responding to member grievances were anathema to contractors. For trades other than the operating engineers, union jurisdictional demarcations sometimes required that unskilled work be performed by highly skilled journeymen, or caused delays because work could not be assigned to employees who were immediately available at the site. For the engineers, the equivalent was limitations on the number of small machines a worker could operate or requirements that automatic equipment be staffed. Restrictions on working hours meant interruptions because of weather or materials shortages that had to be made up at overtime rates. Most of these practices, it is true, were characteristic of building projects and were rarely found in heavy and highway agreements. That was part of the reason building tradesmen were often reluctant to organize earth-moving work. But the reputation besmirched everyone. It wasn't until mid-1980s, when the extent of open shop incursion was fully realized at both the national and the local levels, that policy changes regarding such work rules became universal.

Labor Law Administration

From the passage of the National Labor Relations Act in 1935 until Taft-Hartley in 1947, labor law and its administration generally favored union organization. Even Taft-Hartley adhered to the basic premise of employee right to choose whether and by whom to be represented for collective bargaining with employers. It did allow states to deny that federal right, and it did prohibit some mutually accepted practices that made sense within the context of certain industries but were misunderstood by the uninitiated—such as union hiring hall arrangements in industries of casual employment. But primarily the change was to recognize the possibility of union wrongdoing parallel to that of management. The preconceptions of appointees to the National Labor Relations Board and the Department of Labor were more persuasive than the law itself in the fluctuating policies of the Roosevelt/Truman, Eisenhower, Kennedy/Johnson, Nixon/Ford, and Carter administrations. But the basic commitment to the right to organize stayed strong throughout. The first real sign of wavering was Ford's repeal of the carefully crafted trade-off of "common situs picketing" against wage stabilization, for political rather than substantive reasons. The next came during the Carter administration, not from the executive branch but from a Democratic Congress that was unable, when confronted by filibuster, to deliver mild reforms in labor law administration designed to shift the balance in the increasingly negative results of NLRB certification elections. The tide was beginning to turn but didn't come full circle until the election of Ronald Reagan in 1980. The NLRB became hostile territory, and an erosion of labor expertise occurred in the one agency supposedly dedicated to the well-being of working men and women—the Department of Labor. The department was downgraded during the following two administrations and was often ignored or bypassed in major decisions regarding labor-management relations and collective bargaining.

Prevailing Wage Legislation

As noted earlier, starting in 1960, Davis-Bacon came under increasing attack, and as the open shop movement grew, efforts to either limit the Act or repeal it altogether increased proportionally. Nine states repealed prevailing wage legislation during the 1970s and 1980s, and one's law was declared unconstitutional. By 1980, there were thirteen bills before the U.S. Congress calling for either repeal or substantial amendments to Davis-Bacon.

Early in 1971, the General Accounting Office prepared a report to Congress that severely criticized the methods used by the Department of Labor to determine prevailing wage rates. Later in 1971, the Department of Labor began to demand more evidence before issuing the determinations. Because of a lack of Department of Labor staff to conduct the required surveys, various contracting agencies, particularly the Departments of Transportation and Housing and Urban Development, conducted their own surveys and gave the data to the Department of Labor. However, the regulations promulgated by Madame Perkins were not substantially changed until 1981, when President Reagan's New Jersey campaign manager-turned-secretary of labor Raymond J. Donovan issued new regulations that altered the manner in which prevailing wages were established and their conditions determined. The Donovan regulations were fought bitterly and litigated unsuccessfully by the construction unions. The unions won in the lower court but were reversed by the Appellate Court, and the Appellate Court's decision was upheld by the Supreme Court.

The Donovan regulations called for the following changes:

1. Elimination of the 30-percent rule and the substitution of a formula for calculating the prevailing wage on 50 percent of the workers in a geographical area doing the same type of work.

2. The exclusion of wage rates of nearby metropolitan areas from consideration in determining rates for county and rural areas.

3. Inclusion of the job category "helper," a provision that, according to the building trades, would undermine labor-management apprenticeship programs.

4. The exclusion of prior federal projects from consideration in determining prevailing wages for building and residential construction projects "unless it is determined that there is insufficient wage data to determine the prevailing wages in the absence of such data."

5. The elimination of weekly payroll reports—the act's chief enforcement provision—from submission to the Department of Labor.[10]

There were valid arguments for each of these, depending upon where one stood in the various conflicts of interest involved. What was significant was that the same arguments had been around since the 1930s, yet the prevailing wage laws had remained essentially prounion and sacrosanct. Now, what had not been achievable through legislation was simply accomplished by a stroke of the pen, or through administrative fiat. Few doubted that the new regulations would make it easier for open-shop contractors to win government-supported jobs, but the full effect of the regulations in eroding union power and control has not as yet been determined.

At the end of the 1980s a new weapon was leveled at state prevailing wage legislation. The passage by Congress of the Employees' Retirement Income Security Act (ERISA) preempted all overlapping state pension regulations. Employers across the nation were able to convince state and federal courts that the preemption covered all related state regulation such as prevailing wage laws, apprenticeship regulations, mechanics' lien laws, surety bond requirements, and other state rules that affected the level of, or collection of, payments to ERISA-covered pension and health and welfare plans.[11] When appeals courts upheld state and federal district interpretations and the U. S. Supreme Court denied further appeal, the Building and Construction Trades Department took the case to Congress, arguing that the courts had gone far beyond congressional intent.[12] The issue had not been resolved at this writing.

OSHA Administration

From its passage in 1970, OSHA has been a target for the proponents of deregulation. During the period of 1970–80, the defenders of OSHA were successful in fending off legislation designed to cripple, if not destroy, the act, but they were not as successful in gaining adequate appropriations for effective administration. With the advent of the Reagan administration, the assault on OSHA through administrative restraint accelerated. OSHA's 1980 budget amounted to only $2.60 per covered worker.[13] With some 6 million workplaces eligible for inspection, the skeleton cadre of some 2,500 federal and state inspectors was decreased below 2,000, limiting the already deficient number of safety and health inspections. The number of citations and amount of penalties for violations declined accordingly.

Equally important, OSHA's development of safety and health standards all but ceased. Between 1984 and 1988, the only standard-setting activity of any consequence was the enactment of a revised asbestos standard in 1986. This resulted directly from an asbestos program moderated by Dr. Irving J. Selikoff at the IUOE's Eighth Annual Safety and Health Conference in 1983. Members of the Building and Construction Trades Safety Committee were the principal witnesses at the rule-making hearings.

The Mine Safety and Health Administration suffered a similar but less drastic decline in the quantity and quality of the safety and health protection of miners. The National Institute for Occupational Safety and Health also had many of its activities and services curtailed as a result of reduced budgets. Disabling workplace injuries, which had been reported as 2.2 million (by an admittedly inadequate estimating system) in 1970, the year of OSHA's passage, had risen to 6.8 million by 1990 with construction still vying with underground mining to lead the pack at 14.1 injuries per 100 workers. Following a rash of cave-in deaths on construction sites in the mid-1980s, OSHA began a series of inspections that found two out of three excavations to be out of compliance.[14]

Some resurgence of OSHA activity occurred under changed Department of Labor leadership during the Bush administration, with an increase in inspections, citations, and the level of fines. But the Operating Engineers joined with the rest of the labor movement in demanding OSHA reforms, including mandatory safety and health programs governed by labor-management safety committees, workers' rights to challenge weak citations and penalties, authorization for OSHA inspectors to shut down dangerous jobs without delay, a guaranteed right of workers to refuse unsafe work without penalty, mandatory health and safety training for all workers, and increased penalties, including jail terms for those knowingly putting their employees at serious risk.[15] Committed to those reforms, the IUOE, along with the remainder of organized labor, was waiting at the door to welcome the incoming Clinton administration.

Section 10(K) and Jurisdiction

The passage of the Taft-Hartley Act in 1947 made strikes or threats of strikes over jurisdictional disputes illegal under Section 10(K). The act subjected unions to penalties and authorized the NLRB to determine and award jurisdiction unless the parties either adjusted or agreed upon a method for the voluntary adjustment of disputes. In response, therefore, the Building and Construction Trades Department, the Associated General Contractors (AGC), and other major contractor associations developed and put into effect, in May 1948, the National Joint Board for Settlement of Jurisdictional Disputes. As the name implies, representatives of both labor and management were involved in the decision-making and administration procedures. Under the previous forums, employers had the opportunity to express their position. Under the new procedure, employers were directly and equally involved with the unions in determining trade jurisdiction.

Decisions of the Joint Board were to be based on historic union jurisdictions and on recorded previous decisions and agreements. Since

NLRB members and staff and administrative judges had little knowledge of the construction industry or of historic union jurisdictions, NLRB decisions were far more likely to be based on employer preference. The Joint Board continued until 1973, when the AGC withdrew because it was unable to eliminate previous decisions and agreements as criteria for decision-making. The AGC decision was based to a great extent on the increasing influence and power of nonunion contractors, especially the ABC, within the organization. Other mechanisms were created after the AGC withdrawal, but they were largely ignored as contractors realized that it was to their advantage to have jurisdictional problems settled through the NLRB, thus rendering labor-management jurisdictional-disputes machinery unworkable.

The NLRB jurisdictional-dispute bias, which became flagrant during the Reagan-Bush years, was apparent even in 1968, at the end of an eight-year Democratic era. As is true with most policy makers, NLRB members are more familiar with industrial settings wherein work assignments are the sole responsibility of the employer and are subject to challenge through the grievance procedure in case seniority or other individual rights are violated in the process. In the case of the construction industry, the very life of a union and the working careers of its members are often on the line, as well as a choice among different subcontractors who are employers of the various crafts.

An ironic example of the NLRB bias, though outside of construction, occurred when the board rejected a Newspaper Guild charge of unfair labor practices in favor of the Communist Party USA, the behind-the-scenes employer in the case.[16] The actual employer, *People's Weekly World,* instituted an editorial policy whereby certain officials of the Communist Party USA or their designees would review articles written for publication. When the managing editor protested the new policy, he was fired and barred from the premises. Subsequently, twenty employees of the paper struck in protest of the new policy and the firing of the managing editor. All twenty employees were then discharged. The guild, which did not have a contract with the paper, nevertheless agreed to represent the managing editor and the fired employees before the NLRB. The board responded, "This is a subject which has been deemed by the board and the courts to be within the sphere of management control."[17] The guild's charge of unfair labor practices was rejected, and the employer's right to institute an editorial policy whereby all articles must first be reviewed by a representative of the Communist Party USA was affirmed.

The IUOE was sometimes successful in defending its jurisdiction before the NLRB in the 1960s, but from the Nixon administration on, even during the Carter administration, the board's decisions on 10(K) matters virtually always were based on employer preference. It "takes two to tango," and why should an employer participate in a bipartisan jurisdictional-disputes settlement scheme when an appeal to the NLRB would invariably result in assignment according to the employer's choice? And what is the incentive for unions to try to maintain machinery employers disdain? Members of one or the other of the unions involved in a jurisdictional dispute, after all, will be selected by the employer and will be favored by the NLRB decision. Of course, a choice between two crafts generally implies a choice between two subcontractors or between work being performed by the employees of the general contractor as an alternative to subcontracting to another employer, but there is no mechanism for getting that issue before the NLRB.

The result, therefore, is that jurisdictional disputes, once endemic in the construction industry, now occur infrequently. But a minor 1992 Wisconsin dispute between the Laborers and the Operating Engineers serves as an example of the continuing issue. A bricklaying subcontractor assigned the operation of a mason-tending forklift to members of the Laborers' local. The Operating Engineers local struck because of its claimed jurisdiction over all construction machinery. The contractor appealed to the NLRB, which agreed that the assignment was a uni-lateral employer choice. In earlier years, the decision would have gone to the two international presidents to "bump heads" or to the bipartisan jurisdictional-disputes mechanism of the time, where the impartial umpire would have been most likely to assign the task to the Operating Engineers under the 1909 AFL jurisdictional grant. The issue is not the correctness of either procedure but the marked change over past norms.

The Department of Labor

The Department of Labor, which had served as the keeper of the collective bargaining flame since the passage of the Wagner Act in 1935, suffered a tremendous loss in prestige during the Reagan and Bush administrations. With the exception of one defeated politician, every secretary of labor since the 1930s, Democrat or Republican, until the

Reagan-Bush era, brought expertise and relevant experience to the position—as labor leaders, management personnel representatives, or academic neutrals. Most Reagan-Bush secretaries were amateurs. When Reagan fired 11,400 striking air controllers in 1981, it was not to his secretary of labor that he turned for advice but to his transportation secretary. Late in the Bush administration, the Department of Labor dismantled its Bureau of Labor Management Cooperative Programs, the lone remaining agency within the department that dealt with collective bargaining issues. The duties of the bureau, to the extent that they were to be continued, were to be taken over by a bureau whose name might have been coined on Madison Avenue: the "New America Workplace Agency." Nor was the Department of Labor involved in the decision to reexamine the Railway Labor Act, which governs railroad and airline labor relations. That task was also assigned to the Department of Transportation .

"The Department of Labor," said AFL-CIO Secretary-Treasurer Thomas Donohue in 1992, "has become the Department of Employment. The Department of Labor has destroyed the [collective bargaining] expertise it had. I don't think you have anyone in the Department of Labor today who could write a credible paper on the state of collective bargaining."[18] IUOE President J.C.Turner said in 1984:

> The Department of Labor has become a mockery of its name. It has been stripped of people who were advocates and defenders of working people. In their place, Reagan has appointed champions of employer causes, not a few of whom were recruited from the ranks of the National Right to Work Committee and other groups dedicated to the destruction of the labor movement.[19]

Turner referred to the appointment of a staff attorney for the Associated Building and Contractors of America—the voice of the open shop movement—as Deputy Assistant Secretary for Employment Standards. The department was also criticized for its administration of the Landrum-Griffin Act. In 1984, the House Subcommittee on Labor-Management Relations charged that the Department of Labor had "systematically dismantled" the employer disclosure program since Reagan took office.[20] The budget for that program, which requires employers to disclose their expenditures for union-related activities (including the hiring of professional union busters) dropped from $306,000 in 1980 to a mere $22,000 in 1984—an amount too small to sustain a single employee. During the same four-year period, the budget allocation to conduct audits of union accounts jumped from $386,000 to more than $750,000. So much, the unions thought, for labor advocacy within the president's cabinet.

Contractor Policies

As the open shop movement gathered momentum in the mid-1970s and the 1980s, many union contractors began exploring ways to recapture some of their lost market. One method, which mushroomed during the 1980s, was "doublebreasting," or dual-shop operation. Contracting firms formerly employing only union crafts reconstituted themselves as holding companies each with two wholly owned subsidiaries. One operated as previously under union contracts, primarily on publicly financed projects, especially where prevailing wage laws were in force; the other operated nonunion in competition with other open shop contractors, in situations where adherence to union agreements might substantially reduce the chances of successful bidding.

The unions unsuccessfully attacked doublebreasting in the Congress and through the NLRB as a subterfuge to avoid union contracts and the courts. The board's position on common ownership of two companies is that unless there are other indications of common control, the same corporation can maintain 100 percent financial control of two companies engaging in the same type of business in the same locality without subjecting the second company to the terms of a collective bargaining agreement entered into by the first. The crucial criterion appears to have been whether or not the two firms have a "common management." But common management by itself is not enough to outlaw doublebreasting; it has to be proven that the day-to-day operations of both companies are integrated. Thus if the contractor can show that the two companies have separate management operations, not related to each other in personnel, office space, or transfers of workers from one company to the other, it may be determined that common management does not exist, even though the parent company has 100 percent financial control.

The IUOE was a party to one of the most significant dual-shop decisions rendered by the NLRB—a case involving Local 627 (Oklahoma) and the Peter Kiewit Sons' Company.[21] Kiewit, Incorporated, a holding company, owned two subsidiaries—Kiewit and South Prairie —both of which performed general and highway construction. Kiewit had operated for many years as a union contractor in Oklahoma; South Prairie operated nonunion in other states. Kiewit, Incorporated, decided to activate South Prairie in Oklahoma in order to avoid its collective bargaining agreement with Local 627. The local filed charges with the NLRB seeking to have its contract with Kiewit apply to South Prairie.

The board determined that although there was common ownership and similarity in type of business, these factors were not controlling. Because there was no substantial evidence of interrelation of operations or common labor-relations policy, the board concluded that Kiewit and South Prairie were separate entities, rather than a single employer.[22]

On appeal, the Court of Appeals for the District of Columbia reversed the board's decision.[23] Agreeing with the argument advanced by Operating Engineers General Counsel J. Albert Woll, the court found that the act of establishing a company that would operate nonunion "constituted a very substantial qualitative degree of centralized control of labor relations." The court also cited the shift of management personnel from Kiewit to South Prairie's Oklahoma management and supervisory staff, in addition to evidence of some rank-and-file interchange. The court also pointed out that after the activation of South Prairie in Oklahoma, Kiewit's bidding activity declined, thus demonstrating that Kiewit's employees would lose work because of the activation of South Prairie.

Both Kiewit and the NLRB petitioned the Supreme Court for review of the case, and it was here that General Counsel Woll and the Operating Engineers won the battle but lost the war.[24] The Court affirmed the Court of Appeals finding that Kiewit and South Prairie constituted a single employer. However, the Court found that the lower court had overreached itself in concluding that the employees of both firms should be included in one collective bargaining unit. That decision, the Court concluded, should always be made by the NLRB. Therefore, the lower court's judgment, which held that employees of the two firms constituted one collective bargaining unit the case was vacated, and remanded to the board for determination. In a subsequent decision, the NLRB decided in favor of Kiewit.[25] The upshot of Kiewit was that, even if it is determined that a dual operation is, in effect, a single employer, there must be a sufficient commonality of interest between the employees of the two firms for the board to include all in a single bargaining unit.

However, in most NLRB decisions regarding doublebreasting, the decisions have revolved around "day-to-day personnel operations." If it can be demonstrated that control over such matters as hires, discharges, transfers, wages, hours, and working conditions are integrated, or that a common owner dictates and actually participates in day-to-day operations, the board is likely to find that the two companies constitute a "single employer." On the other hand, if it can be shown that the two firms have separate personnel offices and that there is no interchange of management staff and rank-and-file workers, even though there may be common ownership, the board is likely to find that the two companies constitute "separate employers."

In September 1976, the *Engineering News-Record* reported on an AGC conference designed to show members how to go open shop, including sessions on how to meet NLRB guidelines regarding doublebreasting.[26] According to the article, the AGC estimated that 40 percent of its 8,400 members operated either open shop or double-breasted. In the years ahead, that percentage would grow even larger. Since doublebreasting was adopted by many of the largest construction companies in the United States—companies that once operated solely union—it struck at the heart of prior union-contractor relations and was ample proof, in and by itself, of the gains made by open-shop contractors.

The Consequences

The combination of factors described above forced a retreat by the construction trades unions—a retreat that led to across-the-board membership losses. In 1970, 42 percent of construction workers reported to the Current Population Survey that they were union members, down from 85 percent at the end of the Second World War (see Figure 6.1). By 1987, that proportion was 22 percent.

In 1978, 38 percent of all employees in the industry were covered by collective bargaining agreements, compared to 24 percent in 1991.[27] The Business Roundtable claimed in 1983 that open-shop construction had increased from 30 percent of the total in 1973 to 60 percent by 1980. Construction union membership, the Roundtable noted, had de-

Figure 6.1 **The Union Construction Wage Premium and Unionization within Construction**

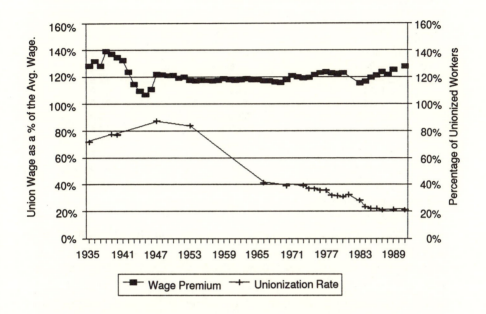

Sources: Union Construction Wages: 1907–1978, *Historical Statistics of the United States, Colonial Times to 1970,* p. 171; U. S. Department of Commerce, 1979–1992, *Statistical Abstract of the United States,* pages vary by year; *Average Construction Wage: Employment, Hours and Earnings, United States, 1909–90,* Volume I, U.S. Department of Labor, Bureau of Labor Statistics.

clined by 125,000 over the same years, totaling 1.6 million in 1980. Meanwhile, "those identifying themselves as nonunion workers had risen by 400,000 to nearly three million."[28]

Historically, younger workers had moved sporadically in and out of the construction industry, had become more solidly committed to the industry in their thirties, and then remained for life. Apprentices, for instance, are primarily in their mid- to late twenties, even older than university graduate students. Union membership has risen by age along with industry commitment, as shown in Table 6.1, but during the 1970s and 1980s fell precipitously in the age groups for which it historically had been the highest—those with the greater financial responsibilities. From an industry of career-committed craft workers, the construction industry was increasingly employing the un-

Table 6.1

Construction Worker Union Density by Age

Age	May 1977–78	1989
Under 20	11.2	5.1
20–24	22.6	14.6
25–29	36.4	19.9
30–34	44.4	21.8
35–39	49.2	26.2
40–44	55.0	33.9
45–49	52.0	38.1
50–54	59.0	37.1
55–59	56.1	46.5
60–64	57.4	39.5
Over 64	31.2	16.3

Source: CPS Public Use Tapes.

committed, who were just passing through to something better or had little interest in permanency.

Proportions of organized construction workers fell across all age groups. Given the differences in wages and fringe benefits between union and nonunion employment (see Figure 6.2), it is difficult to attribute this decline to worker choice. The union-nonunion differential for the industry, estimated at 38 percent in 1967, had risen to between 50 percent and 55 percent in the mid-1970s, then dropped back to 39 percent by 1981. Pension coverage remained unchanged at 90 percent for union employers and 33 percent for nonunion. Health insurance coverage dropped from 89 percent to 80 percent among union members in the industry between 1979 and 1989 while rising for nonunion construction workers from one-half to two-thirds.[29] But the differentials were still substantial. The union-nonunion choice was being made on the basis of employment opportunities. And, of course, these numbers do not account for the proportions of workers maintaining their union membership while working on the available nonunion jobs.

Construction-union density also fell most in those areas where it had been the highest, the Pacific Coast, and the lowest, the South (see Table 6.2).

The union membership decline was not totally a product of a decline in employment opportunities. Employment in the industry rose from 4.8 million in 1970 to 6.2 million in 1980, 7 million in 1985, and 7.7

Figure 6.2 **Average Real Wages: Construction and Unionized Construction**

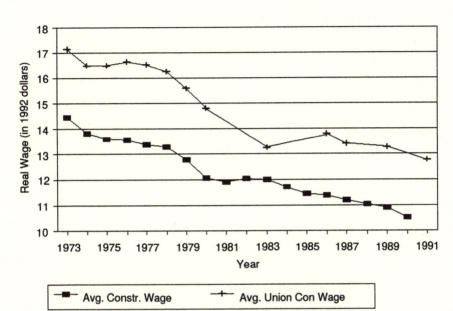

Sources: Union Construction Wages: 1907–1978, *Historical Statistics of the United States, Colonial Times to 1970,* p. 171; U. S. Department of Commerce, 1922–1979, *Statistical Abstract of the United States,* pages vary by year; Average Construction Wage: *Employment, Hours and Earnings, United States, 1909–1990,* Volume I, U.S. Department of Labor, Bureau of Labor Statistics.

million in 1989. The issue was which contractors were displaying "help wanted" signs.

The Operating Engineer's losses were not as great as those suffered by other building trades unions (see Figure 6.3), but they were still major.

Table 6.3 is based on the average per capita paid membership of the AFL-CIO for the two-year period ending in June of the year shown and reflect only actively employed members, as well as union policy

Table 6.2

Union Density by Census Division

Census Division	1977–78	1989
New England	28.7	20.8
Middle Atlantic	54.3	38.2
East North Central	57.8	43.1
West North Central	34.4	27.6
South Atlantic	22.5	8.7
East South Central	30.9	14.8
West South Central	25.5	9.8
Mountana	34.5	18.6
Pacific	57.6	34.8

Source: CPS Public use tapes.

Figure 6.3 **Changes in Union Membership**

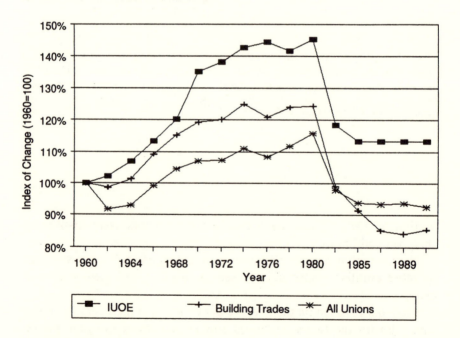

Source: CPS public use tapes.

Table 6.3

Membership (in thousands) of Selected Building-Trades Unions, 1979–1989

Union	1979	1985	1987	1989	Inc/Dec
Carpenters	626	616	617	613	−2%
Bricklayers	106	95	84	84	−21%
Electrical (IBEW)	825	791	765	744	−10%
IUOE	313	330	330	330	+5%
Ironworkers	146	140	122	111	−24%
Laborers	475	383	371	406	−15%
Painters	160	133	128	128	−20%
Plumbers	228	226	220	220	−4%
Sheet Metal	120	108	108	108	−10%
Totals	2,999	2,822	2,745	2,744	−9%

Source: U.S. Membership in AFL-CIO Affiliated Unions, Selected Unon: 1979–1989, *Statistical Abstract of the United States 1990*, p. 24 (table 695).

decisions concerning financial commitments to the federation. Table 1.1 in chapter 1, on the other hand, based on actual IUOE membership figures, includes both active members and retirees. Table 6.3 shows an overall decline of nine percent for the nine unions. The only union that did not suffer a decline was the Operating Engineers, which actually showed a five-percent increase over the ten-year period. However, the figures in Table 1.1 are far more indicative of the Operating Engineers' losses during the 1980s, and we can assume that the losses suffered by the other construction trades were also proportionately greater than shown here. Nevertheless, though the absolute numbers are doubtful, the interunion comparisons of membership loss are meaningful.

Two Theories

There are two major theories concerning the open shop movement in the construction industry that might be described as the conspiracy theory and the "just desserts" theory. The first sees the open shop movement as but one component in a concerted campaign to destroy labor unions in the United States. Led by the Business Roundtable and other conservative organizations, this theory holds that immediate economic considerations are secondary and that the major purpose is to eliminate unionization and, thereby, reap long-term economic rewards from generally lowered wage levels and greater employer discretion in control of the work force. This theory posits that the very existence of unions forces even nonunion employers to pay higher wages and (to a lesser extent) fringe benefits in order to recruit and retain workers than if labor unions were not around exerting upward pressures. Likewise, the existence of unions forces employers in competition to allow employees a greater voice in workplace decisions, restricting employer discretion. In pursuit of unrestricted and unchallenged control of the workplace, even unorganized establishments, according to the conspiracy theory, have an incentive to eliminate unions from the industrial landscape. Financial pressure has been exercised through campaign contributions to recruit government into this antiunion crusade.

A second theory is that the open shop movement is merely a reaction to union excesses—jurisdictional disputes, wage and fringe-benefit raises well above the inflation rate, and work rules that reduce productivity. The fact that over the past ten to fifteen years, the unions have given back much of what they had previously gained is cited as proof of this reaction theory. The unions also have been accused of complacency, of failing to organize the unorganized, and of ignoring changes in the economy that called for dramatic new initiatives. Accordingly, labor has suffered a temporary setback that may be reversed if the unions themselves act to reverse it, aided perhaps by a change in the national government.

There are elements of truth in both theories; no doubt there are individuals and organizations who would like to see the American trade union movement crushed, and the continued downward trends in organization encourage them to consider this to be a realistic option. On the other hand, complacency and occasional union excesses have damaged the cause of employee organization in a number of industries and reduced public acceptance. Individual unions and their federation have responded with concerted attempts to restore both public acceptance and political and economic power. Whether there will be a trade union resurgence in the last years of the twentieth century depends on the union counterattack in the fields of organization, economics, and legislation.

Opportunities Lost

It has been suggested that if some form of tripartite planning had been continued after the demise of the Nixon economic stabilization program, the open shop incursion would have been a good deal less successful than it turned out to be. Bargaining is primarily a local respon- sibility, but the local viewpoint is often narrower than that of the na- tional one. That narrower viewpoint would, in this case, have dire consequences for the organized sector of the construction industry. Without any effective constraint from the national level, local unions pressed for as much as they could get, leading to unsupportable wage and fringe benefit increases and, finally, a revolt by the purchasers of construction services.

Thus Ford's veto of the Economic Rights of Labor in the construc- tion industry legislation was one of the key factors contributing to the rise of the open shop movement. That, together with the hostile politi- cal atmosphere of the Reagan-Bush years, resulted in serious labor union losses in the construction industry. Although the IUOE was not hurt as badly as other construction trades unions, it was hurt, and corrective action was required. The trials and accomplishments of the union's counterattack are the subjects of chapters 7 and 8.

Chapter 7

COUNTERATTACK

J.C. Turner and Larry Dugan began the counterattack against membership decline during the 1980s, laying the groundwork for what was to follow. The decline was checked in the late 1980s, and 1991 and 1992 were the primary years of renewed growth. Aggressive local actions in the United States and Canada were critical, as they always are, in a decentralized organization. That combination of local initiative and Frank Hanley's administrative acumen and aggressive organizational initiatives have been the primary causes of the union's embryonic resurgence during the early nineties.

The Will to Organize

Although the IUOE has always had an organizing program, it is understandable that, between 1960 and 1974, when the union's membership was growing at the rate of 6,000 a year, organization was not considered a high priority. Most of the growth was due to top-down organizing in the expanding construction industry. In that setting, the international had difficulty in convincing member-rich locals to extend their organizing activities to such promising fields as highway construction; quarries; and the rock, sand, and gravel industry, among others. The policy of most local unions was protectionism—that is, protecting present members from job competition from new members. For example, locals engaged primarily in commercial construction, where the work is relatively clean, well paid, and close to home, were reluctant to recruit lower-paid workers employed in outlying areas in highway construction or related industries. The new members would become competitors in the "longest on the bench, the first referred out" hiring hall referral system; the original members might have to accept referral to one of the less desirable jobs or be passed over in rotation. With construction booming and most members of local unions enjoying relatively steady employment, organization was put on the back burner; the need for new organizing activity was not readily apparent. As a result, however, a pool of competent workers and potentially competitive contractors was being created outside the building-trades union/organized employer-association relationship.

Other than a spurt of activity that occurred between 1964 and 1968, there was little action on the organizing front throughout the 1960s and 1970s. Organization was not a subject of the general presidents' reports to the 1968, 1972, and 1976 conventions. In 1980, however, as the union's membership loss became more pronounced, Turner announced a reorganization of the Department of Organization and offered monthly subsidies to local unions when, in the general president's judgment, their financial conditions were not adequate to fully develop an effective organizing campaign and when the potential for new membership warranted the expenditure. But it wasn't until membership began to decline at an alarming rate after 1980 that organization once again became a high priority, a priority calling for new methods, new initiatives, and resort to bottom-up organizing.

Membership Potential

Table 7.1 shows total U. S. employment of hoisting and portable operating engineers in 1988 and projected employment for the year 2000. Coming from Bureau of Labor Statistics data, these are not limited to the construction industry or to the IUOE's claimed jurisdiction. In 1988, a total of 927,000 operating engineers were employed in the United States. Of these, 231,098, or 24.9 percent, were U. S. members of the Operating Engineers union. Although this figure is well above the national percentage of unionized workers (16 percent), the potential for new membership is nevertheless great. Of course, the potential varies by region, with the South being the major area of nonunion employment in the construction industry and the area where the union suffered its greatest membership loss.

Table 7.1

U.S. Employment of Hoisting and Portable Operating Engineers, 1988, and Projected Employment, 2000

Category	Total Employment 1988	Total Employment 2000
Operating Engineers	158,000	179,000
Crane and Tower Operator	60,000	66,000
Excavation and Loading Machine Operators	76,000	84,000
Grader, Dozer, and Scraper Operator	86,000	96,000
Mobile Heavy Equipment Mechanic	108,000	124,000
Diesel Engine Specialists	269,000	312,000
Surveyors	100,000	112,000
Paving and Surfacing and Tamping Equipment Operators	70,000	82,000

Source: International Union of Operating Engineers Labor Market Analysis, prepared for the US. Department of Labor, Internaitonal Union of Operating Engineers, Washington, D.C., October 1991.

Thus the South became a priority area for the IUOE's organizing program, especially for the hoisting and portable engineers.

The potential for stationary engineers, of course, is even greater. Stationary engineers could be employed in every commercial building, school, hospital, factory, utility, etc., in the United States and Canada. Given the falling membership and that organizing potential, the answer for the union was obvious.

Renewed Organizational Efforts

In 1986, General President Larry Dugan made organizing the number one priority of the IUOE. Between 1975 and 1983, the union had lost over 36,000 members, and by 1987 the loss had grown to over 58,000. Clearly, the union's existing organizing techniques were not working. Financial aid and the assignment of International representatives to local unions for organizing purposes were not producing results. All too often, local unions were using International-paid subsidies and organizers to fund or staff other local activities. New approaches were needed. Dugan pledged the International to address thirteen targets, including the hiring and training of full-time International organizers and personnel from cooperating local unions in the latest techniques of organizing.

Organizer training became the foundation upon which the new organizing program was built. The initial training of International and cooperating local organizers took place at the AFL-CIO's George Meany Labor Studies Center in early 1986. The course content was designed and taught by members of the IUOE headquarters' staff, assisted by outside experts on such subjects as communications, public relations, specific organizational techniques, and response to employer antiunion activities.

Between the announcement of the program and the initial training, the Department of Organization, with the assistance of the Department of Education and Training (later called the Department of Research and Education), reviewed local union organizing programs and evaluated the programs of other unions, as well as the organizing courses offered at the Meany Center. From this analysis, the union was able to distill many qualities that were needed to meet the specific challenges facing local unions.

The course content, originally designed by Reese Hammond when he was director of education and training, and refined by James Van Dyke, subsequent director of organization (now special assistant to President Hanley) includes case studies of prior successful and unsuccessful organizing campaigns, among them actual materials used by employers to combat union organizing campaigns, techniques in choosing a "target," researching the target, contacting and polling employees, dealing with the media, combating employer antiunion propaganda, and the law as it applies to organizing.

Each U. S. region was asked to recommend one International representative, and Canada was asked for two to be trained as organizers. After training, they were given the responsibility of assisting in the development of local organizing programs and campaigns, field training local organizers, and developing organizing leads throughout their assigned regions. New tactics were developed and field tested, including polling and surveying, extensive campaign planning, and the use of community minority support groups. The creation of voluntary organizing committees and internal organizing committees and programs was encouraged. Targeted employers were researched, project organizers were used, and cooperative programs were entered into with other unions.

Extensive record keeping allowed the Department of Organization to track organizing campaigns, thus making possible statistical analyses and evaluation. From the introduction of the program until late 1987, IUOE locals, mostly stationary, were involved in 103 elections, winning sixty-six and losing thirty-seven. The winning percentage of 64 percent is 16 percent higher than the AFL-CIO's average of 48 percent. Through those election successes, Operating Engineers locals won the right to represent 4,085 workers, or 47 percent of the potential. That compares favorably with the AFL-CIO's average of between 30 and 32 percent.

Since the introduction of organizer training in 1986, there has been an annual increase in the union's membership. Overall, the increase experienced between 1987 and 1992 has been small (about 2.4 percent), but the downward decline has been stopped. Jim Van Dyke, who designed and was the driving force behind the organizing program, attributes the gain primarily to organizer training:

> One of the reasons I am a very strong believer in organizer training is because in 1977 when I was hired as an organizer, I was handed a group of authorization cards and a small copy of the National Labor Relations Act and was told to go sic 'em! And I said, "Sic who? What am I suppose to do?" Because of the cost of having people on the payroll and the limited resources available to local unions, we can't afford that luxury any more. We need well-trained people in the field who can get something done.[1]

Upon becoming general president, Frank Hanley continued and strengthened the organizing program, including the addition of two new organizing initiatives: the grant program; and a special campaign in the South.

The Organizing Grant Program

As its name implies, the Organizing Grant Program consists of subsidies to local unions for additional new members recruited during a given year. For example, a local whose membership increased by 100 at the end of a given year received a grant of $5,000, an amount more significant to small locals than to the larger ones. There is no paperwork involved; the grants are automatic. Since the start of the program, $484,000 has been awarded to local unions under the program. That translates into 9,680 new members. Grants were increased to $75 in 1993 and will go to $100 in 1994. It is expected that by means

of improved organizer training and the grant program's paper-free subsidies to local unions, the upsurge in membership that has occurred
since 1988 will continue.

Marketing Union Labor in The South

When Hanley assumed the presidency, he decided to do something
about a pervasive problem—the lack of organizing in the heavy and
highway field in the South. Commercial and industrial building construction had long been reasonably well organized in the larger cities
of the South, but suburban and rural organization was virtually nonex-
istent. The largest open shop contractors in the nation, such as Brown
and Root from Texas and Daniel Construction from South Carolina,
were southern firms. Therefore, practically all heavy and highway
work was going nonunion. Nevertheless, with the exception of Louisiana, there were few attempts by southern locals to organize in the
heavy and highway sector. Hanley's idea was to attract union contractors to bid on southern heavy and highway projects. The union would
supply the labor at wage rates and other conditions of employment
competitive with nonunion contractors. But, where were the workers to
come from? The International engaged in a major recruiting drive, and
one of the major sources was the labor employed by nonunion contractors. Another source was the suspended or unemployed members of
southern locals.

With the International taking direct responsibility for the negotiations, union contractors were the winning bidders on bridge jobs in
North Carolina and Georgia, two tunnel jobs in Texas, and five highway jobs in Florida. These International organizing successes, limited
though they were, had several additional beneficial effects on union
conditions in the South. First, where successes have occurred, local
unions have seen the light and have expanded their organizing activities. Second, in at least one area of Texas, the IUOE effort resulted in
increasing the prevailing wage for highway work. A contract was negotiated with a tunnel contractor for wages and fringes five dollars
above the prevailing rate—thirteen dollars an hour plus a two-dollar
fringe package. Qualified nonunion mechanics and operators were recruited to work on the job. The nonunion response was to offer wages
and benefits even higher than the union rate in order to prevent losses
of skilled help. The combination of higher union and nonunion rates

then became prevailing. But in the long run, the higher prevailing rate works to the advantage of union contractors because it prevents under-bidding based on wage cutting.

These organizing initiatives were an important part of the union's counterattack. Organizing, the life blood of any labor union, became once again a high priority for the International and its local affiliates. Stepped-up organizing occurred for both stationary and hoisting and portable engineers. The successful California public-employee organizing drive described later in this chapter was largely due to cooperation between hoisting and portable and stationary locals and unprecedented support from the Hanley administration. Since Hanley has stated more than once that he will commit all possible resources to organizing, it is likely that the accelerated organizing program will continue throughout the foreseeable future.

A Time for Concessions

Historically, successful organizers among Operating Engineers locals had been those that had been willing to make whatever concessions were necessary to enable union contractors to win the bids that offered employment to the membership, then push the wage up, as all major competitors became organized. The 1980s and 1990s were no different in that regard. The heady days of the growth years were over. The open shop challenge was real and wasn't about to disappear. Wage and fringe benefit increases far above the inflation rate were no longer supportable. Concessions had to be made.

The severe recession of 1981–83, together with the increase in non-union competition, led to reductions in negotiated wages and fringe benefits in the construction industry. In 1983, the Construction Labor Research Council, funded by major contractors, found that wage and benefit settlements that covered close to 720,000 construction workers averaged 40 cents per hour, or 2.2 percent—the smallest hourly rate recorded in over twenty years.[2] Involved were both the inability of the local unions to win more and their willingness to make concessions in order to enable union contractors to successfully bid and offer employment. Since 1980, concessions on wages and fringe benefits have been made in areas where the nonunion incursion was greatest. One way of accomplishing this was through amendments to national agreements and the granting of concessions in project agreements.

National Agreements

As noted in chapter 3, when the agreement with the National Constructors' Association broke up in 1972 over local violations, the International continued to pursue national agreements with individual contractors, of which there were 201 in 1984 and 171 in 1988.[3] In 1978, eight major building trades unions, including the Operating Engineers, entered into a national agreement with the National Constructors' Association to shorten construction time requirements on heavy industrial projects, restrain costs, and provide greater stabilization for the industry as a whole. Called the National Industrial Construction Agreement (NICA), it initially involved fifty of the nation's major industrial contractors. Turner told the 1984 convention:

> The pact is openly and frankly a response by the unionized sector of the construction industry to recent open-shop advances in the area of industrial plant construction and preserving jobs for union members. A 1978 study to highlight industrial construction projects awarded to nonunion contractors that had in the past most commonly [been] awarded to union contractors . . . reviewed some 270 nonunion projects in 29 states. The total projected cost of the work is more than $28 billion, of which $25.5 billion is located in the 11 states falling within the initial implementation area of the agreement. Translated into craft employment per year, it means more than 290,000 jobs are lost to union employees in industrial construction alone.[4]

The agreement established a Joint Administrative Committee, which had the authority to establish procedures of operation and areas of responsibility, review grievances, expand the agreement to other areas, establish travel or subsistence for remote projects, adjust holidays, and amend the agreement on a regional or local basis to obtain a more competitive posture. Among its provisions were a standard flexible day and work week, time-and-one-half (rather than double time) for most overtime work, limits on travel and show-up time, elimination of paid nonworking time during working hours, standardized shift premiums, and the prohibition of slowdowns, standby crews, and featherbedding. Although the agreement recognized wage rates prevailing in local areas, there were no provisions for premium pay for high work, special skills, etc., and contractors were exempt from paying into industry promotion or administrative funds. The original agreement covered the states of Alabama, Georgia, Florida, Mississippi, Louisiana, Oklahoma, Texas, and Virginia (excluding the Washington, D.C., metropolitan area), reflecting the nonunion dominance in the South, but it was subsequently extended to other states.

Similar concessions were made in the pipeline, maintenance by contract, railroad, off-shore/on-shore, bridge, and other national agreements. Most national agreements stipulated that the wages, fringe benefits, and working conditions existing in local union jurisdictions would be honored to the extent that they did not conflict with the provisions of the national agreement. However, the General Presidents' Contract Maintenance Agreement and the Nuclear Power Agreement both established their own wages, fringe benefits, and work rules without regard to other local or national agreements. If such clauses were to be contained in other future agreements, the power of local unions to negate or frustrate the implementation of national agreements would be neutralized. However, because the nuclear agreement applied only to the construction of nuclear power plants, and because the wage rates were bound to be at least as high as local rates (and perhaps even higher), there were no objections from local unions. The later cessation of nuclear construction, of course, made that agreement moot. The General Presidents' Contract Maintenance Agreement, on the other hand, is of increasing importance. However, because the work is not in the construction field and maintenance employment is year round in nature, there is little or no objection to the concessions involved.

Project Agreements

In 1979, the Building and Construction Trades Department instituted a uniform system for the review and approval of project-agreement requests and established a Project Agreement Review Committee composed of representatives of each international union to oversee its operation. Contractors must receive union approval to begin negotiations prior to bidding work on a project. After approval has been given, negotiations are then conducted between the contractors and local unions involved through the local building and construction trades councils. This system has worked well to prevent owners and contractors from pitting local building trades councils against one another in an effort to bid down the terms of an agreement to attract large construction projects to their areas. Project agreements ban jurisdictional disputes, reduce the number of nonworking stewards, permit management to select their own supervisors, reduce overtime rates, and eliminate travel time and standby crews. Wages and fringe benefits in local areas are generally not affected (although some wage concessions have been made). As of July 1987, there were 118 project agreement requests worth a total of $25.6 billion of construction work granted or pending approval promising approximately 62,200 jobs for building tradesmen.[5]

Re-establishing Relationships

The metamorphosis of the Associated General Contractors (AGC) from totally union to primarily nonunion had been a prime symptom of the rising power of the open shop movement. The organization, for its own survival, could only respond to the preferences of its membership. But enough AGC members continued to operate under collective bargaining agreements in various states to continue an interest at the national level. Paradoxically, it was the Business Roundtable, owner-representing parent of the open shop movement, that offered to the new committee an attractive vehicle for joint action—review of criticisms leveled at construction unions by that body. Re-establishment of a working, though not exclusive, relationship became a high priority objective of the Hanley administration. Working with other BCTD unions, an AGC-Basic Trades Joint Labor-Management Committee, cochaired by Hanley and Francis Madigan of the AGC Collective Bargaining Committee, was organized in 1992 to work at removing obstacles to a restored relationship. Its first effort was to review criticisms of union conduct leveled by the Business Roundtable in its Construction Industry Cost Effectiveness Project and determine progress toward their alleviation.

In the late 1970s, the Business Roundtable undertook a Construction Industry Cost Effectiveness Project "to develop a comprehensive definition of the fundamental problems in the construction industry and an accompanying program of resolution of those problems leading to an improvement of cost effectiveness in the industry." Included were studies of project management, construction technology, and regulations and codes, but two areas consisting of twelve separate reports focused on union-related topics: "labor effectiveness" and "labor supply and training."[6] A report entitled "Constraints Imposed by Collective Bargaining Agreements" focused on those collective-bargaining contract provisions which the Roundtable perceived as imposing unacceptable construction costs.

The 1982 Roundtable report identified overtime premiums beyond the legally required time-and-one-half, time paid for but not worked, substinence and travel benefits, shift premiums, restricted daily hours, crew size restrictions, off-site fabrication restrictions, and show-up pay as sources of $861 million in excessive costs in 1980.[7] Other provisions that the report criticized without estimating a cost figure involved selection and utilization of foremen, exclusive hiring halls, restrictions on the use of subjourneymen, and limitations on scheduling flexibilities such as four ten- hour shifts and Saturday makeup of lost shifts.

After passage of a decade, the AGC-Basic Trades Committee undertook as a joint project a review of progress made in reducing those costs, implying acceptance of the validity of much of the criticism. A review of collective-bargaining contracts undertaken for the committee by the Construction Labor Research Council concluded that the costs estimated at $861 million in 1980 had been reduced to $508 million by 1992, a 41 percent improvement. Source of the savings was reduction in the incidence in collective bargaining agreements of every item objected to with the exception of crew size restrictions.[8] Other unquantified changes declared to be "positive" and "widespread" were use of subjourneymen, flexible start and stop times and shift lengths, and Saturday straight-time makeup days. The growth of project agreements eliminating many of the objectionable practices was cited, as was the fact that no parallel study of the costs of nonunion construction had ever been made.

The AGC-Basic Trades Committee introduced its 1992 report with the comment:

> The union sector of the industry has been and will continue to be assiduous in improving its competitive position by building on its strengths—highly trained workers, competitive and flexible agreements, and quality job-site performance. We submit that this update of the original BRT report is a solid objective bellwether for the future. We can now point to data showing what we know to be the fact—union labor and construction firms that operate with collective bargaining agreements are committed at the local and national level to meeting the strenuous demands of a competitive marketplace.

Committing themselves to the continued pursuit of competitiveness, the cochairmen added that

> we are hopeful that we can build the achievements of the AGC-Building Trades Committee into a model of positive relations that has a real effect on project performance for the benefit of the industry and the economy. Moreover, we are keenly aware of the coming challenges in economic, political, and regulatory affairs that will demand a responsive structure to maintaining the momentum toward enhanced competitiveness documented in this report.

Since the implied cost reductions had been primarily the result of negotiated concessions at the local level, they ended by "commend[ing] local bargaining teams across the country for the sound judgments documented in this report."

Report C–5 of the Business Roundtable's Construction Industry Cost Effectiveness Project Reports had focused on inefficient local labor practices going beyond the requirements of the collective-bargaining agreements. For this the Roundtable criticized the employers as well as the unions:

> In attempts to appease labor, recruit employees, or avoid confrontation, contractors and owners have relinquished their right to manage their business by allowing the continuation of these practices. Alarmingly, in many instances such practices occurred despite existing prohibitive language in labor agreements. This reflects the loss of a bargained-for gain through work-site concessions of inattentive management.[9]

"Management ineptness and weakness" were cited as the primary source of such extra-agreement practices. A list of fifty-seven such practices was then cited with the cost impact estimated as 15 percent. No corresponding estimate of costly practices on nonunion jobs was provided, but a softening of attitudes opposing costly practices rather than employee organization as such was implied. Among other recommendations, prejob conferences between owner and contractor and contractor and union to agree upon job rules, work practices, and labor relations strategies were advised. Contractors were advised to use the contractual grievance procedure rather than settling disputes by concessions on work practices. Owners were urged to choose contractors on the basis of their previously demonstrated ability to avoid such concessions.

The AGC-Basic Trades Committee has on its agenda a follow-up of the Local Practices Report to assess progress in pursuit of those complaints. Roundtable specification of objectionable practices and the joint committee's declared intention to continue their elimination can only be read as positive steps toward reestablishment of once-productive relationships on a more cost-conscious basis.

Training as Counterattack

The IUOE's program of apprenticeship and training, begun reluctantly in the early 1960s, also became a major weapon in the union's counterattack. Realizing that its greatest asset was the skills of its members, the International expanded its training activities, even as its membership declined. "We must train and retrain our members," Frank Hanley told the delegates to the thirty-fourth convention, "so they have the skills to do the job better, safer and more efficiently than their competitors."[10] The Business Roundtable confirmed Hanley's admonition in a complaint to its construction-purchaser members:

> Current construction industry training efforts are inadequate to meet the needs of the industry. Training that is being done is largely concentrated in the union sector where training is supplied through charges on labor hours which in turn are passed on by contractors to the ultimate user or client. ... Although the open-shop sector does 60 percent of all construction, it has no comparable method available for funding of training. Less than 10 percent of all funds going into construction craft training is directed toward open-shop training. Likewise, less than 10 percent of those individuals completing construction craft training are in the open-shop program. If the open-shop sector of construction remains at 60 percent without a significant increase in its training, there could be a deterioration in the quality and quantity of the construction work force.[11]

What little training was under way by open-shop contractors was largely limited to carpentry, electrical, plumbing, and sheet metal, with occasional ironworking, bricklaying, and cement finishing "geared to housing, commercial, or light industrial work"—hardly a challenge to the operating engineer craft.[12] The possibilities of vocational education as well as on-the-job training were being neglected. The Roundtable did not note the complaint of vocational educators whose programs in the construction field tend to be undersubscribed. Few students are interested in preparing for a career in a component of an industry that can promise only sporadic employment without compensating wages and the customary benefits of health insurance and pensions.

On the other hand, the union's apprenticeship, retraining, National Training Project, and Job Corps programs continued, and several new programs were initiated. Two of the most important of the new projects were training in the hazardous-waste industry and training and retraining for stationary engineers.

The "HAZMAT" Program

Clearing up and disposing of the hazardous materials and waste buried in and adorning the land will be, by necessity, a decades-long undertaking that will require thousands of highly trained workers. Recognizing the employment potential in this industry, the IUOE sought ways of preparing its members for work in the field. With a 1987 grant from the National Institute of Environmental Health Sciences, the Operating Engineers established a comprehensive hazardous materials—hazmat for short—training program for its members. Participants received in-depth classroom instruction in a variety of hazmat-related topics, including industrial hygiene, toxicology, the use of respirators, protective clothing, recognizing and identifying the properties of hazardous materials, medical surveillance, radiation, and emergency entry and egress procedures, among others.

Special emphasis was given to hands-on training at a simulated hazardous-waste job site. These field exercises taught maximum protection and production in handling and removing or disposing of hazardous materials and waste while outfitted in protective clothing and with supplied air. Here, too, emergency entry and egress procedures and the decontamination process were taught.

To provide this training, the union established an intensive eighty-hour "train the trainer" program at the National Mine Health and Safety Academy in Beckley, West Virginia. Here, IUOE training instructors receive a combination of classroom instruction and simulated hands-on exercises to familiarize them with all aspects of the proper and safe handling of hazardous materials under the guidance of recognized professionals from the fields of labor, government, and industry.

These instructors then returned to their local unions where they conducted forty-hour training courses for members who would be working in the hazmat industry. Members completing the forty-hour course met the U.S. Department of Labor's (OSHA) training requirements for hazmat work. They were required to take an annual eight-hour refresher course to remain qualified. The instructor-training program at Beckley, supplemented by local union hazmat programs, has resulted in over 35,000 operating engineers being certified as skilled workers in Hazmat cleanup and disposal.

The hazmat program not only provides highly skilled workers in a field that will be with us well into the twenty-first century, but it also helps protect the health and safety of IUOE members. Graduates of the program learn how to recognize potentially hazardous materials and conditions as well as the proper procedures for protecting their fellow engineers on the job. Finally, it provides contractors with highly skilled workers in a growing field.

Stationary Training

The craft of stationary engineer underwent radical changes during the period between 1960 and 1993. Today's stationary engineer is, in the words of Lionel Gindorf of Local 399, a "composite mechanic," with skills cutting across all craft lines—a far cry from the traditional operator of power plants. Stationary engineers are no longer "stationary"; they move throughout buildings and plants "replacing, remodeling, and repairing"; the emphasis is no longer on "operation" but on "maintenance."

The introduction of new technology into the stationary jurisdiction increased the need for new training and retraining programs. Plants and buildings were being robotized, computerized, operated, and monitored with no one present. The only work left to humans was maintenance, which could be performed either by owner-employers or by contractors. The traditional position of the Operating Engineers has been "what we operate, we maintain."

The International emphasized two factors that could have had a deciding effect on whether or not the IUOE retained jurisdiction over power plants in both the public and private sectors. The first was the necessity to organize service maintenance contractors and to include in the collective-bargaining agreement language that would insure Operating Engineer jurisdiction after robotization or computerization took place. The second was to prepare stationary engineers for the jobs of the future. The former was the responsibility of the organizing department; the latter was a matter for action by the Stationary Committee.

Hanley directed the Stationary Committee to develop, in cooperation with the Training and Apprenticeship Committee, a comprehensive set of training modules for use by stationary locals. The resulting curriculum has been adopted either in whole or in a modified form by local stationary unions throughout the country. Stationary engineers, properly trained, would become the natural heirs of the new work requirements.

A Question of Productivity

The primary purposes of the IUOE's training activities are to make it the preferred source for employers seeking competent employees and to increase the productivity of its members, thus justifying the higher wages and fringe benefits paid to union workers. Herbert Northrup cites several studies purporting to show the cost differences between union and nonunion construction, some favorable to the open shop and some favorable to the union shop.[13] There does not seem to be any argument as to whether nonunion contractors have lower hourly labor costs; they do. The argument revolves around whether union productivity makes up for the higher wage and benefit costs.

A study performed by the Operating Engineers in 1991 compares labor work hours and cost per project mile on federally aided highway construction contracts over $1 million.[14] All data in the study were compiled from unpublished Federal Highway Administration Survey Forms FHWA–47. Comparisons were made between four predominately nonunion states (Texas, Georgia, Florida, and Virginia) and six union states (Illinois, Pennsylvania, New York, Michigan, California, and Missouri). The data indicate that the union cost per mile was 10 percent lower than the nonunion cost and that the union workers completed their projects with 56 percent of the work hours.

Using the same data, Ruttenberg, Kilgallon, and Associates compared labor hours per project mile in ten predominately nonunion states with the national average.[15] The ten-state group required from 42 percent (1987) to 65.4 percent (1988) more labor hours per project mile than was the norm for all the states combined. If the ten states are extracted when calculating the national average (in order to remove the influence of the ten-state group on the national average), the differences are significantly larger. They range from 70.8 percent in 1987 to 122.6 percent in 1988, with a four-year average differential of 91.2 percent, or almost double the norm.

The highway figures do indicate that union labor is more productive than its nonunion counterpart, but the data are inadequate to determine whether that added productivity is sufficient to offset the union-nonunion wage differential. Highly trained workers are highly productive workers. Historically, construction-industry training has been union driven. Few nonunion contractors have significant training programs, relying instead on their ability to recruit unemployed union-trained or experienced workers or upon informal on-the-job learning. Recognizing that relative advantage, the theme of the IUOE's thirty-fourth convention was "Training for the Future," indicating that training will remain a vital concern in the years ahead.

Stationary Engineer Initiatives

The problems faced by the stationary branch of the IUOE were of a different sort from those of their hoisting counterparts. The industries in which stationary engineers traditionally had been employed were declining and, in some cases, even disappearing. The advancing technology of the stationary craft demanded new training and retraining programs. The organizational efforts of stationary locals were hampered by AFL-CIO antiraiding provisions. Many of these locals were too small to be economically viable. NLRB decisions against small stationary units within larger maintenance units, and the necessity of organizing entire multioccupational public employee groups designated as bargaining units by state agencies, forced the stationary engineers to abandon the so-called blood lines and organize "wall-to-wall" in many instances.

Stationary Membership Trends

Stationary membership experienced only a slight decline during the mid-1980s (Table 7.2). With that exception, the stationary branch continued its slow but steady growth, aided by supportive International policies and extremely effective legal representation.

Table 7.2

Hoisting and Portable/Stationary Membership, 1977–1991

Year	Total	Stationary	Percent	H & P	Percent
1977	402,184	93,058	24	309,126	76
1980	419,937	98,053	24	321,884	76
1983	382,818	98,342	27	284,476	73
1986	362,033	97,923	28	264,110	72
1989	365,536	99,637	28	265,899	72
1991	366,766	99,109	28	267,657	72

Note: Extracted from official IUOE statistics.

Many of the stationary battles were decided in the courts and are illustrative of the time-consuming and complicated procedures of the NLRB. One of these, a legal challenge to separate bargaining units of stationary engineers in health care institutions, which began as a threat and finished as an opportunity, illustrates these developments. The other constituted the IUOE's first large-scale venture in public employee bargaining. Both are described below, preceded by discussions of the support stationary locals received from the International in several key areas.

Amalgamation and Mergers

The primary *raison dêtre* for any labor union is to serve the membership once they are organized. In today's world of complex labor relations, it is difficult for small locals to adequately service their memberships with part-time help and limited resources. Employer resistance and the seemingly endless procedures of the NLRB take time and money. Since the stationary branch of the union included many small locals without full-time staff, and because a great deal of geographical and industrial territory was not covered by any local, the International sought to bring about mergers of small stationary locals within geographic and jurisdictional areas.

Actually, the merger of stationary locals had begun in the 1940s and 1950s. For example, nine northern California locals were merged to form Local 39 in 1949, and in the southern part of the state, Local 501 was formed by means of the merger of eight locals and a San Diego independent welders' union in the early 1950s. The merger movement was renewed in the mid 1970s. Between 1976 and 1980, the merger of more than twenty stationary locals took place. Still, in 1984, there were forty-eight stationary locals with full-time staff and sixty-nine without. Of the sixty-nine, thirty locals represented employees in a single establishment whose employees had been organized "wall-to-wall." Nine incorporated the stationary engineer employees of a single school district, and fifteen represented similar units of public employees in public buildings. Two represented supervisors and inspectors only, whereas the remaining thirteen were small locals representing employees in a few small units. The general president's report to the 1984 convention advocated that at least twenty of the sixty-nine be merged, an objective largely accomplished within the remainder of the decade.[16]

Permanent Stationary Committee

Turner established a permanent Stationary Engineers Committee, chaired by Robert Fox, general vice president and business manager of Los Angeles Local 501, and composed of vice presidents and business managers from stationary locals. The committee's agenda included the aforesaid amalgamation and mergers, education and training, interlocal communication, territorial jurisdiction, industrial surveying, and organization in the health care industry. (The latter would prove to be the most complicated, difficult, expensive, and time-consuming initiative of the post-1960 years.) A newsletter, *Intercom,* was authorized to inform all locals of what was happening in the stationary field. A map was created that showed the territorial jurisdiction of each stationary local. A computerized industrial survey was begun that, coupled with the use of the *International Union Directory,* would provide each local with the location of all stationary agreements on file in the United States and Canada, thus providing a tool for stationary locals in both organizing and servicing the membership.

Two Major Battles

The intricacies of NLRB procedures, including the vagaries of federal district court decisions, and internecine warfare between AFL-CIO affiliates, are well illustrated by two jurisdictional and organizational battles—one involving health care facilities throughout the country and the other, state employees in California.

The Health Care Battle

Prior to 1974, stationary locals had organized skilled maintenance or craft units within more than 250 hospitals and other health care facilities, many with a handshake rather than a formal election procedure. At that time, hospitals were not covered by the National Labor Relations Act; thus state legislation, where it existed, governed labor relations in the health care industry. In 1974, Congress passed the health care amendments that extended the National Labor Relations Act to all private health care employers—legislation that was actively sought and supported by the IUOE. An issue soon arose, however, as to the appropriate bargaining units in hospitals. The dispute was generated by comments in the Senate and House Committee reports on the legislation that the NLRB should give consideration to avoiding proliferation in bargaining units. These comments would be used by the American Hospital Association in its battle against skilled maintenance units, arguing that only the largest possible units were appropriate.

Over the following years, stationary locals frequently encountered difficulty in having their skilled maintenance units found appropriate. For example, in 1975, Local 39 petitioned the NLRB to establish a five-member stationary engineer unit in a small San Francisco Shriners hospital.[17] In a split majority decision, the NLRB decided that "in the hospital industry the only appropriate unit for collective bargaining which encompasses stationary engineers is a broad unit consisting of all service and maintenance engineers." In effect, the NLRB was opting for a limitation to two units—one professional and one nonprofessional. Thus, janitors, orderlies, and other relatively unskilled workers were lumped together with skilled and apprentice stationary engineers. The decision was hailed not only by hospitals but also by industrial unions, which attempted to organize all workers in a facility regardless of skill or craft. The decision threatened the very existence of stationary engineers in the health care industry and inevitably would affect other industries in which the IUOE traditionally has represented small units of stationary engineers. However, in other cases the NLRB found craft or skilled maintenance units appropriate. These findings often followed protracted hearings and were sometimes overturned by the courts on review. During those years of confusion, the IUOE took an active part in litigation on behalf of local unions.

By 1984, nine years after the Shriners decision, there were thirty health care cases concerning skilled craft units before the NLRB, more than half of which involved Operating Engineers locals. Finally, in 1987, the NLRB moved to put an end to the uncertainty about appropriate units in the health care industry by engaging in rule making, as contrasted to case-by-case determination. The NLRB proposed a rule that would include skilled maintenance workers with clerical and service employees in a single unit but called for hearings on the question.

In response, the IUOE's legal department, led by General Counsel Michael Fanning, coordinated a major effort with the local unions to provide testimony and other evidence to the NLRB. Over the next months, local business managers, training directors, and rank-and-file maintenance employees testified at the fourteen days of hearings across the country and also provided affidavits and other evidence to support the union's argument that skilled maintenance employees constitute an appropriate bargaining unit.

The IUOE sought to distinguish skilled maintenance employees from unskilled service employees for purposes of unit determination. According to IUOE-prepared testimony, *all* maintenance employees in hospitals should be combined in a single unit:

> There should be no confusion or concern over combining skilled workers with those less skilled, because all maintenance employees, whether skilled stationary engineers and electricians or unskilled maintenance mechanic helpers and assistants, are dedicated to the performance of skilled labor. To the extent that they all work together in skilled maintenance, whether as journeymen and women or helpers, it is accurate to identify the unit as a skilled maintenance unit. But regardless of whether it is called maintenance or skilled maintenance, the unit we seek is one which includes all skilled physical plant operation and maintenance classifications as well as those lesser skilled helper and assistant classifications engaged in physical plant maintenance and operation.[18]

The NLRB speculation that "service and maintenance employees generally do routine work, are not normally skilled or trained, and are paid less than technical employees," was termed flat-out, dead wrong . . . a slap in the face to the pride and aspirations of those who strive through training and experience to attain skills. Let there be no mistake—every member of the maintenance unit, whether the stationary engineer first class at the top of the scale or the maintenance mechanic helper at the bottom, has either achieved, or is seeking to achieve, mastery of the skills necessary to operate and maintain physical plant systems.[19]

Thus the IUOE sought a bargaining unit of skilled workers and apprentices engaged in the operation and maintenance of the health care industry's physical plants.

In April 1989, the hard work of the IUOE and its local unions culminated in the NLRB's issuance of its Final Rule on Collective Bargaining Units in the Health Care Industry, in which it found a separate skilled maintenance unit to be appropriate in all acute-care hospitals. However, the board's rule was enjoined by the District Court for the Northern District of Illinois. The IUOE joined the AFL-CIO and other affiliates in appealing that ruling, and in April 1991, the Seventh Circuit Court, on appeal, reversed the district court and found the board's rule to be valid but stayed the effect of its order until the case was reviewed by the Supreme Court. Finally, on April 23, 1991, the Supreme Court unanimously affirmed the decision of the Seventh Circuit Court, and the 16-year legal battle was over.

The NLRB rule that was affirmed by the Supreme Court specifies eight bargaining units, including:

all skilled maintenance employees (generally includes all employees involved in the maintenance, repair, and operation of the hospital's physical plant, as well as their trainees, helpers and assistants); classifications which generally should be included in such units are carpenter, electrician, mason/bricklayer, painter, pipefitter, plumber, sheetmetal fabricator, automotive mechanic, HVAC (heating, ventilating, and air conditioning) mechanic, chief engineer, operating engineer, fireman/ boiler operator, locksmith, welder, and utility man.[20]

The NLRB found that skilled maintenance employees were distinguishable from all other hospital employees in their common function and supervision; their high skill, training, and wage levels; their separate labor markets and cross-industrial career paths; their distinct organizing and bargaining interests; and their history of separate representation.

Since the Supreme Court decision upholding the rule, the International legal staff has coordinated with the local unions on petitions filed in the hospital industry to assure that the units in question display the characteristics of the skilled maintenance unit as defined in the NLRB rule. The IUOE legal department has advised and represented local unions in NLRB and court cases in which the rule has been applied; these efforts, for the most part, have been successful.

The California Triumph

The prize was 10,500 California state employees all in one state-determined bargaining unit, Unit 12, and all dispersed throughout the state in blue-collar occupations associated with several state agencies. Unit 12 originally was represented by the California State Employees' Association (CSEA), an independent union that boasted that none of its members' dues was sent to a large Washington, D.C.-based national or international union. However, in 1983, when the IUOE and the International Brotherhood of Electrical Workers (IBEW) began circulating authorization cards among Unit 12 members, and other AFL-CIO affiliates mounted organizing drives in other units CSEA represented, CSEA forgot all about the financial advantages of non–AFL-CIO affiliation and sought affiliation with an AFL-CIO union. The reason was to obtain protection under Article XX against the raiding efforts of these unions. After auditioning several unions, including the Operating Engineers, CSEA reached an affiliation agreement with the Service Employees International Union (SEIU).

Under the leadership of Art Viat, a proposal had been made for all four California IUOE locals to jointly represent Unit 12. When the four-local coalition continued its organizing efforts after CSEA affiliated with SEIU, SEIU responded by filing Article XX charges against the Operating Engineers. The basis of SEIU's charge was that, once CSEA affiliated with SEIU, CSEA's preexisting collective bargaining relationship with the State of California became protected by Article XX and the IUOE's ongoing organizing efforts violated the AFL-CIO's nonraiding constitutional provision. In its defense, the IUOE cited the criteria that the AFL-CIO had established, which an affiliation agreement had to meet in order to gain Article XX protection for the former independent union's collective-bargaining relationships. The IUOE argued that the CSEA-SEIU affiliation did not meet those criteria, particularly the requirement that the former independent's membership must be granted the full rights of membership in the AFL-CIO affiliate. The AFL-CIO arbitrator assigned to the case rejected the IUOE's arguments, finding that, although the affiliation agreement waived certain SEIU membership rights for CSEA members, the SEIU similarly had waived certain of these rights for its own local unions and, therefore, the CSEA members were treated no differently than other SEIU members. Thus the four-local coalition was obliged to cease its organizing activities.

Enter ATAM. Subsequently, another independent union, the Alliance of Trades and Maintenance (ATAM), began a successful campaign to decertify CSEA-SEIU as the bargaining agent for Unit 12. As an independent organization unaffiliated with the AFL-CIO, ATAM was not constrained by the no-raiding provision of Article XX. ATAM actually was a front for a consultant firm, and had no superstructure or field staff to service its members. Basically, what ATAM proposed was professional representation, low dues, and freedom from contributing to the treasuries of national organizations. What ATAM tried to hide, however, was that 90 percent of its income went directly to the consultant firm for services rendered. Viat tried to put together another coalition of the service employees, electrical workers, and operating engineers to oppose ATAM. For various reasons, the coalition broke down. ATAM prevailed in its campaign against CSEA/SEIU and was certified as Unit 12's bargaining agent.

Enter the Teamsters. As it turned out, ATAM did not have the necessary resources to adequately represent the Unit 12 employees. Because the 10,500 employees were so widely dispersed throughout the state, it was extremely difficult to service them without any field offices or staff equally dispersed. As a result, Unit 12 employees became dissatisfied with ATAM. In early 1990, some of the dissatisfied ATAM members contacted the Teamsters about the possibility of Teamster representation. When the business managers of the four IUOE California locals got wind of that, they immediately alerted Frank Hanley, who contacted John Sweeney, general president of the SEIU, in an attempt to form a coalition to decertify ATAM. Hanley had several meetings with Sweeney and William McCarthy, then president of the Teamsters, but for a variety of reasons, not the least of which was that McCarthy was having his own internal political problems, the Teamsters decided to drop out, and Sweeney agreed to allow the IUOE to proceed without the SEIU. SEIU's authorization to proceed was crucial because, by virtue of its former representation of Unit 12 as the parent body of CSEA, Article XX still protected SEIU's relationship with Unit 12; SEIU, therefore, could have filed Article XX charges to prevent the Operating Engineers from proceeding to decertify ATAM.

Enter the Laborers. After Hanley had received SEIU's waiver of its Article XX rights, the four California IUOE locals, with the full assistance of the International, signed up 4,000 Unit 12 employees, more than enough to file a petition to decertify ATAM in November 1990. When ATAM realized that the IUOE's petition was about to succeed, it went the way of CSEA and sought affiliation with an AFL-CIO union in order to obtain Article XX protection. No longer was the independent status of ATAM considered important; if it was to remain the bargaining agent of Unit 12, it would have to affiliate with an AFL-CIO union. ATAM chose to affiliate with the Laborers International Union of North America (LIUNA). Despite efforts by Frank Hanley to dissuade the Laborers, the importance of the "numbers game" won out, and the Laborers agreed to become the parent body of ATAM. The prize of 10,500 members was too inviting to pass up.

Immediately upon reaching the affiliation agreement with ATAM, the Laborers filed Article XX charges against the Operating Engineers, basically advancing the same theory on behalf of ATAM's collective-bargaining relationship with the State of California that SEIU had advanced on behalf of CSEA's contract in 1983. This time the Article XX situation was much more complicated, however, since SEIU still had Article XX protection for Unit 12, and the Laborers had not obtained a waiver from SEIU before striking the affiliation bargain with ATAM. SEIU responded by filing Article XX charges against LIUNA, and LIUNA filed a countercharge against SEIU, in addition to its charge against the IUOE.

In the meantime, the California Personnel Board refused to defer the decertification election pending the resolution of the Article XX cases, so hearings on the Article XX charges proceeded while the ballots were being mailed to the Unit 12 members. The legal situation was complicated further when certain ATAM members, with full IUOE support, sued ATAM in the California courts alleging, among other things, that the ATAM officers did not have the authority to agree to the ATAM-LIUNA affiliation because they were improperly holding office. The Article XX charges and this lawsuit resulted in multiple contentious proceedings during the months of March and April 1991.

When the legal dust had settled, the Operating Engineers had successfully defended against LIUNA's Article XX charge, and the ATAM members successfully prosecuted their lawsuit. Ironically, the IUOE prevailed in the Article XX case on the same argument that it had unsuccessfully advanced in the 1983 Article XX proceeding with SEIU. The IUOE argued that the LIUNA-ATAM affiliation agreement was inadequate to convey Article XX protection because the agreement did not meet the AFL-CIO requirement that full rights of membership in LIUNA be given to ATAM members. The AFL-CIO arbitrator, University of Pennsylvania law professor Howard Lesnick, agreed that the affiliation agreement left ATAM members as second-class citizens within LIUNA. He, therefore, found that the IUOE's continued organizing after the ATAM-LIUNA merger did not violate Article XX.

Victory at Last. Arbitrator Lesnick issued his decision on April 30, 1991. On May 3rd, the California Personnel Board counted the ballots in the Unit 12 election. The four-local IUOE coalition triumphed, receiving 3,271 votes to ATAM's 2,736 votes. Thus, in 1991, the Operating Engineers gained 10,500 new public employee members. They were divided by craft and geographical location between the four California locals—Locals 39 and 3 in the north and Locals 501 and 12 in the south—stationary and hoisting and portable, respectively.

The Name of the Game. The battle for Unit 12 involved five national or international unions and two independents (which eventually became "dependent") in a contest with a prize of 10,500 new members. Craft jurisdiction was not a primary factor in the battle; Unit 12 was composed of so many different crafts that, if craft jurisdiction were the deciding issue, as many as eight or more different unions would represent the membership. The California contest was about organization in the public sector where craft demarcations are, for the most part, ignored. In the interunion struggle against membership decline, many of the rules of the past governing interunion relationships appear to be in abeyance. The new name of the game is "numbers," and everyone, especially public employees, are fair prey. Because so many public sector job classifications normally fall within the jurisdiction of both the hoisting and portable and stationary jurisdictions, the IUOE became a major contestant in the "game."

The Implications

The stationary engineers were forced to abandon the pure-craft bloodlines and expand their jurisdiction into new areas, particularly the health care industry and the public sector. Membership in the stationary branch continued to grow, aided by improved education and training programs and wall-to-wall organizing when necessary. Although somewhat limited by AFL-CIO antiraiding regulations, the stationary branch was strengthened through amalgamation and mergers and several successful litigation battles.

Reorganization

These successful organizing efforts of both stationary and hoisting and portable locals were products of steadily improving communication and coordination between the International union and the locals. One of Hanley's first moves as general president was to revamp the general executive board, which had been made up of vice presidents drawn from both International staff and local business managers. As employees of the international union, the International representatives were likely to represent the views of the general president and perhaps the general secretary-treasurer, leading to criticism that the board was a rubber stamp for the incumbent administration. Several resignations from the board occurred concurrent with Hanley's ascendance to the presidency in 1990. He exercised his presidential political influence to have none but local business managers elected to the vice-presidency and, therefore, to the board. During the elapsed three years, the relationship between the president and the board has been as amicable as it was during the years when substantial numbers of the board members were International employees. But when a divisive issue arises, greater independence on the part of the board should be manifest.

At the same time, Hanley undertook a reorganization of the International staff. Some departments were merged, others eliminated, and considerable personnel changes were made. As in many not-for-profit institutions, occasionally the International office employed staff or elected officials who had outlived their usefulness at the local level.

Under Hanley, only staff who had demonstrated themselves in other capacities, in and out of the union, to be dedicated, competent, and hardworking were selected for International assignments.

To assist local unions in their organizing and negotiating efforts, Hanley instituted an electronic "information exchange," providing local unions with computerized access to information on all pending public agency project planning and construction-bid openings; all identifiable private construction projects, relevant job opportunities, apprenticeship materials, organizing data, Davis-Bacon and state prevailing wage determinations, health and safety material, relevant government documents, and other material. Local unions, in turn, were able to transmit back to the international materials, feedback, or corrections on matters of concern.

Financial Initiatives

The IUOE, like many contemporary unions, has been learning during the 1990s to use its financial powers as a weapon that does not require the membership to risk either jobs or pay. According to General President Frank Hanley, the international union controls approximately $15 to $17 billion in investment funds from pension and fringe benefit plans. These funds, combined with potential investment funds of other unions, both construction and nonconstruction, constitute a significant investment portfolio. The IUOE joined in the AFL-CIO drive to use these funds to encourage unionization and provide work for union members. The major thrust of the "corporate campaign" is to direct union investments into projects on condition that the projects be union-built. Of course, in following this policy, the unions must make certain that the primary purpose of pension funds—income for the retired—is met, or the unions could be in violation of the Employee Retirement Income Security Act of 1974 (ERISA). Thus far, the unions have been successful in meeting both objectives—income for retirees and jobs for union members.

Industrial unions negotiate pension benefits, but then they leave it to the employer to either provide and administer the pension or contract with some financial or insurance company to do so. The employers are generally large enough to provide a separate plan for their nonunion employees. The employers of the craft unions, generally relatively small, are not capable of either unilateral funding or unilateral administration, necessitating union participation in pension administration. And in the casual labor markets of the construction and similar industries, the employees move frequently among employers, requiring multiemployer involvement to create a viable pension system. In fact, the creation and preservation of a private pension system in an environment of small employers and frequent job change is one of the major attractions of unionization in such industries.

The building trades unions, including the Operating Engineers, were therefore instrumental in the enactment of the Multiemployer Pension Plan Amendments Act, which included provisions to make employers withdrawing from multiemployer plans liable for the unfunded vested liabilities occurring during their period of contribution to the plan. Withdrawal from a multiemployer plan in the construction industry is defined as occurring only if the employer ceases to have an obligation to contribute to the plan and continues to perform the same type of work in the jurisdiction of the collective bargaining agreement, or resumes such work within five years without then renewing the obligation to contribute. To thwart double-breasted companies that maintain a small operation subject to the plan in order to avoid withdrawal liability assessments, the law also provides that a partial withdrawal occurs when "the employer's obligation to contribute under the plan is continued for no more than an insubstantial portion of work in the craft and area jurisdiction of the collective bargaining agreement of the type for which contributions are required."[21] This was a union-sponsored provision aimed at doublebreasted organizations.

Finally, President Hanley has started a process that he calls "stock tracking." He has assigned a full-time staff member, Tim James, to track where the union's funds have been invested. The stock tracker has been trained in how corporations invest their money and what takes place at the stockholders' meeting. Hanley puts it this way:

> I am talking about where a contractor or an owner has a policy of making their jobs nonunion. We are going to determine how much stock we have in that company. We are going to ask for a meeting. . . . All we want to know is why the company is making that nonunion decision. If it is an intelligent decision and there is reason for it, so be it. But if it's merely to keep unions out, then we're going to see you at the stockholders' meeting. And we are going to get other people to come with us.[22]

Hanley says that he may never see the complete benefit of the program, "but the general president after me is going to see a first-class operation when it comes to how to handle a stockholders' meeting."

To what extent these initiatives will be effective remains to be seen, but the ability to use hard-gained funds to affect corporate attitudes toward unions is generally recognized as a potent future tool in providing work for union labor.

Canadian Growth

One year after the 1896 founding of the National Union of Steam Engineers, the parent organization of today's IUOE, the union's jurisdiction was expanded to include Canadian stationary locals. From that point on, the National Union of Steam Engineers, and eventually its successor, the IUOE, became an International union. The internationalization had strong economic motives. United States contractors and corporations were active on both sides of the border; thus agreements negotiated in the United States needed to be applied to Canada as well, and vice-versa. Canadian workers gained the support of a larger and potentially more powerful "International" union, and the union could exert pressure to keep its contractors honest on both sides of the border.

The question of Canadian representation within the International union, or the adequacy of such representation, became an issue in the 1950s when some Canadians began to pressure then President William Maloney for a vice-presidency and a seat on the International's general executive board. Maloney resisted the creation of a Canadian vice presidency, but did agree to appoint a Canadian regional director. He asked for and received nominations for the position but took a long time in making up his mind. Finally, Rowland Hill received a telegram from Maloney asking him to report to the International office. According to Hill:

> I went to see Maloney. After hours of waiting, I was able to see him in his office. He said that the names he had received were not acceptable to him. And he told me that my name had been suggested and asked me what I thought about it. Well, I was not prepared at that stage to make a commitment. So, I said, "Well, Mr. President, I was not aware that my name had been submitted," and asked him to tell me who was my

sponsor. He did not answer me but said that I was the only one who was acceptable to him. I asked him whether I could go back and talk to our people. He said, "No, you have five minutes to make up your mind!" Well, things were going around in my mind—I really didn't want it that badly. And at the same time, I didn't want to roll the thing out of the water because we would end up worse than we were at the time. So, I told him that I would accept the appointment. And so I became the Canadian regional director in 1952.[23]

Herb Ingham, who succeeded Hill as regional director, says that Hill was primarily responsible for improving Canada's status within the International. "He went to the executive board meetings and fought for Canada. As far as I am concerned, Rollie is the father of the International Union of Operating Engineers in Canada."[24] Certainly, Hill was instrumental in the creation of a Canadian Conference in 1958, and in 1972 he became the first Canadian to be elected vice-president and gain a seat on the general executive board. Ingham's successor as regional director, Budd Coutts, was selected by J. C. Turner and later was appointed by the executive board as secretary-treasurer when Hanley was elected to the presidency in 1990. Both were elected to their respective positions at the 1993 convention.

Canada has its equivalent of the AFL-CIO, the Canadian Labour Congress (CLC), but the Canadian IUOE and most of the other building trades left the organization in 1982 and formed a new organization—the Canadian Federation of Labour (CFL)—creating a split between the primarily craft and primarily industrial unions in Canada. Thus the Canadian labor movement went in the opposite direction from its counterpart in the United States, where the craft-oriented American Federation of Labor and the Congress of Industrial Organizations had merged in 1955 as the AFL-CIO. The major reason for the Canadian split was that the craft unions opposed the close alliance between the CLC and the National Democratic Party (a third party, which gained considerable strength in Ontario and British Columbia). The crafts believed that the industrial unions were trying to gain through legislation the bargaining power the craft unions had already achieved by exercise of economic power. There was also the feeling that the legislation sought by the CLC, controlled by the big industrial unions, could make it easier for the industrial unions to absorb workers already organized by the craft unions. Jim Biddle, the current IUOE Canadian regional director, says that only the carpenters of all of the building trades have defected and rejoined the CLC.

The modest long-term growth of the Canadian IUOE locals helped to a small but significant degree to offset some of the U.S. hoisting and portable membership decline, especially during the late 1970s and the 1980s (Table 7.3). Nevertheless, that growth has not been without its fluctuations and its own troubled times, three of which are especially worthy of note.

In the early 1960s, a group of stationary engineers split from the International Union of Operating Engineers and formed the Canadian Union of Operating Engineers (CUOC). The dissidents claimed that they were not getting enough attention from the IUOE, but Rowland Hill believes that intraunion politics was the major reason for the split; the local leaders wanted to run their own show without interference from the International. The CUOC still exists, but is declining in both membership and influence.

The peculiar politics of Quebec led to a split within the hoisting and portable ranks in 1982. As a result of the separatist political movement which sought to break Quebec away from the other provinces as an independent state, Local 791, along with most of the building trades local unions in Quebec split from their international unions and formed independent local unions. The IUOE did not oppose Local 791's departure because that local had already been under government-imposed trusteeship for several years as a result of government investigation into allegedly corrupt influences in the local. The International replaced 3,000-member Local 791 with Local 905, which by 1993 had 1,500 members.

Canadian Operating Engineer locals function under a different set of legal rules and regulations than their U.S. counterparts. In Canada, provincial rather than national labor legislation has the greatest effect on the building trades in general and the Operating Engineers in particular. The primary reason for the 1983–86 hoisting and portable membership loss, displayed in Table 7.3, was an open shop movement in Alberta and British Columbia promulgated by the antiunion Construction Labor Relations Association (CLRA). That organization took its cues from the Business Roundtable and the Associated Builders and Contractors of America, leaders of the open shop movement in the United States. Doublebreasting, which did not appear in other Canadian provinces, made an appearance in Alberta. Throughout most of

Table 7.3

Canadian IUOE Membership, 1977–1991

Year	Total	% IUOE Total	Stationary	H & P
1977	31,530	7.8	5,871	25,659
1980	34,360	8.2	6,492	27,868
1983	37,060	9.7	6,742	30,318
1986	31,443	8.7	6,529	24,914
1989	34,246	9.4	7,215	27,031
1991	36,559	10.0	6,991	29,568

Note: Extracted from official IUOE statistics.

the Canadian provinces, unions which could show that they represented a majority of any contractor's employees could generally be granted bargaining rights for them without elections. As a result of CLRA lobbying, the labor laws of both western provinces were changed to require elections for all bargaining rights applications. The delay inherent in exercising the election requirements gave the employer time for antiunion counter initiatives, as in the United States.

In fact, however, the Alberta-British Columbia open shop movement had the effect of increasing the intensity of organizing activities of all of the Canadian building trades, including the Operating Engineers. Eventually, the British Columbia law was repealed, whereas the Alberta unions learned to effectively counter employer tactics in certification elections. Thereafter, the IUOE conducted organizing classes in British Columbia, Saskatchewan, and Ontario, which had the effect of improving organization success rates. Increased organization efforts accompanied a post-1982 construction boom in Alberta and Ontario and an increase in pipeline construction across the entire nation and resulted in continued growth despite the open shop disruption from 1983 to the present. By 1991, Canadian membership was just short of the 1983 record and still climbing. The 14 percent gain in Canadian membership between 1977 and 1991 helped to offset the 13 percent loss of U.S. hoisting and portable members and brought the Canadian proportion of IUOE membership from 7.8 percent in the former year to 10 percent in the latter.

Jim Biddle believes that Canada's modest growth rate will continue during the nineties. He rates the relationship between the Canadian locals and the headquarters' office as "above nine" on scale of one to ten and believes that Canada's new government is a move to the political center (from the previous administration's position on the right of the spectrum), which, in turn, should make organizing a bit easier. "There won't be a return to the heady days of the 1960s," he says, "but our house is in order and we expect to experience a steady climb in membership during the remaining years of the twentieth century."[25]

Limited Growth

For the union as a whole, the recession of the early 1980s stalled any quick recovery in membership growth. Unemployment in construction reached 20 percent in 1982 and fell only slightly to 18.4 percent in 1983. From that point until 1988, construction unemployment dropped, reaching a decade low of 11.6 percent in 1987, only to rise again during the recession of the early 1990s. Yet by 1993, the union could boast:

> At a time when most unions are suffering devastating losses in membership, the IUOE is growing. While other unions are having to increase dramatically their per capita tax . . . the IUOE is keeping its per capita low and its services high. While other unions see little, if any, hope of growth, the IUOE is positioned to take advantage of the growing trend among underrepresented workers to seek unionization as the only means of achieving decent wages and working conditions.[26]

Although gratifying, the renewed growth was too limited and narrow for comfort. Between 1987 and 1991, 82 IUOE locals experienced gains totaling 21,763, and 112 locals suffered losses totaling 15,639, for a net gain of 6,124. However, only nine locals with 2,000 or more members accounted for 67 percent of the net gain. Actually, two locals with memberships greater than 15,000 accounted for 27 percent of the gain. These two locals, Local 3 in the west and Local 150 in Illinois, together with the Canadian locals, accounted for over half the total IUOE gain between 1987 and 1991. By the end of 1992, the IUOE had added an additional 2,399 members, thus recording a net gain of 8,523 since 1987.

Growth and Containment

The IUOE counterattack included concessions to increase the competitiveness of union contractors, aggressive organizational activities in both the public and private sectors, the training of operating engineers in areas of future demand, legal defense of health care unit determination, and financial initiatives designed to increase employment opportunities for both hoisting and portable and stationary engineers. Membership decline was turned around in the stationary and Canadian jurisdictions, and new fields were opened in public employment. But no more than containment can yet be claimed in the construction industry. The counterattack at the local level is the subject of chapter 8.

Chapter 8

THE VIEW FROM THE LOCAL LEVEL

The counterattack was not solely an International undertaking; local unions developed their own means for coping with the open shop incursion and technological change. The case histories below provide a view from the local level, including the actions taken by local unions to meet the challenges of a difficult period in the Operating Engineers' history.

The Largest Local

Local 3, headquartered in the San Francisco Bay area, is not only the IUOE's largest local in terms of members but also one of the largest in the entirety of organized labor in terms of its geographical scope. The local has 35,000 members, and its jurisdiction includes northern California, Utah, Hawaii, and most of Nevada.

Since 1956, when the local was led by Business Manager Victor S. Swanson, it has experienced a series of political upheavals, including a period of International supervision, that might have left a weaker union shattered, but they had little lasting effect on Local 3. The first upheaval came when Swanson unsuccessfully challenged Maloney for the International presidency at the 1956 convention. Swanson, who according to one of his successors, Dale Marr, "preached hate of the International,"[1] was the subject of an International audit that indicated that he and several of his cronies had their hands in the till. He was removed from International and local office (he had been an IUOE vice-president) and eventually served a term in prison for using cars, a boat, and an airplane (bought with local funds) for his own pleasure, and for speculating in real estate with union funds.

After a period of International supervision under International Vice-President and native San Franciscan Newell Carman, Al Clem was elected business manager in 1960. There followed twelve years of growth and internal political warfare, which came to a head when the U.S. Department of Labor threw out the results of the 1972 election, allegedly because of tainted ballots from Hawaii and Guam. (The latter, at the time, was part of Local 3's jurisdiction.) Clem, who had won the disputed election, then decided to retire and supported Dale Marr as his successor in the rerun. Marr, whose career in construction began as a supervisor for the Peter Kiewit Construction Company, was up against Clem's opponents Norris Casey, Stapleton, and Paul Edgecombe—the latter president of the local. Somehow or other, another Casey—Martin Casey—who was completely unknown to the membership, was put on the ballot. Martin drew 1,500 ballots away from his namesake (Norris), enough to give Marr the victory. The word around the local was that if only one Casey had come to bat, he wouldn't have struck out.

Marr, who led the union through the 1974 and 1981 recessions, decided to retire in 1983 and supported Robert Mayfield as his successor. Mayfield's (and Marr's) opponents eventually settled on Thomas Stapleton, who had served as a business agent from 1956 to 1964, became recording secretary in the latter year, then lost out in a bid for business manager in the disputed 1972 election. Stapleton won a close election and immediately fired seventy-five business agents, replacing them with his own appointees.

The political infighting within Local 3 represented the attractiveness of its financial and membership strength rather than any general dissatisfaction based on hard times. The local's membership actually increased slightly during a period when most other IUOE locals were in a decline. Recently, it moved into a new, modern facility in the East Bay, and its pension plan is now worth more than $2 billion. Its training facility at Rancho Murieta, California, has gained a worldwide reputation, and its totally computerized operation is as efficient in tracking finances, contractors, and construction coming into the jurisdiction as any in the construction industry.

Membership Growth

In 1960, Local 3 had 12,000 members—virtually all hoisting and portable engineers working in construction. By 1993, the local's membership stood at 35,000, but of the total, 7,000 were retirees and 8,000 were public employees engaged in a variety of activities, mostly outside of construction. Thus only about 20,000 are active private-sector construction workers, a gain of about 8,000 since 1960. However, since the mid-1970s, the membership's gain has been primarily in the public sector; there has been a slight loss in the private-sector hoisting and portable membership during the same period.

The major period of growth, of course, was from 1960 to 1974, when heavy and highway construction was booming in California and, as Tom Stapleton says, "we called the shots." The recessions of the mid-1970s and early 1980s and 1990s took their toll; thousands of Local 3 members became unemployed and available to work for nonunion contractors. Success in organizing government workers neutralized the loss of construction workers, but clearly, action was required if the union was to offset the inroads being made by open shop contractors. A computerized system for tracking all new construction coming into the local's jurisdiction was set up. District representatives were alerted well in advance to the nature, dollar volume, and scope of proposed new construction projects, as well as to the names of the contractors (both union and nonunion) who were bidding on the projects. Where necessary, changes were made on an ad hoc basis in the local's master agreements in order to make union contractors more competitive with their open shop competitors. But it wasn't until the mid-1980s that the local established a more orderly means for dealing with the problem.

Market Area Committees

Under the leadership of Tom Stapleton, market area committees were established, composed of three employer representatives (union contractors), three local union representatives, and three rank-and-file employees performing work in the designated market areas. The areas so designated were those where work "has been substantially lost or is rapidly being lost to nonunion employers."[2] The role of the committees was to review employer requests for changes in the terms and conditions of the master agreements believed necessary to preserve and protect work opportunities for both union members and employers. The committees were authorized to approve such changes where they were deemed necessary. The committees were limited to projects of $1,000,000 or less, the idea being that projects over $1,000,000 probably would be performed under the existing master agreements without changes or would be performed "union." The committees are unique in that one-third of their memberships are composed of operating engineers working at the trade as opposed to salaried, full-time employees of the local. Stapleton believes that the concessions granted by the committees have helped preserve low dollar-volume construction work for both union members and union contractors. To date, the open shop incursion in northern California has been greatest in the area of smaller construction projects. Nevertheless, convinced that the Associated General Contractors organization had become dominated by nonunion contractors, Local 3 played a major role in the development of an alternative association—Associated Engineers and Contracting Employers (AECE)—made up entirely of contractors operating solely within a collective bargaining structure. Concerned that a cutback in state personnel was leaving prevailing wage and other regulatory enforcement inadequately staffed, the local took the lead among the building trades in establishing the Foundation for Fair Contracting to provide private policing of those laws.

National Contracts

Victor Swanson's 1956 rebellion was triggered by President Maloney's National Pipeline Agreement, which called for a wage and benefit package less than that called for in Local 3's master agreement. Prior to the pipeline agreement, all national agreements recognized local wage and benefit scales while eliminating or lowering overtime pay provisions and other work rules. Swanson felt that the International did not have the right to overturn locally negotiated wages and fringe benefits and/or work rules. Many other locals throughout the country agreed with him, even with regard to changes in work rules to eliminate costly overtime provisions, featherbedding, and other rules that affected the competitive position of union contractors. The 1970–74 construction wage freeze gave the International temporary control over local negotiations, but as soon as controls were lifted, wages once again began to climb. However, the economic downturns of the mid-1970s and early 1980s, together with the open shop incursion, reduced local resistance to national contracts.

Under Stapleton, a reevaluation was made of the construction industry in Local 3's jurisdiction. Work rules that made union contractors less competitive were thrown out of the master agreements. "We made up forms," Stapleton says, "that included all contract stipulations, safety provisions, overtime, work rules, etc., and asked superintendents, engineers, and others responsible for the work to evaluate each stipulation. We changed our contracts based on these evaluations. Our goal was to make our employers more competitive with the nonunion contractors."[3] National contracts were no longer viewed as an infringement of the rights of the local; in most cases, they were seen as benevolent. Stapleton also points out that when times were good, back in the halcyon days of the 1960s and early 1970s, the contractors were as much responsible for featherbedding work rules as the unions. "They had these cost-plus-25-percent contracts, whereby they could make more money if projects were overmanned."[4] Dale Marr, Stapleton's predecessor, puts it more bluntly:

> I was teaching classes in labor relations at Bechtel, and one of the things they wanted me to talk about was featherbedding. And I told those budding supervisors that the king of featherbedders was sitting upstairs, John O'Connor [a Bechtel and AGC official]. My first introduction to a compressor operator was when I was oiling on a big rig in Richmond. There was this guy carrying a little pump and another guy walking along right behind him with a Local 3 button on. I asked the manager, "Who is the guy following the guy with the pump?" The manager said, "He's the pump operator." I said that I could urinate a bigger stream than that thing could pump. So why was the pump carrier there? Because of cost-plus-25-percent. Those compressor and pump operators started during the war and they [the companies] didn't want to give them up.[5]

Marr might have added that they didn't want to give them up until the boom days were over and the open shop contractors were breathing down the necks of the union contractors. Then, featherbedding was blamed unilaterally on union work rules.

All of these changes came too late to prevent a loss of membership and work, but they did stem the decline and set the stage for a renewal, when and if the expected upturn in construction activity was to occur.

The Civil Rights Challenge

Another effect of the loss of hoisting and portable membership was the inability of the union to extricate itself from the consent decree that was issued against Local 3 in 1972. The local's attempts to increase its minority membership were thwarted by negative economic conditions. Since the late 1960s, the union's apprenticeship program has ranged from 27 percent to 33 percent minority, and other minority members have been enrolled outside apprenticeship. The problem was that during economic downturns, younger engineers tended to leave construction in favor of more stable jobs in other industries and, of course, minorities were among the younger engineers. As for apprentices, when openings dried up, apprentices dropped out of the program. "We always have too many apprentices when we don't need them," according to Stapleton, "and not enough when we do need them."[6] The result is that Local 3 is still operating under the 1972 consent decree. The fact that the union's minority membership has increased mainly through organization in the public sector has no effect on the court. "The court only considers our construction membership," Stapleton says, "they couldn't care less about our government members."[7]

The situation has changed a great deal since the 1960s in that today there are far more options available to minorities. "I have never worked at anything except construction," Stapleton says, "When times were good, I made good money; when times were bad, I was laid off. But today, when the layoffs come in construction, people move on to more stable employment, and the opportunities available to minorities in other fields have multiplied, so it's difficult to hold them. God knows we have tried, but so far we haven't succeeded."[8]

On the Open Shop Doorstep: Baltimore

A continent and more away (if Hawaii is considered) from Local 3's jurisdiction, Local 37 in Baltimore, Maryland, copes with the changing nature of labor relations in the construction industry. Located in the birthplace of the Associated Builders and Contractors of America (ABC), the driving force behind the open shop movement, Local 37 fights to maintain its share of the construction market. Ron DeJuliis, business manager of Local 37, admits that nonunion contractors have negatively affected organizing in Maryland, but "not to the extent that you might think."[9] He blames the open shop incursion on the short-sightedness of local building trades leadership. "They still want to do things that they did twenty years ago," DeJuliis says.

> They prevent their contractors from being competitive. But the operating engineers have always been innovative, and we try to be that way here. But our hands are tied with the other trades. So, we enter into more independent types of agreements [without the other construction trades]. Remember, though, that the nonunion movement is still based on greed and selfishness and, in the long run, that is going to hurt them. We are already increasing our membership by bringing in nonunion workers.[10]

Actually, Local 37 is a mixed local—that is, made up of hoisting and portable and stationary engineers. Its membership totals 2,800—a far cry from Local 3's 35,000, but it is up about 500 since 1977. Approximately 75 percent of the members work in construction; the remainder are stationary engineers. The union has experienced an increase in membership despite the decline of one of the area's largest industries—Bethlehem Steel—and the loss of work to open shop contractors. Although small in size, Local 37 has been involved in several initiatives of national significance.

Apprenticeship

DeJuliis claims that close to 50 percent of the hoisting and portable membership are graduates of the local's apprenticeship program. That is a good deal higher than the national figure, but, as DeJuliis explains, the program is twenty-five years old, operates year-round, and has a certain built-in flexibility that allows trainees to spend less time in training, if their skills are evaluated as advanced at the time of entry. The program is located on a seventy-five acre plot a few miles north of Baltimore and employs six full-time instructors.

A unique illustration of how apprentices can be put to work on a public project occurred in Baltimore County. A stump dump—that is, a burial ground for tree stumps—caught on fire. The dump was huge; it covered 1,500 acres and was 150 feet deep. The dump was smoldering for two years, causing complaints from homeowners in the neighborhood who exerted pressure on the county to correct the situation. Experts were called in, and it was finally decided to capsulate the dump with dirt. The county asked for bids, and the cost of the first proposals received averaged between $5 million and $6 million. As a result, the county changed the specifications and put the job out for bids a second time. The cost of the new proposals averaged between $1 and $2 million.

DeJuliis approached the county and proposed that Local 37's apprentices be put to work on the job under the supervision of the program's six instructors. He said that not only would the job be done well, but that the county would be saved a good deal of money. After watching the apprentices build access roads to the site, the county accepted DeJuliis's offer. According to DeJuliis:

> I literally shut down the school and the whole operation. We rented the equipment from a union contractor, so that he got something out of the project too. My instructors were put on the county payroll during the course of the project, thus saving me money. My apprentices received practical, hands-on experience, and we did the job in three and one-half months for less then $500,000, thus saving the county more than a million dollars.[11]

Local 37 received an award from the county for its work on the tree-stump dump.

Bethlehem Steel

A good example of the conflicts that arise between unions when employment is declining occurred at Bethlehem's Baltimore steel plant and involved the United Steel Workers and Local 37. At one time, the Bethlehem plant employed 30,000 workers, including 2,000 members of the construction trades, of which 325 were operating engineers. Today, the plant employs only 5,000 workers, and the construction trades total is down to about 300, of which sixty are operating engineers. As employment declined, the steel workers' union demanded that the company refrain from contracting out maintenance work without first obtaining approval from the steelworkers' local. The purpose, of course, was to place steelworkers in the maintenance jobs. A 1986 arbitrator ruled against the company and in favor of the steelworkers on the issue. Thus, if the company continued to contract out maintenance work, the steelworkers could approach management and demand that steelworkers be placed in those maintenance jobs.

Local 37 had a contract with a maintenance company, which, in turn, had a contract with Bethlehem Steel, that involved sixty operating engineers. The steelworkers demanded that the operating engineers employed by the maintenance company be replaced with steelworkers. Attempts to settle the dispute at the local level failed. Local 37, therefore, filed an Article XX complaint against the steelworkers. Hearings were held where both sides presented their arguments before an arbitrator. In early January 1992, the AFL-CIO arbitrator ruled in favor of Local 37.

The decision is significant in that it establishes a precedent in an on-going dispute between craft and industrial unions. Craft unions generally have contracts with outside contractors to maintain industrial facilities. The arrangement presents no problem as long as the plants are operating at full capacity. But when employment declines, the industrial unions, as in the Bethlehem case, demand that the maintenance jobs be turned over to in-plant workers. Thus Local 37's victory could be applied to similar disputes occurring throughout the country.

Targeting

Nowadays, everybody expects to get a "rebate" when they purchase a new car. The building trades have latched on to this concept in their attempt to make union contractors more competitive with their non-union counterparts. The idea was first advanced by an Illinois electricians' local and has spread throughout the country, especially in areas where the building trades unions are losing their share of the market. Targeting involves the establishment of an "industry advancement fund," financed by an assessment of local union members, for the purpose of supplying union contractors with a "rebate" for hiring union labor. In Baltimore, for example, Local 37 members are assessed 50 cents an hour (of their hourly on-the-job wage). These moneys are placed in a special fund to be used in connection with "job targeting." Certain projects or jobs are targeted by the building trades acting together or by any one building-trades union acting alone.

If, for example, a proposed job requires 1,000 work hours and there is a five-dillar difference between the union and nonunion wage, the union proposes to the contractor that, at the completion of the project, the union will provide the contractor with a rebate of $5,000, thus allowing the union contractor to bid on the same level as the nonunion contractor. DeJuliis says that Local 37 has won seventeen or eighteen projects involving 44,000 work hours by means of the job-targeting program.

Needless to say, the Associated Builders and Contractors of America do not look with favor on job targeting. They see it as nothing more than a kickback, and they sued in federal court to have the program outlawed in projects involving federal funds. ABC contended that the program was a violation of the 1932 Copeland Act, which prohibits employers from accepting kickbacks from employees as a condition of their employment. It is ironic that a nonunion organization would use a prolabor statute in order to thwart a local union initiative, but that is what happened, and the federal judge's decision was in favor of the ABC.

That decision applied only to federal contracts, not to contracts in the private sector. Local 37 is one of only two IUOE locals that have adopted the job-targeting program, but DeJuliis sees it as a potentially powerful weapon in the battle against the open shop. "There is another face to it," he says.

> If we lose the contract, I can say to the owner, "Look, we lost this job by only $5,000. If you use our people or our contractor, I'll give you a grant of $5,000 and I'll guarantee that you're going to get top quality labor at the price you want." Or I can tell him that otherwise he might see a picket line out there.[12]

He hasn't been able to turn an owner around yet, nor have there been any picket lines, but he and most of the other building trades in Baltimore (all but the Laborers have industry advancement funds) have high hopes for the future.

Licensing

Although stationary engineers must be licensed in many counties, municipalities, and states, and the licensing of heavy-equipment operators is mandatory in most Canadian provinces, licensing has never been required for heavy equipment operators in the United States. In the city of Baltimore, however, Local 37 was instrumental in passing an ordinance requiring the licensing of all heavy equipment operators.

The law, passed a year and one-half ago, covers nine pieces of equipment, including cranes, loaders, and bulldozers. Thus far, however, because of budget shortcomings, the law has not been implemented. DeJuliis serves on a six-person board that is charged with the responsibility of developing the licensing program. When the law becomes effective, all contractors working on City of Baltimore projects will be required to hire only licensed operators. Local 37, with its training program geared to licensing indentured apprentices and upgrading the skills journeymen and journeywomen, will be in a good position to provide a source of licensed operators.

At any rate, thanks to the efforts of Local 37, Baltimore is the only political jurisdiction in the United States that requires the licensing of *all* heavy equipment operators. (Crane operators must be licensed in some cities, counties, and states.) Whether this will redound to the benefit of Local 37, only time will tell.

Prevailing Wages

Local 37 deals with three sets of prevailing wage laws: the Davis-Bacon Act covering federally financed construction; Maryland's "Little Davis-Bacon Act," and the city and county of Baltimore's, "Little, Little Davis-Bacon Act." However, the state and local laws are not well policed because of budget cutbacks, and the federal law often causes problems for union members and their contractors because of the "fringe-benefit factor." The nonunion contractors pay the union wage and then add, in cash, the equivalent of the value of the union fringe benefit package. Human nature being the way it is, the workers believe that they are being paid more working nonunion than if they were working under a union contract. The fact is that they may earn more cash but have far less medical protection (if any), little or no life insurance, and no pension contributions. Davis-Bacon works best in a highly unionized area; in areas such as Baltimore and eastern and western Maryland, where nonunion competition is strong, its impact is not quite so benevolent.

The unions fought a long and hard battle to obtain medical insurance and other fringe benefits for their members. It is ironic that many of today's blue-collar workers, ignorant of past union battles, forgo these benefits for cash, thereby jeopardizing their own and their families' future security. It is less surprising that employers save money wherever they can, even at the expense of leaving their employ-ees uncovered in the face of inevitable family and life exigencies.

Local 37's jurisdiction also covers western Maryland and the state's eastern shore. Its membership is 40 percent minority and 3 percent female. Beside the headquarters office in Baltimore, there is one office each on the eastern shore and in western Maryland. The local has an executive board, three trustees, and three auditors and employs six full-time business agents who service both construction and stationary contracts. Thus Local 37 is a small but vibrant union operating with considerable success in what is generally accepted as hostile territory.

Minnesota's 49ers

A sharp contrast in philosophy characterizes Local 49. Its sobriquet is "The 49ers," but the members root for the Minnesota Vikings rather than the San Francisco team. Local 49, headquartered in St. Paul, covers the states of Minnesota, North Dakota, and eastern South Da-kota. Its business manager, Fred Dereschuk, became a member of Local 49 in 1952, its dispatcher in 1960, president in 1982, business manager in 1984, and International vice president in 1989. Part of the union's jurisdiction (Minnesota) is one of the most highly organized areas in the country; the remainder (the Dakotas) is "right-to-work" territory and a good deal less friendly to trade unions. However, most of the members reside in Minnesota where, Dereschuk estimates, Local 49 controls about 70 percent of the hoisting and portable potential.

The Membership

At the present time, the union's membership stands at 10,200, down from 14,000 in 1977. Local 49 lost 1,100 state highway maintenance workers in 1979, when the Minnesota Legislature passed a bill consoli-dating union representation in the state, which, in effect, transferred the highway workers from Local 49 to the American Federation of State, County and Municipal Employees (AFSCME). Similarly, some electri-cians who had acquired IUOE membership in similar fashion were turned over to the IBEW. The remainder of the loss was due to down-turns in the construction industry. The union responded by organizing county highway maintenance workers, thus making up for some of the loss that occurred at the state level.

The majority of the local's members are employed in the heavy and highway and building sectors (6,500). Approximately 2,000 are government workers, and the remainder are employed by equipment shops and sand and gravel pits all within the operating engineers craft. The union is constantly organizing, not so much to increase its membership but to replace those who die, retire, or withdraw from the union for other reasons. The local has considered organizing several big groups outside the construction industry but has not followed through, mainly because of the change it might make in the union. "You have to be very careful," Dereschuk says, "because the mixture might overturn the whole organization and the new group could gain control."[13] The result of this conservative policy is that the union's membership has remained constant, at slightly over 10,000, for the past five years. But that membership is well served.

The Competition

Although there has been some nonunion activity in suburban and rural areas, it has not been significant and has not been the cause of the local's slight decline in membership; that decline was due primarily to a decrease in construction activity. There has been no doublebreasting in Local 49's jurisdiction, and the local has made few changes in its master agreements to bolster the competitiveness of union contractors. Given his local's strong bargaining position, Dereschuk objects to any national agreement designed to support union contractors in open shop areas that might be used to pursue concessions where, as he sees it, they are not needed.

The local negotiates its own project agreements, some of which are covered by national agreements, at wages higher than those called for in the national agreements and without other concessions granted in the national pacts. "So far," Dereschuk says, "our contractors have not rebelled and demanded to be covered under the national agreements."[14] As far as project agreements are concerned, the wages, fringe benefits, and working conditions are set at prejob conferences. Another means of maintaining good relations with contractors is the local's Liaison Committee, composed of contractors and union representatives, which meets once a month to discuss problems and propose changes in master agreements. Evidence of the local's good employer relations is that there has not been a strike in the jurisdiction since 1969—twenty five years ago.

Training

Local 49 is very much involved in training, especially an "upgrading program" to improve the skills of journeymen and journeywomen and to keep the members up-to-date on new technological developments. the local's training center is open to all members during the off-season (February to April). Courses are offered on changing crane technology, hazardous waste operation, tower crane operation, and the operation of backhoes, bulldozers, scrapers, and small equipment. The latest equipment, rented from equipment supply companies or borrowed from contractors, as well as simulators, are used. Local 49's upgrading program is considered one of the best in the country.

Despite a strong commitment to training, the local manifests a traditional pre-1960s attitude toward apprenticeship. Reflecting both employer reluctance to entrust the operation of expensive machinery to inexperienced people and the high dropout rates of apprentices confronted by sporadic employment, Business Manager Dereschuk prefers a less formal approach to on-the-job "learning," in both equipment maintenance and operation.

> We maintain the machines we work with, and learners are assigned to those maintenance machines. Learners are also assigned to operators on the job. When a person has a chance to work with these machines, he learns ... and the operator helps him learn. ... That's how you get a good operator, and that is why we maintain learners on all of our rigs.[15]

The local has an apprentice program, but its size is consistent with the prevailing attitude.

The innate conservatism may be an artifact of the local's history. Local 49 was formed through the merger of members of the Steam Shovel and Dredgemen into the International Union of Steam and Operating Engineers in 1927. Further amalgamation brought in all engineer locals in Minnesota, North Dakota, and eastern South Dakota. Local officers and the executive board are elected by referendum vote. The members of the executive board are elected from five geographical areas throughout the territory. A total of twenty-one business agents service contracts in the heavy and highway, building, well-drilling, pipeline, sand and gravel, supplies, county, municipality, hospital, school-district, and cemetery sectors. Located in a strong union area, Local 49 suffered little from the open shop incursion. As a result, it is more concerned with protecting its present membership than with expansion.

Northern California Stationary Engineers

The movement toward organization in the public sector was given its greatest impetus under the leadership of Art Viat in northern California. When Viat assumed leadership of Local 39, the local was not in good shape. Since its formation by means of a merger of nine local unions in 1947, it has had six business managers and by 1965, the International was considering placing the local under supervision. The problem was that when the merger took place, each of the nine locals was given equal representation on the executive board regardless of the differences in local memberships. For example, San Francisco had a membership of 2,000 while Fresno had only 150, yet both had equal representation on the board. This led to the development of cliques, each seeking control of the union, thus causing periodic upheavals in the leadership of the local. Viat's first order of business was to promote something closer to proportional representation. It took him over a year, but the by-laws were finally revised to provide one executive board member for memberships of 150 or less, an additional member for memberships from 151 to 750, and a total of three representatives for memberships over 750. The result was that control of the local shifted to the San Francisco Bay area, where most of the membership was located.

When Viat took over, the local had 3,000 members, almost all "pure" stationary engineers in the private sector. The only public sector members were a few hundred city of San Francisco stationary engineers —a contract, Viat says, that was accomplished with a handshake. But conditions were changing in northern California, and Viat realized that the local could not survive without broadening its organizational base. Industries were either shutting down or moving out of the area, and the application of high tech to power-generating units was causing changes in the craft of stationary engineer; some jobs were being eliminated altogether, and others required retraining for current engineers and new training for incoming engineers.

Viat appeared numerous times before the general executive board, urging organization outside the pure craft "blood lines," especially in the public sector; but, until the administration of J. C. Turner, he was rebuffed. Even Turner was reluctant to abandon the "blood lines," but he did give a tentative go-ahead. According to Viat, it wasn't until the Dugan-Hanley era that the stationary jurisdiction began to receive the attention and services they needed from the International. Viat, like Gindorf in Chicago, gives Hanley full credit for improving the status of the stationary locals within the international union.

Public Employees

Today, Local 39 has 13,000 members—the largest stationary local in the country, but over half of those members are city, county, and state employees. Art Viat was the first to move on the public sector in a big way and, by so doing, he contributed to a change in IUOE policy. Organization in the public sector required a good deal of groundwork, including convincing the membership of the wisdom of the move. "True-blue stationary engineers do not like public engineers," Viat says. "They had to be convinced that the growth, indeed the survival of the union, depended on organizing in the public sector."[16] The government workers also had to be convinced that a craft union could serve them better than a service union.

One advantage the Operating Engineers had over other craft unions was that only four locals—two stationary and two hoisting and portable —covered the entire state. Other craft unions had locals in every county and, in some counties and cities, more than one. Since California labor relations legislation requires the California Personnel Board to carve out statewide bargaining units, the IUOE was in an excellent position to service those units through interlocal cooperation. Locals 39 and 3 in northern California and Locals 501 and 12 in southern California could divide up the work.

One of Viat's major victories was in convincing then Governor Jerry Brown to carve out a statewide stationary engineer unit. Called Unit 13, it had 428 employees—equally divided between Local 39 in the north and Local 501 in the south. Later, Viat and Bob Fox lobbied to have 2,000 out of 10,500 blue-collar workers in State Unit 12 transferred into Unit 13. The transfer took place, but Article XX charges were brought against the two IUOE locals by the Service Employees International Union (SEIU) on behalf of the California State Employees Association (CSEA). The SEIU won its case, and the 2,000 workers were transferred back into Unit 12, but that would not be the end of the story. Later, as recounted in chapter 7, the four California locals, with the full cooperation of the International, were successful in organizing the entire unit of 10,500 state employees.

Today, Local 39's 7,000 public sector members include stationary engineers, carpenters, electricians, plumbers, and other skilled workers, as well as groundskeepers, janitors, secretaries, and nurses, among others. The last are members of units, which also include either blue-collar workers or technicians carved out by the California Personnel Board. Thus, in meeting the requirements of public sector organization, the so-called blood lines had to be abandoned.

The Private Sector

There are no more boilers in downtown buildings; Pacific Gas and Electric provides the power, so the buildings now have reducing machines, not boilers. The entire stationary engineer craft has changed, and Local 39 has kept up with the changes. Less than 300 Local 39 members are old-time stationary engineers. The local's slogan now is "replace, remodel, and repair," and the union has branched out into the field of electronics. Today, Local 39 has contracts with nearly every major high-rise building, hotel, hospital, wastewater treatment plant, and airport in the San Francisco Bay area. It has contracts with 220 buildings and 74 hospitals and has organized traveling units that maintain smaller buildings, as well as the electronic units in Kaiser Foundation hospitals.

The key has been education and training. According to Viat:

> We spent more money for training and retraining [per capita] than any other local in the country, and we continue to do so. Last year, we graduated forty-one apprentices, put 672 people through upgrading, and reimbursed the membership $105,000 for courses they took in community colleges for computer training. We have buildings where the chief engineer gets up in the morning and, before he steps into the shower, calls the computer, starts the building, runs the flag up, and so forth. Then he gets into the shower and shows up an hour later. That's how high tech we are. And, so, consequently, we have to train our people for the twenty-first century.[17]

Viat claims that Local 39 controls 94 percent of the "replace, remodel, and repair" labor force in the union's jurisdictional area. His members perform not only traditional stationary engineer work but also carpentry, plumbing, electrical, and electronic work. In hospitals, for example, Local 39 members maintain steam sterilizers, nurse call systems, and biomedical units. The biomedical technicians are members of Local 39.

There were times when Local 39 was challenged on jurisdictional grounds by the building trades, but by holding to the "replace, remodel, and repair" policy, an understanding was finally reached. All new construction and all construction under warranty were the jurisdictions of the building trades, but after the construction had been completed and the warranty period had expired, the jurisdictions shifted to Local 39. The jurisdictional disputes did not cause work stoppages and were settled at the local level without resorting to AFL-CIO or NLRB procedures.

Although Article XXI protected stationary engineers where they had prior collective bargaining rights, it hurt their attempts to organize stationary engineers in units where other AFL-CIO affiliates had prior relationships. Local 39 was involved in one Article XXI case. When a new Fairmont Hotel was built in San Jose, Local 39, which already had bargaining rights for the Fairmont Hotel in San Francisco, expected to place their members in the San Jose facility. The hotel, however, entered into an agreement with the Culinary Workers Union, which included stationary engineers. The result was an Article XXI case that was eventually decided in favor of Local 39; the stationary engineers' prior bargaining rights with the Fairmount had to be respected.

Employer Relations

Local 39 has contracts with both individual owners and maintenance contractors. The union is constantly negotiating contracts, organizing, and upgrading the skills of its members. Viat claims that his relations with employers are good because Local 39 members are highly skilled and, as a result, save the employers money. When some employers complained that skilled workers were performing unskilled work such as changing light bulbs, Viat created the position of utility engineer—an unskilled position at a lower rate of pay to perform all unskilled tasks in buildings and hotels. The position is not part of the union's apprenticeship program; it stands by itself as a separate and distinct position intended to relieve skilled workers from performing unskilled work.

A recent strike against the American Telephone and Telegraph Company in the East Bay illustrates the highly skilled nature of Local 39 members. The strike involved outside maintenance contracts; the company wanted the work done in-house. As a result, they canceled the contract with the Local 39 contractor. Two weeks later, the company reinstated the contract because there was nobody in the company that could run the building and because Local 39 members refused to work in-house. (They could earn higher wages by being placed in other positions.) There were five different systems in the AT&T building, which rotated every day of the week. The company lacked the expertise to operate and maintain those systems, so the contract was reinstated.

Local 39 also has been successful with nonunion and even anti-union owners. Although nobody believed that the open shop movement would penetrate the highly organized San Francisco Bay area labor market, today, Brown and Root has an office in San Francisco's Embarcadero Center. A nonunion contractor built a building right in the heart of San Francisco's financial district, but that building is being maintained by Local 39. The reason was that Local 39 controlled the work force with the required skills. The company did not deal with any other union.

Staff

Art Viat has a staff of fifty, including private- and public-sector directors, twenty-six business agents, and two staff members who service the seventy-four hospitals under contract to Local 39. Viat serves on the IUOE Stationary Engineers Curriculum Committee and employs a full-time educational coordinator. The membership reflects the ethnic makeup of the northern California region, an area where fifty-seven different languages and dialects are spoken. As a result of an outreach program, approximately twelve women graduate each year from the Local 39 apprenticeship program.

The union has grown from 3,000 to 13,000 in twenty-seven years. Since the union controls 94 percent of the stationary engineer labor force in northern California, it would seem that growth probably will be slower in the years ahead, but if the organizing base continues to expand, future growth may very well equal or even surpass the rate of the past twenty-seven years.

The Southern California Counterpart

Robert Fox, a native of Cleveland, Ohio, arrived in southern California in 1937. Following his graduation from Hollywood High School, he enrolled in the Kings Point, New York, Merchant Marine Academy. He graduated from the academy in 1944 and spent the rest of the war on merchant ships in both the Atlantic and Pacific. Because of the knowledge of high-pressure steam and power generation that he learned in the Merchant Marine, he went to work as a stationary engineer in 1946. He worked in meat packing houses, hotels, and dairies before he was hired by the University of California at Los Angeles in 1950.

When Fox joined stationary Local 63 (the Los Angeles Basin) in 1946, the local had been under International supervision for several years. Fox, along with many other local activists, were pushing for local autonomy, but the Maloney administration was in no hurry to remove the union from supervision. "The membership had no say in local policy," Fox says, "The appointed supervisor of the local took care of his friends and negotiated contracts without any input from the membership."[18] This was prior to the Landrum-Griffin Act, which contained safeguards against the arbitrary take-over of local unions by national and international unions.

The inciting incident that triggered a local union rebellion against the International was a collective bargaining agreement that was negotiated by the International representative with several hotels in the Los Angeles area. The conditions negotiated were inferior, especially a clause that allowed the hotels to fire employees at will, without grievance or termination procedures. Ray Tucker, who was the local secretary of the union, called the members into a meeting and explained the contract to them. The members rejected the contract. Tucker returned to the negotiations with the International representative but had to leave town on business for a few days. When he returned, he was told by the "rep" that he (the rep) had agreed to the contract and Tucker would have to sign it. Tucker refused and was demoted from secretary to business agent. The International representative signed the contract. As a result, the cry for local autonomy grew into a roar, and the International was forced to allow local elections.

Local 63 regained autonomy, International supervision was discontinued, and Ray Tucker was elected business manager of the union. Tucker asked Bob Fox to join him on the local staff. When Local 63 merged with Local 235 (Orange County) in 1953, the local's number was changed to 501. When Ray Tucker was named special assistant to the general president for Stationary Engineers in 1965, Fox replaced him, subsequently becoming IUOE vice president in 1972 and chairman of the Stationary Engineers Committee before he retired in January 1993.

Industrial Change

Local 501's geographic jurisdiction runs from Fresno to the Mexican border—an area that is far less unionized than the northern part of the state. The city and county of Los Angeles are sprawling areas that extend from the Pacific on the west to the foothills of the San Gabriel Mountains on the east. Organization and servicing of the membership is extremely difficult in such a widespread area, even with the vast and confusing system of freeways that make automobile travel either a pleasure or, during the rush hours, a nightmare in the Los Angeles area.

When Bob Fox arrived in Los Angeles from Cleveland in 1936, the city's population was slightly over one million. Since then, it has become the second largest city and metropolitan area in the United States. Fox has seen the orange groves disappear from Orange County, replaced by high-tech industries and office buildings, and the entire area, from Anaheim to the Mexican border, develop into a huge megalopolis. Population growth meant economic growth and opportunities for union organization, but along with economic growth has come industrial and technological change:

> When I first became a business agent, most of our members were employed in ice and cold-storage facilities, meat and sausage rendering plants, bakeries, and laundries. Those industries have all but disappeared.[19]

Today, the majority of Local 501 members are employed in high-tech office buildings, hotels, hospitals; and city, county, and state agencies. The method of bargaining has also changed. "We used to bargain in political chambers and execute agreements with a handshake; now we have collective bargaining agreements."[20] The whole process has become far more complicated. Stationary engineers have always organized from the bottom up—that is, organizing workers rather than employers. Where the NLRB was involved, the local had to obtain enough "authorization cards" to petition the NLRB for an election. During his first three years as business manager, Fox represented the local before the NLRB. "I handled those cases myself," he said, "because we could not afford a lawyer."[21]

Local 501 has grown from 1,200 members in 1965 to well over 8,000 today, but the potential has not, by any means, been reached. Fox estimates that the local's membership represents only 20 percent of the potential. The other 80 percent either has been organized by industrial unions or are unorganized. Under Articles XX and XXI, the local can't touch those stationary engineers who have been organized by other AFL-CIO affiliates. Where previous collective bargaining relationships exist, it is against the rules for one affiliate to "raid" another. Fox agrees that the no-raiding provisions are good in that they prevent competing unions from "cutting each other up," but he regrets the fact that many stationary engineers working under contracts negotiated with the machinists, steelworkers, and laborers are earning a good deal less than Local 501 members.

Organization And Training

The key to the future, according to Fox, is organizing, education, and training. Prior to the 1980s, many local leaders scoffed at training programs instituted by the International. Reese Hammond, former IUOE director of education, once developed a leadership program for business managers and business agents. Fox recalls that he went east to attend one of these sessions, and when asked where he was going, he replied, "I am going to school." He told his colleagues that he was going to attend Hammond's leadership program. The reaction was one of incredulity. The attitude was, "Why should we go to school? We know everything there is to know about this business." The program was discontinued because of a lack of interest. Since the membership decline, however, attitudes have changed. "The best thing that ever happened to this International," Fox says, "is the organizing program instituted by President Dugan, carried on by President Hanley, and run by Jim Van Dyke. People come out of that program raring to go," Fox says, "not just stationary engineers but hoisters as well."[22]

Like Art Viat, Fox is also a strong believer in training and retraining. Local 501 has two training centers, one in Los Angeles and one in Nevada. He admits, however, that Local 501 "doesn't even come close to training enough new stationary engineers to replace retirees and others who may leave the industry." Still, the potential for Local 501 is far greater than that of its northern California counterpart. Perhaps, with the help of an extended organizing campaign and even more intensive training and retraining, the union's growth will accelerate in the future.

The Midwest Equivalent: Chicago

Lionel Gindorf, IUOE vice president and business manager of Chicago Local 399, offers a new definition of stationary engineer that pretty much reflects the views of Art Viat, Bob Fox, and other stationary engineer business managers throughout the country: "Composite Mechanic." Gindorf says that "the days of sitting around watching the boiler are gone. We do everything, including carpentry, electrical work, computer maintenance, shoveling the snow—everything. We try not to let a contractor into a building."[23]

Gindorf joined Local 399 in 1946 immediately after his discharge from military service. At the time, he was employed as a stationary engineer trainee in the laundry industry. Eventually, he received his license and became a full-fledged stationary engineer. In 1956, he became a member of the local's executive board and business agent. He was named financial secretary and assistant to the business manager in 1977. Upon the death of his predecessor, he was elected business manager in 1980.

Education And Training

Like Viat and Fox, Gindorf has seen dramatic changes in the craft of operating engineer. The union began to prepare for the change when, in 1960, drastic revisions were made in the local's training program. Since computers were the wave of the future, computer training was initiated. Today's program is tied in with a program developed by the International and also with a community college in the Chicago area. The program is two years in length and is open to all incoming members. New trainees start at $7.00 an hour and receive raises every six months. After two years, if they pass the city of Chicago's licensing examination, they are treated as journeymen and journeywomen. The program is paid for out of the union's general fund and is used primarily to pay community college teachers. No training funds are negotiated through collective bargaining.

The local's program is also open to nonunion trainees. Nonmembers are charged for the training because they do not contribute to the general fund. The local sees the enrollment of nonmembers as a prelude to organization. Nonunion trainees often become union members and are instrumental in organizing their own workplaces.

Employer Relations

Local 399 covers 102 counties—nineteen in northern Indiana. The membership has risen from 4,000 in 1960 to 6,700 in 1992. Its largest single unit is composed of 700 employees of the city of Chicago, all covered under one contract, although the 700 workers are employed in several different city agencies and departments. The union also represents state workers in Illinois, all but two of Chicago's hotels, office buildings, hospitals, universities, and pipeline workers in Hammond, Indiana. All told, the local has 450 contracts and, according to Gindorf, not a week goes by that a business agent is not negotiating.

Relations with employers are good for several reasons. First, if the union contemplates organizing campaigns, it first sends letters to the targeted employers explaining exactly what it is the union intends to do. Thus employers are forewarned; this enhances the union's reputation as an "up-front" organization. Second, Local 399's business agents have the authority to negotiate agreements without interference by the local hierarchy. According to Gindorf:

> When we go out to meet the employer, we have the whole package in our hand; the members have already voted on the package. So, anything above our proposals is icing on the cake; if the employer insists on something lower than the proposed package, it goes back to the membership for ratification. Out of 450 contracts, there was need for only two ratifications in 1991.[24]

Local 399's evolving relationship with hospitals, especially Catholic hospitals, is interesting in the light of the IUOE's sixteen-year NLRB and court battles to obtain jurisdiction for maintenance units in health care facilities. When Gindorf started as a business agent, Local 399 represented most of the Catholic hospitals in the Chicago metropolitan area, not with collective bargaining agreements but with handshakes. "At that time, the sisters were the administrators of Catholic hospitals and they were always trying to squeeze the penny," Gindorf says, "and we could make a deal with them."[25] Now the Catholic hospitals have administrators and lawyers, thus putting an end to the era of the handshakes, and introducing an era of antiunion activity. When the health care industry was added to the jurisdiction of the NLRB, conflicting decisions created a labor-relations chaos in the industry. When the Supreme Court finally rendered a decision favorable to the union position, Local 399 was ready for it. "Because we had the handshakes . . . we went after twenty or twenty-two hospitals and we picked up twelve of them . . . and now we are going back this year."[26]

Relations with Hoisting and Portable Locals

Prior to the decline in the membership of hoisting and portable locals in the 1980s, there was very little cooperation between the hoisters and the stationary engineers; they each traveled their separate ways, almost as if they didn't belong to the same organization. Gindorf cites several examples of this. A group of workers who maintained highway equipment approached Local 399 about becoming members of the local. Realizing that the workers were within the hoisting and portable jurisdiction, Gindorf called the business manager of Local 150 (the hoisting and portable local) and advised him of the request. He was told that Local 150 was not interested in the workers, so they were admitted into Local 399. Five years later, when one of the maintenance men was called out to work on a highway job, he was asked by a hoister whether he was a union man. The man said yes and showed him his Local 399 membership card. "But this is highway!" replied the hoister, the implication being that he should belong to Local 150, not Local 399.

In another case, a group of well diggers asked to join Local 399. Again Gindorf called Local 150, and again the hoisters expressed no interest in the well diggers, so they were accepted into Local 399. When the hoisters ran into trouble in the 1980s, they suddenly became interested in the maintenance workers and the well diggers.

Times have changed, however; now the two branches of the IUOE are working closely together. Gindorf says that when a building is completed now, the hoisting and portable local sees to it that the stationary engineers get the opportunity to talk to management about maintenance, something that was never done in the past. And when Local 150 goes out to small villages and towns where the stationary engineers have contracts, Local 399 does its best to help them. According to Gindorf, such cooperative relationships now exist in California, New Jersey, New York, and other areas of the country—a major improvement over the past.

Staff

Local 399 has eleven business agents, two of whom also serve as education coordinators, to service its 450 contracts. "If we organize hospitals, our engineers will get one rate, and if we get carpenters after that, they must come to our school. . . . They must learn the computer, refrigeration, and electronics . . . ."[27] That is what Gindorf means when he calls his members "composite mechanics," a far cry from the old definition of stationary engineer.

A Southern Local

Louisiana Local 406 was formed in 1910, when ten hoisting and portable members of stationary Local 226 petitioned for independent status.[28] It was confined to building, street, and sewer construction within the city of New Orleans, except for a brief flurry into Baton Rouge during the mid-1930s. Construction of Governor Huey Long's new state capitol and other projects in Baton Rouge prompted the area's few hoisting and portable engineers to request a separate charter in 1936. However, the building boomlet was short-lived and, in 1938, they were reabsorbed into Local 406. At the same time, the New Orleans local was assigned statewide status by the International.

Growth Years

The timing was fortuitous. World War II brought the construction of army camps, air bases, munitions depots, shipyards, and expanded port facilities, not only in New Orleans but throughout the state. Following the war, after a brief period of adjustment, there came oil industry expansion, pipelines and petrochemical plants, highways and bridges, and other industries. The 1960 membership of 3,203 rose steadily to a peak of 5,460 in 1981.

The period was one of strong relationships with major employers, rising wages, and increasing involvement with employee benefits. Continuity in internal affairs, policies, and employer relationships were aided by the father/son leadership of Peter Babin, Jr., business agent and recording and financial secretary from 1955 to 1981, and Peter Babin III, who, after ten years as an operator (interspersed with school attendance) and another decade as a union organizer in the public sector, became a Local 406 business agent in 1973 and business manager in 1976. He was elected International vice president in 1992.

A health and welfare plan was negotiated with New Orleans contractors in 1956, then was spread statewide through negotiations with the state chapter of the AGC during the 1960s and was incorporated into the International Pipeline Employees Health and Welfare Plan in 1973. Local 406 was one of the first locals to join the Central Pension Fund after its inauguration in 1960. The local was somewhat slower to follow the International's lead in the initiation of a formal apprenticeship program, but it did so on a statewide basis in 1973. Subsequently, three training sites were established and equipped with used equipment contributed by contractors or obtained from government surplus. The poor condition of much of the equipment lent itself more to the training and upgrading of mechanics before being useful for operator training. Subsequently, given the Louisiana industry mix, Hazmat became an important addition to the local's training activities.

Troubled Times

But like the rest of the IUOE, Local 406 was in for troubled times. Its political influence had been as potent as its bargaining power during the 1950s and 1960s and included a successful campaign to repeal the state's right-to-work law in 1956. During the difficult 1970s, however, the membership of stationary Local 226 fell until it was no longer viable and was absorbed into Local 406 in 1979. Open shop contractors began competing for major contracts, and union contractors doublebreasted to meet the competition. When a nonunion contractor began work on a contract in the formerly tightly unionized city of Lake

Charles, mass picketing erupted into violence, including shooting from both sides. A stray bullet through a trailer house killed its uninvolved occupant and became the publicity flashpoint for a 1976 campaign to reinstate the right-to-work law.

Everybody was suing everybody else in a litigation binge resulting from the violence when, in the midst of the 1976 campaign, a public-relations assistant to an antiunion gubernatorial candidate and right-to-work advocate was killed by a hired assassin. Although it was later proved that the unions had no involvement in the murder, the damage had already been done; the right-to-work law was reinstated.

The results for construction unions not dependent upon the legal enforceability of union shop clauses were indirect. Open shop and doublebreasting employers were encouraged. Workers wanting access to union hiring halls but resenting the payment of union dues were taught that "free riding" was state public policy.

Repeal of the state's construction prevailing wage law was next on the open shop political agenda. Repeal efforts in the mid-1980s were thwarted only by the union-supported governor's veto, but a new governor signed the repeal bill in 1989. Outgunned on both the economic and political fronts, Local 406 watched its membership plunge from 5,640 in 1981 to 2,823 in 1989 (Table 8.1).

Stabilization

If it had not been for several long-term relationships and the General Presidents' Contract Maintenance Agreement, the impact of the open shop movement might have been even more devastating. For example, Boh Brothers, one of the largest contractors in the state with solid commitments from various parishes for whom it did most of their sewer and water work, remained staunchly union. The company found doublebreasting to be unnecessary, mainly because of the unions' willingness to make concessions to maintain the company's ability to compete. The maintenance agreement was an extremely important source of jobs (and therefore union members) because of the prevalence of oil refineries and petrochemical plants in Louisiana. The concessions built into the agreement, eliminating nonproductive time and maintaining flexibility in work rules and crew assignments, along with the availability of International intervention on behalf of the employer when necessary, reduced the effectiveness of nonunion enticements.

Table 8.1

Local 406 Membership Trends, 1960–1993

Year	406	406A	406B	406C	406R	Total
1960	2,459	530	199	15	0	3,203
1965	2,938	696	163	22	0	3,819
1968	3,621	828	165	69	0	4,683
1972	3,243	629	145	2	0	4,019
1978	3,883	845	197	0	26	4,951
1981	4,188	964	213	56	39	5,640
1985	2,967	437	120	84	15	3,623
1989	2,297	281	87	148	10	2,823
1990	2,275	267	77	232	10	2,851
1991	2,244	266	70	222	12	2,814
1992	2,184	254	68	235	14	2,755
1993	2,142	243	67	234	19	2,705

Notes:
Branch Local 406A consists of oilers who are not engaged in formal apprenticeship.
Branch Local 406B's members are staionary engineers.
Branch Local 406C is made up of newly organized units that will later be incorporated into either 406 or 406B.
Branch Local 406R consists of apprentices. All others are enrolled in Local 406.

By 1989, the local had been able to check the hemorrhage and stabilize its membership at about 2,700. Three major efforts were responsible for stemming the membership decline. In the construction industry, where the maintenance of relationships with building contractors was the key to survival, a policy of Market Recovery Agreements was instituted. Essentially, that consisted of offering the same work-rule and work-assignment concessions as those contained in the maintenance agreement and making wage concessions as necessary to enable friendly contractors to become successful bidders. Second, local organizers began an aggressive pursuit of employees in nontraditional industries, especially public employment (where the prior experience of Peter Babin III came in handy), as well as those in industrial establishments. Finally, Louisiana was feeling its way into the gaming industry on both land and water. (In Louisiana, the term "gambling" is never used.) Local 406 was beginning to have success in organizing as stationary engineers those who maintained the necessary machinery and facilities.

Although there have been no great victories since the early 1980s, Local 406 has demonstrated that hard work and flexibility can stave off disaster and set the stage for future successes.

Initiative and Response

The union counterattack has been built around policies to make union contractors more competitive—with renewed organizational activities, an increased emphasis on training to increase productivity, financial initiatives to encourage unionization, and innovative action at the local level. IUOE membership, which suffered a 58,000 decline between 1985 and 1987, increased by over 8,000 between 1988 and 1992—a reassuring source of encouragement. Whether that success is likely to continue is the subject of the final chapter.

Chapter 9

THE FUTURE

The resumption of IUOE membership growth is reassuring to all who value the role of employee organizations in American life, and the lessons therefrom are worth noting. But those lessons are meaningful primarily in the context of craft unionism, the crucible out of which the U.S. labor movement originally emerged but which is largely ignored in most contemporary discussions of labor-management relations policy.

The Role and Values of Craft Unionism

After a near century of subdividing tasks into narrower and narrower specialties—part of the genius of scientific management—progressive industrial employers now tout the values of pay for knowledge as a supplement to pay for output and productivity. The purpose is to facilitate semiautonomous work teams that can be given a production assignment and be left to themselves to decide who is to do what and to rotate tasks among the team members with limited supervision. If that approach is to work, each team member must have the ability to do all the tasks, and, for necessary flexibility, there must be some incentive to maintain a range of skills and knowledge. With that development widely acclaimed in manufacturing industries, it is interesting to see the opposite trend in construction.

Historically, the ideal has been for each worker to maintain the broadest possible range of skills within a particular craft, thereby enabling the employer to make assignments that differ from day-to-day and job-to-job with full confidence that the tasks will be performed competently with a minimum of supervision. That has been the basic philosophy of craft unionism and the premise upon which construction apprenticeship programs have been designed and operated. For contractor/employers, that approach has offered maximum flexibility within the range of craft assignments, though not protecting them from jurisdictional disputes at the boundaries between crafts. Unionized contractors generally have been comfortable with this approach as long as all of their competitors have been party to the same agreements and governed by the same rules. However, open shop contractors have found a short-run advantage in moving toward the scientific-management direction, subdividing craft jobs into specialties performed by less-skilled and lower-paid labor. But the manufacturing industry, where scientific-management first emerged, at least offered long-term employment rather than the contract-by-contract casual relationships existing in construction. The long-run consequences of the open shop approach, in terms of managerial flexibility and employee job security, are just beginning to undergo scrutiny. It was in this context that the IUOE approached its thirty-fourth convention.

The IUOE in 1993

The 1993 convention was one of the smoothest in the union's history. The four minor amendments to the constitution and the thirty-three resolutions were passed on a voice vote with no discussion and hardly a nay being heard. The candidates for office were not opposed and were elected unanimously to their positions. Frank Hanley, who had been appointed by the general executive board to replace the retiring Larry Dugan in 1990, won his first election as IUOE general president. However, since his executive board appointment, Hanley had already taken action to strengthen the union's administration and put some of his ideas, based on thirty years experience as an International union administrator, into operation.

While still general secretary-treasurer in 1988, Hanley established the position of controller—responsible for overall supervision of the bookkeeping, membership, and data-processing department. When he assumed the presidency in 1990, he immediately set about reorganizing the headquarters staff. Departments were eliminated and others were merged to concentrate resources in key areas, and to make certain that qualified people were appointed to top staff positions. He replaced outmoded typewriters and word processors with personal computers and introduced a computerized information-exchange system.

Hanley's executive board is composed of experienced and successful local business managers. He wanted a board made up solely of independent business managers who would be policymakers rather than rubber-stamp approvers, and that is exactly what he got.

In response to declining membership, organization also became a union priority. Hanley not only beefed up the union's organizational training program, but also instituted the grant program as an incentive to increase organizational activities at the local level and developed new organizational initiatives in the south—the area of the country where the union is weakest. Training and organization, together with economic concessions designed to increase the competitiveness of union contractors, were primarily responsible for reversing the membership decline that began in 1976 and ended in 1988.

All things considered, the Operating Engineers union emerged strong from a difficult period in its history. Its membership in 1993 stood at 367,775, 59,000 below the 1975 record but 62,000 more than in 1960 and 8,523 more than in 1988.[1] Its net worth had almost doubled between 1987 and 1992—from $44,403,000 to $83,667,000.[2] Its three pension plans were in solid financial condition,[3] and the cooperative relationship between the International and its local affiliates was never better. The union's priorities appeared to be in order, and the overall management of the union, including the organization and quality of the International staff, was at its peak. Thus Hanley appeared to be justified in predicting a bright future for the union. "Our task will be difficult," he reported to the convention, "but we will prevail. We will succeed because our cause is right and just. And because we enter the fray well-prepared."[4] Hanley acknowledged, however, that there will be a "fray"—a battle that will be won only if the mistakes of the past are not repeated.

Lessons from the Past

The foremost lesson to be learned from the open shop movement of the past twenty years is "don't price yourself out of the market."

Cost Competitiveness

The construction unions had depended on taking wages out of competition by versions of the closed shop and prevailing wage legislation. As long as each contractor could know that competitors could not obtain labor at cheaper rates, they had no reason to worry about the level of those rates and the costs of production. But the purchasers of construction services did have cause for concern, and when the unions and contractors let wages get out of hand in the late 1960s and early 1970s, they attacked, and the open shop took root. The line can be held against competition for a time, but sooner or later, if costs get too extreme, there will be an adjustment.

Centralization and Decentralization

Local unions may not have the breadth of vision to foresee such a nationwide phenomenon. And even if they do, in the ferment of local union politics, union business managers who forgo current wage and benefit increases in the interest of protecting future employment opportunities are subject to becoming has-beens; opponents are apt to crucify them for their restraint. It is up to the International officers, positioned for a broader vision, receiving support from many locals under many circumstances, in contact with the larger national contractors, and generally politically secure, who must find ways of restraining the locals. Putting the union into a tripartite planning scheme would have been a considerable achievement, but that opportunity is gone for the foreseeable future. Nevertheless, the IUOE, throughout its history, has searched for the appropriate balance between centralization and decentralization and must continue to do so. Consolidation gives locals a broader vision and set of responsibilities, but it also makes them less dependent on the International for support and therefore more independent. The IUOE must continue to struggle to find the right balance between national policy and local autonomy. A strong executive board, made up of experienced and diversified business managers, interacting with the general president and his staff, may be the answer to this problem.

Open Shop Limitations

The open shop is not without its own internal problems. The fact that the Business Roundtable, which sparked the movement, appears to have shifted its focus from antiunionism per se to cost containment in general, including opposition to cost-generating union practices, is encouraging. In its 1983 summary report of the Construction Industry Cost Effectiveness Project, the Roundtable calls on "organized labor to act in its own job-creating interest by increasing productivity." Although not overly optimistic about the union response, the Roundtable noted that there were some signs of hope:

> There are some signs of changing attitudes. In half a dozen cities in recent years, voluntary local labor-management groups have had heartening success at reducing jurisdictional strikes, improving productivity on unionized projects and thereby making their communities more attractive places in which to build. This appears to be a promising route for future progress.[5]

The following also indicates a softening Roundtable attitude:

> The study teams make no overall endorsement of open shop contracting, concluding that a vigorous construction industry requires its union sector with its experienced and capable contractors and pool of skilled workers. Moreover, the study teams meticulously point out that many open shop contractors do not appear to manage their labor force as adroitly as they might, with a corresponding lack of productivity. More than half the time wasted, the study teams found, is attributable to poor management practices.[6]

J.C. Turner is quoted favorably as assuring "that building-trades unions are willing to do our share in a cooperative venture to improve productivity. . . . We are well aware that the standard of living of our members rises and falls with the profits of our employers." A decade ago, even talk about such cooperation with management was all too seldom heard from union leaders."[7] But now, another decade has passed and the message is not unusual from either local or International construction union leaders.

The Roundtable studies and reports have given the construction unions targets upon which to focus, and the activities of the AGC-Basic Trades Committee cited in chapter 7 indicate the promise of that bipartisan approach. Many open-shop and doublebreasting-contractors also appear to be having second thoughts about the consequences of deunionization. One of the most fervent of open shop contractors, Theodore C. Kennedy of B E & K Construction Co., Birmingham, Alabama, put it bluntly in a speech before the delegates to the 1993 Engineering and Construction Conference of the American Institute of Chemical Engineers. Calling contractors "whores" and owners "pimps and procurers," he lambasted "merit-shop" personnel practices:

> The average increase in the merit shop industry over the last ten years is less than ten cents per hour per year. Few craftsmen have any kind of meaningful retirement program. Fewer still have any kind of medical or hospitalization plan, beyond workmens compensation. And, if they have a heart attack, we'll have to take up a collection for the burial.[8]

Kennedy was even more scornful of merit-shop job security:

> As long as the sun is shining and there's a weld to be made, [there is job security]. But if either stops, your severance pay is just as long as it takes you to get to the gate. We'll train you—on your own time—and we'll send you to jobs that are hot, cold and certainly dirty. You'll have to leave your family and likely share less than desirable living accommodations. You'll be exposed to one of the more dangerous occupations, but if the law doesn't protect you, in all likelihood, we won't either. And for all of this goodness, what do we ask in return?—enthusiasm, loyalty, hard work, initiative, and a hearty smile. And, oh yes, we'll give you a belt buckle and a ball cap if you don't get hurt. Yo! Ho! Way to go![9]

And to the owners who contract with Kennedy's and other open shop construction companies, he had this to say:

> You owners are sitting there watching us degrade what is supposed to be our most valuable commodity—our people. And, as the wages fall, the benefits disappear, and more and more leave the industry, you take refuge by saying, "It's the American way—the competitive marketplace at work—the free enterprise system in action."[10]

As to the future, Kennedy poses this question:

> How in the world do we attract bright, energetic young people into a business where they can't earn retirement; they can't expect to work a full year; they may get ten cents per hour per year raise; and other benefits are virtually nonexistent? What will we attract into the 21st century?—those who can't get a job elsewhere?—those who may be willing to look at it as a stepping-stone to a *real* career?[11]

Kennedy was not advocating a return to collective bargaining; instead, he argued that the necessary improvements could be made by open shop contractors supported by a change in owner policy:

> As long as owners believe that efficiency and cost effectiveness are directly related to low wages and minimal fringe benefits, we are going to have continuing high turnover and a constantly changing work force. As long as contractors continue to treat their employees as seasonal harvest hands instead of skilled professionals, we cannot expect to maintain a work force of skilled 20-year veterans because they will continue to leave the industry by age 40 when we offer them no career future.[12]

Industry Responsibility

But it is exactly that sense of responsibility to the industry and cynicism about the possibility of persuading competitive contractors to invest in long-term human resource development that convinces other contractors to put up with the pressures and frustrations of collective bargaining. Hal Clyde, recently retired part owner of Utah contractor W.W. Clyde Company (Jeanita Martin's employer) puts it this way:

> Why do we stay union when most of our competitors have gone open shop? We've been in this business for over seventy years. My uncle and dad started the business and now we, their sons, have turned it over to our sons to manage while our grandsons learn the crafts. This industry has been good to us and we want to put something back. Training and high ethical standards are the keys. However, too many ignore the responsibility if they can get away with it. Unions can be exasperating, but there seems to be no other way in a competitive industry to force us all to act responsibly in our own long-term self-interest. . . . We fight plenty with our unions and we never agree to a demand we cannot afford to live with. If they send us out a worker who can't cut the mustard, we just send him or her back. But I still think unions are important to the discipline of the industry.[13]

The Role of Training

The theme of the IUOE's thirty-fourth convention was "Training for the Future," an appropriate theme under the circumstances. As noted in earlier chapters, the primary reason the Operating Engineers were less vulnerable to open shop competition than the other construction trades unions was the inability to substitute lesser or partially skilled workers as operators of expensive equipment. The primary source of cost saving with respect to other crafts was the substitution of "helpers" for journeymen and journeywomen.

Open shop contractors have been able to hire skilled operating engineers and members of other trades because of the scarcity of employment opportunities. They sometimes compete, as noted, by paying competitive wage rates, but they skimp on benefits. But as soon as jobs are available, those with skills exercise their preference for the better-paid union jobs accompanied by health insurance, pensions, and other benefits.

The Associated Builders and Contractors of America has prepared curriculum materials and encouraged its members to undertake training, but with only limited success. In a casual labor market, with employees moving frequently among employers, no individual employer can afford to train those who will then move on to work for competitors; it pays to train only those few key employees who are to be retained permanently. Smaller open shop contractors, not having access to union hiring halls, offer fairly steady employment by limiting the size, scope, and geographical range of their operations, but that also keeps them too small to afford a unilateral training effort. Competing employers could join together to sponsor and finance training programs, but the advantage of avoiding training costs altogether by pirating skilled workers or picking them up off the unemployment rolls is too much of an enticement for the individual contractor to resist. There are rarely common interests strong enough to hold competitors together for joint action in the absence of unionization.

Hence unions historically have been the moving force behind apprenticeship and training in the construction industry. As long as the unions demand and negotiate equal training contributions from each competitor and allow none to escape, there is no competitive penalty and all benefit equally. The majority of construction craft workers still pick up their skills through work experience rather than formal training. But apprenticeship, by producing supervisors, instructors, and key personnel, is the glue that holds the system together. It represents a career investment for the employee as well as a human capital investment for the employer. It also represents an investment in the industry's future by union journeymen and journeywomen, since some portion of the funds negotiated to support apprenticeship programs might otherwise have been bargained into the basic wage rate.

Nonunion employers can operate by hiring a few skilled workers (other than operating engineers) and reorganizing the work to allow them to supervise partially skilled helpers. Public vocational schools also can be persuaded politically to provide training for those crafts that combine substantial academic components with hands-on skills that can be learned in a shop setting, but only if an adequate number of students respond to the course offerings. As noted in chapter 7, vocational schools face an increasing student reluctance to enroll in training for occupations in industries that cannot offer the career promise of relatively steady employment and satisfactory annual earnings that are accompanied by the customary benefits.

The vocational school alternative is even less relevant for operating engineers. There is a substantial academic accompaniment to the operating engineers skill, in terms of familiarity with the directions of surveyors, with understanding the principles of hydraulics, and being able to calculate the angles at which the boom of a crane or drag line can safely lift a load. But all of that is for the purposes of hands-on operation, which can be learned and practiced only in the open on an expensive machine. The lesson is the same for all skill trades: A craft union survives by being the source and repository of scarce skills. Therefore, there is no substitute for training.

Training is also extremely important to the stationary engineers, as the experiences of stationary business managers throughout the country illustrate. If the IUOE is to be successful during the last decade of the twentieth century and on into the twenty-first, the union's ability to supply highly skilled workers to employers will be one of the key factors. The emphasis on training begun in the 1960s has expanded through the years to include nuclear energy, hazardous materials, pipeline construction, worker safety, Job Corps, and other programs for the disadvantaged, as well as training for headquarters staff, business agents, and organizers. The increasing cost of heavy equipment and liability insurance, together with technological change in the stationary sector, means that the demand for skilled mechanics, operators, and maintenance personnel will continue to grow. The IUOE's ability to meet that demand will be a measure of its future success.

Training is also the key to "being there first with the most" when new technologies or employment opportunities arrive on the scene; the hazmat program is a critical example for the operating engineers and other building trades unions. If union members are the first available with a newly emerging set of skills, they will be in on the ground floor.

Meeting Skill Demands in a Fluctuating Casual Market

The training challenge is a formidable one. Despite the union's renewed emphasis on training, there is an immense gap between those efforts and projections of the future need for operating engineers. An IUOE labor market analysis, prepared for the Department of Labor in April 1992, projected that employment for nonstationary operating engineers would rise from 945,540 in 1990 to 1,055,000 by the year 2000.[14] Not all of these would be employed in the construction industry, but most of them would. A compilation of statistics from state occupational information departments and related construction industry employment projections reveals an annual turnover of current workers in the operating engineer field due to retirement, disability, and career change of about 2.6 percent.[15] During the years 1990 to 2000, over 395,000 workers are projected to need training in the operating engineer craft; this amounts to an average of over 35,000 new workers annually (see Table 9.1).

IUOE locals were training a total of 5,800 apprentices in 1990, and over 1,000 individuals successfully completed IUOE programs in that year. Experience has shown that only one out of three apprentices reach journeyman or journeywoman status.[16] Nonunion employers are making little or no contribution to the training challenge, and few operating engineers, whether stationary or hoisting and portable, are trained by either public vocational schools or private proprietary schools. The union and its unionized contractors stand almost alone against a formidable challenge. Yet the IUOE recognizes as its primary source of strength and its promise for the future the ability to supply on short notice productive workers of unimpeachable skill who are able to earn their wage and benefit differential without endangering the competitiveness of their employers. It does not expect to meet the entire economy's demand for operating engineers. But it is determined to see that no hiring hall request from a union contractor or production challenge to a stationary engineer goes unfilled for want of adequate preparation. To meet that commitment will require continued strenuous effort in an atmosphere of erratic employment fluctuations and membership fear of overstaffing.

Table 9.1

Operating Engineers Training Needs, 1990–2000

Job	Employment 1990	Employment 2000	Gain	Separation 1990–2000	Need 2000
Operating Engineers	161,160	179,000	17,840	46,269	64,109
Crane Operators	61,200	66,000	4,800	17,570	22,370
Excavation & Loading Machine Operators	77,520	84,000	6,480	22,256	28,736
Grader, Dozer, & Scraper Operators	87,720	96,000	8,280	25,184	33,464
Mobile Heavy Equipment Mechanics	110,160	124,000	13,840	31,627	45,467
Diesel Engine Specialist	274,380	312,000	37,620	78,774	116,394
Surveyors	102,000	112,000	10,000	29,284	39,284
Paving, Surfacing, & Tamping Operators	71,400	82,000	10,600	20,499	31,099
Total	945,540	1,055,000	109,460	271,463	380,923

Source: International Union of Operating Engineers Labor Market Analysis, prepared for the U.S. Department of Labor, International Union of Operating Engineers, Washington, D.C., October 1991.

Apprenticeship as a transition from school to work has never been as accepted in this country as it has been in Europe. Education as it has evolved in the United States has not instituted a formalized process whereby noncollege-bound students are prepared for entry into the labor force. Many of the nation's antipoverty programs have amounted to an after-the-fact recognition of a problem of structural unemployment, that is, the surplus of underprepared workers lacking required skills. The problem has been exacerbated by an adversarial relationship between unions and employers and a general lack of cooperation among government, industry, and the schools.

Training and retraining opportunities are in scarce supply, but they are still more abundant than the number and proportion of people who take advantage of what is available. Enrollment is a hit-or-miss affair; some individuals do enroll; others do not even know that training opportunities exist, or they lack the basic skills to qualify. The result contributes to a persistent youth unemployment problem and to a lack of a sound basis for managing the nation's human resources.

In that context, the fact that two-thirds of German workers enter the labor force through apprenticeship between the ages of sixteen and nineteen has not gone unnoticed in this country. The long history of apprenticeship in Europe is based upon a generally more cooperative relationship between government, industry, and labor that makes possible a more systematic linking of education and jobs. But, more important, apprenticeship assumes both early career choice and limited mobility among, as contrasted to within, occupations. No youth wants to invest years in preparation for an occupation that, upon experience, may prove unattractive, nor are many employers prepared to accept the expense of training those who are not committed to the occupation, industry, and employer. U.S. youths, confronted by a wider range of occupational choices, generally require a longer period of career exploration before making a definitive career choice. Other characteristics of U.S. society contribute to this extension of adolescence, high youth mobility, and delay of career decision making. The relatively few apprentices in the United States are generally in their early twenties before indenture and their late twenties before completion. Those who argue for large-scale youth training programs are either overlooking the prevailing career immaturity of U.S. youths or advocating programs of career exploration based on work experience that leads to but does not necessarily incorporate permanent commitment.

With a few notable exceptions, it has been the craft unions that have pushed for apprenticeship against employer resistance. Employers are reluctant to train workers who have the option to resell their new skills to the highest bidder. Left to employer initiative, there would be little training for other than firm specific skills, and employers often attempt to shift even those training costs to public-education budgets.

It is in the interest of craft unions to assure a sufficient inflow of skilled people under union auspices and control without creating a surplus of workers competing for the limited and fluctuating number of jobs available. But both the limited ability to predict need and the inherent fluctuations in labor demand threaten the process. Even if it were possible to accurately predict long-term need, incumbent members would object and resist when the needed flow of trainees exceeded current demand. That inherent fear of labor excess and job shortage provides a downward bias to union recruitment and training decisions. New labor-market entrants are also reluctant to make the long-term commitments that apprenticeship requires, typically entering only after years of labor-market floundering result in a greater personal commitment to orderly skill preparation. Employers, in turn, are reluctant to support apprenticeship until the applicants have demonstrated their maturity and readiness to commit. But with fluctuating employment opportunities, otherwise committed apprentices, old enough to have family responsibilities, are forced to drop out in pursuit of more dependable sources of employment during the crucial years. When times are good, the number of indentured apprentices rises; when times are bad, the number declines. That is the major reason for the high dropout rates of most U.S. apprenticeship programs. When apprentices are laid off, they seek other work; when journeymen and journeywomen are unemployed, no new apprentices are indentured.

A few large-scale manufacturing firms conduct their own in-house apprenticeship programs, but beyond that, apprenticeship in the United States is primarily the responsibility of joint labor-management committees and has been restricted to the traditional craft union structure—that is, separate programs for each craft. Only the International Brotherhood of Electrical Workers and the United Association of Plumbers and Pipefitters, along with their employer associations, have traditionally produced the bulk of their membership through formal apprenticeship programs. Other crafts have trained substantial proportions, but apprentice-trained craft workers have remained a minority.

Not that apprenticeship has been unimportant to them. As argued by construction-labor expert Daniel Quinn Mills:

> Apprenticeship appears to supply a core of key journeymen, foremen, supervisors, and even contractors in most trades. In this sense it can be as much a management training mechanism as a means of training the work force itself.[17]

He well could have added instructors for apprentice programs to the list.

Open-shop contractors and their associations have complained that the Bureau of Apprenticeship and Training is reluctant to approve nontraditional programs—e.g., multicraft programs and "task training," or the training of workers to accomplish specialized tasks—both of which are favored by open-shop contractors. The critics charge that BAT is dominated by ex-union officials, whose sole purpose is to perpetuate craft-union apprenticeship policies. According to open shop contractors and some scholars in the field, notably Herbert R. Northrup, these policies discourage innovation and limit the ability of the industry to meet its future replacement needs.[18] But the fact remains that the objective of apprenticeship is craftsmanship, a philosophy that disputes the value of narrow specialization. Whatever the previous affiliations of its practitioners, the original premise and continued dedication of BAT has been to the broader scope.

Since the early 1980s, BAT has approved a few apprenticeship and training projects proposed by open shop contractors, but the results have been limited. Open shop contractors are generally no more eager than union contractors to undertake the costs of apprentice training, and they have no unions to compel their participation. The advocacy stems from the promoters of the open shop movement, the Business Roundtable and the Associated Builders and Contractors of America, not the contractors themselves.

The International Union of Operating Engineers, which largely avoided formal apprenticeship until 1960 and gave it strong impetus thereafter, was, by 1993, committed to place itself among those select few labor organizations that put training among their highest priorities, as reason for its being and its route to survival. That commitment is not limited to apprenticeship. Other programs administered by the IUOE and funded by itself, employers, or federal agencies may play an even greater role in training new operators for future employment opportunities—the hazmat program being a prime example.

As noted previously, the NLRB decision that forced the Operating Engineers into the apprenticeship field was a blessing in disguise. The union's apprentice programs, both formal and informal, provided the means for producing skilled hoisting and portable and stationary engineers. But the NLRB decision also had the effect of expanding the union's training activities into training arenas outside of apprenticeship. The union used federal funds to establish a national training program, become deeply involved in the Job Corps, and increased considerably its skill upgrading. Although the IUOE was late in entering the apprenticeship and training field, training has now become one of the union's foremost weapons in combatting the incursions of open shop contractors.

There is no doubt that as long as Frank Hanley remains president of the IUOE, the commitment to training and retraining will continue; and this is as it should be, for the union's greatest resource is the skill of its members. As long as the membership is better prepared for present and future jobs than those available outside its numbers, the union will remain a viable economic force in the industries where operating engineers are employed.

From a reluctant beginning, training had become a major undertaking and lasting commitment of the IUOE. No one expects it to be easy. The IUOE does not expect, by itself, to meet the demands implied by the projections of future operating engineer employment. But it does intend to fulfill the training requirements of its membership, a challenge toward which it has a considerable distance to travel but toward which it is making substantial progress. On the way to that elusive goal, there is, in the case of rising demand, a growing repository of experienced operators employed by open shop contractors who can be attracted back into unionized employment, as needed, by the superior wages and benefits generally available there.

The Question of Productivity

Union training commitments are designed not only to give the union a corner on the market for skilled personnel but also to justify and defend a pay differential. It is not enough to claim that union productivity offsets the higher union scale. That must be proved in practice the only way it counts—that is, by enabling union contractors to become the lowest bidders and the lowest cost producers commensurate with quality.

Thus the IUOE must see to it that its members are not only the most skilled workers but also those willing to work most efficiently. Training must encompass efficiency and high production as well as operating skills. The union may also have to pressure its contractors to improve their engineering and managerial competencies. National and project agreements of all kinds were great accomplishments in the immediate postwar period because they gave the union an "in" with the most capable and rapidly growing of contractors. That "in" was partially lost in the 1970s when the unions priced themselves out of the competitive market, and contractors resorted to doublebreasting in order to survive. Again, the union must make profitable survivors out of its employers, enabling them to prosper in a tough, highly competitive environment, then winning a share of those profits for its members after the fact of success.

The critical question facing the construction trades unions is whether their members can be persuaded to invest in the future by granting concessions until union contractors are successful. Union efforts to make doublebreasting illegal have not succeeded, and there is nothing on the horizon to indicate that future efforts will be any more successful. Thus the initiative must come from the unions without relying on help from Congress or the courts.

Until 1960, the operating engineers union had grown by taking advantage of technological change and the mechanization of the construction industry. There is now less to be gained from those quarters in construction. The issue today is cost control and keeping union-controlled technology out of the hands of the open shop. The IUOE's recent growth has come from recognizing and capturing niches in hospitals and public employment. The hazmat program is geared toward future growth. If the engineers remain alert to such opportunities, their future strength and growth, though not assured, will have a higher probability.

Union Visibility

Unions found themselves operating in a goldfish bowl during the 1950s. The Kefauver crime and McClellan labor-management hearings fed the public a steady diet of alleged union corruption. The stereotype of the "labor baron" emerged—a beefy man with a cigar in his mouth and ashes on his vest. But although the image of unions suffered from what was obviously a distorted picture, there was also a good deal of objective reporting about the labor movement. Labor unions were considered newsworthy organizations with a good deal of political clout. Today, the unions suffer from the opposite problem—lack of visibility.

For example, thirty years ago, every major newspaper and wire service in the United States had a reporter covering the "labor beat"; today only two are left—Harry Bernstein of the *Los Angeles Times* and Frank Swaboda of the *Washington Post*. The problem now is not bad publicity but little or no publicity.

This low visibility, together with the public's lack of knowledge of the past contributions of the labor movement, makes organization difficult. Labor history has been given short shrift at all levels of the nation's educational system. Today's baby boomers take for granted benefits such as social security, unemployment compensation, workers compensation, health insurance, and pensions, not to mention the eight-hour day and extra compensation for overtime; many of these were the direct result of collective bargaining and union lobbying activities. By the same token, these labor union successes appear to have had the opposite effect of making labor unions less necessary. To the extent that most workers are covered by health, safety, and welfare legislation, the need for organizations that bargain for those benefits decreases.

The Union Role

However, the primary reasons for labor organization remain: to provide employee leverage in workplace rule making and to enlarge the employees' share of the firm's revenues. Many employers seek to provide an employee voice, but voice is not power. Management giveth and management taketh away. Blessed be the name of management! But even a powerless voice is unavailable to employees who have only a brief passing relationship with any individual employer in a casual labor market. Only an employee organization to which the individual has a continuing relationship can provide an effective communication channel.

Industrial unions in stable employment situations can provide a voice that is reinforced by an independent power base for labor-management cooperation. But that is also unavailable for a craft union in a casual labor market. The employee's leverage must be with the industry rather than with the individual employer, and only some representational organization bargaining with all competing employers in the same labor market can meet that need.

Similarly, as essential as wages are in the short run, just as essential under modern industrial conditions are family health insurance through the working years and a pension to supplement Social Security at the end of the working career. Once again, large employers in industries of

relatively stable employment, accompanied by legal vesting requirements, can meet those needs with or without unions, though actual or
potential union demands may be the motivating factor. But for a casual
labor market, health insurance and pensions must be provided on a
marketwide basis with all employers paying into a pool based upon
their proportion of the total employment provided. What glue for such
a system exists other than collective bargaining or government fiat?

There have been endless arguments about the extent to which collective bargaining increases wages, but there is no doubt that some
differential exists, and there is a strong likelihood that nonunion wages
are maintained at levels higher than they would otherwise be in order
to prevent further unionization. Open shop wages would, no doubt, be
a good deal lower than they are now if the construction trades unions
went out of existence. Given the persistent differential of approximately 20 percent between union and nonunion wages in the construction industry, the limited extent of health insurance, and the near absence
of pensions for other than the few permanent employees, it is specious
to argue that employees prefer nonunion employers. The availability of
employment opportunities is the obvious issue. If the union was the
repository of all the important craft skills and if the skilled refused
to work under less advantageous conditions—a closed shop—there
could be no open shop contenders. But workers and their families
have subsistence needs and mortgages. Family incomes must continue, whatever the sacrifice. The skills will follow the employment
opportunities. Over time, union conditions will prevail in the private
sector only as long as they remain cost competitive and in the public
sector only as long as the cost differentials do not outweigh political
influence.

And the Future

These are the problems that face the entire labor movement and under-
lie such dire predictions about its future viability as that made by
Professor Leo Troy of Rutgers University:

> The recent past for private-sector unions ... was bad. But the future
> will certainly be worse. By some time in the next century, the private-
> sector unions that once ruled the city will be extinct.[19]

In contrast, Jeff Faux, president of the Economic Policy Institute,
responds:

If you got rid of all unions in the country tomorrow, you would have to reinvent them the day after tomorrow, because unions are basic to the way you get representation, respect, and communication with the labor force. . . . They are also the engine of social progress in this country. It is no accident that, at a time when labor unions have been weakened and their influence has waned, it has also been a period of reversal of social gains. As we go into an era of continued wage and income problems, more people are going to be willing to join a union, and maybe not just in blue-collar occupations either."[20]

There is no doubt, however, that the labor movement in the United States is at a crossroads. Labor union membership, as a proportion of the labor force, has been in a steady decline for a third of a century. And in recent years, that has included decline in absolute numbers as well as in relative terms. Lower membership means reduced resources and a good deal less clout, both in the halls of government and at the bargaining table. Much of the decline has been outside the control of labor—for example, the loss of manufacturing jobs—but much also has been due to outdated policies, moribund organizing activities, and a resultant indifference toward unions on the part of the general public. The labor movement is attempting a comeback. Fewer resources are being spent on interunion battles for already organized workers, and more on organizing the unorganized, wherever they may be. Unions seek more aggressively to ally themselves with those organizations that promote social reform. But at the same time, although the historic aim of the labor movement to provide "more" for its members cannot be discarded, there must be realism in determining "how much" constitutes "more."

The Continuing Struggle

"More" meant "too much" for the IUOE and its sister building- and construction trades unions during the period 1960–75. As a result, they experienced a consumer rebellion and the challenge of the open shop—a challenge supported during the 1980s by antiunion federal policies. The operating engineers union took a hit during this difficult period in its history, but it was one less damaging than those suffered by its sister unions.

But then the IUOE began to make the right moves in counterattack. Its national contracts and project agreements provided a means of granting economic concessions where they were called for, and the union's training and organizing programs were expanded and strengthened. The necessity of offsetting superior wages by superior performance and productivity became recognized, but it remains to be institutionalized. Alliances with social-reform groups in Alabama and Mississippi and on the Navajo Reservation, together with its Job Corps program and increased minority representation in the union, has made the operating engineers union an integral part of what Faux calls "the engine of social progress in this country." Finally, the union streamlined its administration and strengthened its general executive board. A strong president interacting with an equally strong executive board may result in finally attaining a workable balance between centralized policy and local autonomy.

The IUOE emerged from the competitive battle of the eighties smaller and leaner but in good shape. Based on past performance, the union should continue to prosper in the future. Although it may never again experience the rate of growth of the 1950s and 1960s, there is also no reason to expect a resumption of membership decline. The most likely scenario is a continuation of the modest growth rates of the early 1990s. But that recent growth has been from outside the union's traditional areas of strength. Continuation of growth among stationary engineers will require further adaptation to new technologies. Resumption of growth in the construction industry will require the union, while continuing to serve its members in pay and job protection, to assure that their employers remain economically viable through attention to productivity and costs.

The future of other craft unions depends on the same considerations. Industrial unions may grow or decline with the levels of employment in their industries. Craft unions, on the other hand, survive and grow when they control the supply of labor or can supply superior skilled labor to employers in a cost-efficient manner. Meeting member needs is essential and is a union's reason for being. But member needs cannot be met without employer survival. Craft union survival depends on playing to strengths, on adapting successfully to constantly changing conditions, and, above all, on being the source of the most productive labor at competitive costs.

Doing all of those things at once is not unreasonable; it will guarantee that the International Union of Operating Engineers will remain a positive force in the industries where its members are employed. If it does, it will also provide to other labor organizations an instructive example of union resilience in troubled times.

NOTES

Chapter 1

1. Interview with Lionel Gindorf, March 30, 1992.
2. Garth L. Mangum, *The Operating Engineers: The Economic History of a Trade Union* (Cambridge, MA: Harvard University Press, 1964).
3. *Officers' Report to the 26th IUOE Convention,* Bal Harbour, FL, 1960.
4. Selig Perlman and Philip Taft, *History of Labor in the United States, 1896–1932,* Vol. IV, The MacMillan Company, NY, 1935, pp. 489–514.
5. Steven G. Allen, *Developments in Collective Bargaining in Construction in the 1980's and 1990's,* North Carolina State University, Bureau of Economic Research, February 1993.
6. J. C. Turner (referring to a report of the House of Representatives Subcommittee on Labor-Management Relations), *Officers' Report to the 32nd IUOE Convention,* Hollywood, FL, April 9, 1984, p. 22.
7. *Training for the Future, Officers' Report, 34th Convention of the International Union of Operating Engineers,* April 5, 1993, Chicago, IL, p. 35.

Chapter 2

1. This entire chapter is drawn without further attribution from Garth L. Mangum, *The Operating Engineers: Economic History of a Trade Union* (Cambridge, MA: Harvard University Press, 1964).

Chapter 3

1. Interview with Billy Hurt, May 29, 1993.
2. *Officers' Report to the 28th IUOE Convention,* Bal Harbour, FL, April 1, 1968, pp. 24–25; *Officers Report to the 30th IUOE Convention,* Bal Harbour, FL, April 5, 1976, p. 105.
3. Interview with Peter Babin, Jr., October, 1992.
4. *Officers' Report to the 34th IUOE Convention,* Chicago, IL, April 5, 1993, p. 68.
5. John T. Dunlop and Arthur Hill, *The Wage Adjustment Board: Wartime Stabilization in the Building and Construction Industry* (Cambridge, MA: Harvard University Press, 1950).
6. D. Q. Mills, "Construction Wage Stabilization: A Historic Perspective," *Industrial Relations: A Journal of Economy and Society,* Volume II, no. 3, October, 1972, pp. 351–52.
7. Statement of John T. Dunlop, Secretary of Labor, before the House Committee on Education and Labor, September 10, 1975, p. 8.
8. Ibid., pp. 8–11.

9. Hunter B. Wharton, *Officers' Report to the 1972 IUOE Convention,* Washington, D.C., April 24, 1972, p. 26.

10. Interview with John Dunlop, January 19, 1993.

11. Garth L. Mangum, *The Operating Engineers: The Economic History of a Trade Union* (Cambridge, MA: Harvard University Press, 1964, p. 3).

12. Ibid, p. 8.

13. Statement by Albert L. Lake before the National Labor Relations Board, August 17, 1987.

14. Ibid.

15. Ibid.

16. Interview with Art Viat, March 26, 1992.

17. President's Task Force on Employee-Management Relations in the Federal Service, November 30, 1961; Executive Order 10988, January 17, 1962.

18. Service Contract Act of 1965.

Chapter 4

1. Interview with Joe Neeley, June 1993.

2. Interviews with Nick Matoris and Bill Snow, June 1993.

3. Interview with Billy Hurt, May 29, 1993.

4. Ibid.

5. Based on an interview with N. Budd Coutts, February 20, 1993.

6. Based on an interview with Larry J. Dugan, March 23, 1992.

7. See "The Key to Craft Status," *Officers' Report to the 26th IUOE Convention,* Bal Harbour, FL, April 11, 1960, p. 49.

8. Ibid., p. 49.

9. *Officers' Report to the 27th IUOE Convention,* San Francisco, CA, April 13, 1964, p. 58.

10. *Officers' Report to the 30th IUOE Convention,* Bal Harbour, FL, April 5, 1976, p. 78.

11. Based on an interview with Al Lake, March 2, 1992.

12. Based on an interview with Art Viat, March 26, 1992.

13. Interview with Dan Goodpaster, August 1993.

14. Hunter B. Wharton, *Officers' Report to the 27th IUOE Convention,* San Francisco, CA, April 13, 1964, p. 63.

15. Ibid., p. 64.

16. Interview with Orlando Sanchez, June 1993.

17. Interview with Steve Brown, February 28, 1993.

18. *Officers' Report to the 30th IUOE Convention,* Bal Harbour, FL, April 5, 1976, p. 84.

19. *Evaluation of the Economic Impact of the Job Corps Program, Third Follow-Up Report,* Mathematica Policy Research Study, Report MEL 82–10, Contract Number 23–24–76–06, Princeton, NJ, September 1982.

20. Based on an interview with Jeanita Martin, August 1993.

21. Based on an analysis of IUOE follow-up report to the U. S. Department of Labor, Section 292 of Contract Number 53–3187–7–28, Heavy Equipment Operators Training, Washington, D.C., June 30, 1990.

Chapter 5

1. Joseph J. Delaney, *Address* before the 26th IUOE Convention, April 11, 1960.

2. *Officers' Report to the 26th IUOE Convention,* Bal Harbour, FL, April 11, 1960, p. 10.

3. Right-to-work laws currently in force: Alabama, Arkansas, Florida, Georgia, Iowa, Kansas, Louisiana, Mississippi, Nebraska, Nevada, North Carolina, North Dakota, South Carolina, South Dakota, Tennessee, Texas, Utah, Virginia, and Wyoming.

4. *Officers' Report to the 26th IUOE Convention,* Bal Harbour, FL, April 11, 1960, p. 12.

5. Herbert R. Northrup, *Open Construction Revisited,* Industrial Research Unit, The Wharton School, University of Pennsylvania, Philadelphia, PA, 1984, p. 39.

6. Amendment to Davis-Bacon Act, 1964, PL 88–349.

7. In re: Guy F. Atkinson Co., 90 NLRB 27, June 18, 1950.

8. United Association of Journeymen and Apprentices of the Plumbing and Pipefitting Industries, Local 231, 115 NLRB 594.

9. Mountain Pacific Chapter of the Associated General Contractors, 119 NLRB 126A, 41 LRRM 1460.

10. Ibid.

11. U. S. Bureau of Labor Statistics, *Occupational Injuries and Illnesses in the United States by Industry; Statistical Abstract of the United States,* 1991, Table 693, p. 423.

12. *Officers' Report to the 28th IUOE Convention,* Bal Harbour, FL, April 1, 1968, p. 37.

13. Interview with Al Lake, March 2, 1992.

14. Interview with Billy Hurt, May 29, 1993.

15. Ibid.

16. Executive Order 10988, January 16, 1972.

17. Garth L. Mangum, *The Operating Engineers: The Economic History of a Trade Union* (Cambridge, MA: Harvard University Press, 1964, pp. 233–34).

18. IUOE General Executive Board Resolution, May 8, 1961.

19. See *Officers' Report to the 29th IUOE Convention,* Washington, D.C., April 24, 1972, pp. 92–94.

20. Ibid., p. 93.

21. Official IUOE statistics.

Chapter 6

1. "IUOE's Turner Plans Two-Pronged Campaign for Jobs," *Enqineering News-Record,* February 26, 1976, cover and p. 16.

2. *Engineering News-Record,* September 23, 1976, p. 60.

3. *Engineering News-Record,* June 12, 1975, p. 18.

4. *Engineering News-Record,* August 21, 1975, p. 18; September 23, 1976, p. 60.

5. Ibid.

6. The Business Roundtable, "More Construction for the Money," Summary Report of the Construction Industry Cost Effectiveness Project, New York, 1983, p. 1.

7. *Officers' Report to the 31st IUOE Convention,* Honolulu, Hawaii, April 14, 1980, p. 87.

8. "1984 Construction Labor Rate Trends and Outlook," Construction Labor Research Council, July 1, 1980, Bulletin 2091, February 1984, p. 2.

9. Communication from Henry Landau, President-Business Manager, Local 83, Sheet Metal Workers' International Association, Albany, New York, to membership, October 5, 1972, as cited by Herbert R. Northrup, *Open Shop Construction Revisited,* p. 98.

10. Regulations issued by Raymond J. Donovan, Secretary of Labor, 1983.

11. *Hydrostorage, Inc. v. Northern California Boilermakers Local Joint Apprenticeship Committee,* 891 F.2d 719 (9th Cir. 1989), *cert. denied,* 111 S. Ct. 72 (1990); *General Electric Co. v. New York State Department of Labor, et. al.,* F.2d 25 (2d. Cir. 1989), *cert. denied,* 496 U. S. 912 (1990).

12. "House Education and Labor Panel Approves ERISA Preemption Bill," *Employee Relations Weekly,* Bureau of National Affairs, June 6, 1993, p. 708.

13. *Officers' Report to the 31st IUOE Convention,* Honolulu, Hawaii, April 14, 1980, p. 94.

14. Garth L. Mangum, "Murder in the Workplace: Criminal Prosecution and Regulatory Enforcement," *Labor Law Journal,* Vol. 39, No. 4, April 1988, p. 223.

15. Colleen M. O'Neill, "Fight for Living Spotlights OSHA Reform," *AFL-CIO News,* March 15, 1993, p. 1.

16. *Newspaper Guild v. Long View Publishing Co.,* NLRB, Case #2-CA-25587, 1992.

17. Ibid.

18. Frank Swaboda, "Labor Loses the Strike Weapon," *Washington Post,* July 5, 1992, pp. H1 and H10.

19. *Officers' Report to the 32nd IUOE Convention,* Hollywood, FL, April 9, 1984, p. 21.

20. Ibid., p. 22.

21. Peter Kiewit Sons' Co., 206 NLRB 562 (1973).

22. Ibid.

23. *Local 627, International Union of Operating Engineers v. NLRB,* supra, n. 5.

24. *South Prairie Construction Co. v. Local No. 627, International Union of Operating Engineers,* 425 U.S. 800 (1976).

25. Peter Kiewit Sons' Co., NLRB 76 (1977).

26. "Conference Shows AGC Members How to Go Open-Shop," *Engineering News-Record,* September 2, 1976, pp. 10–11.

27. Steven G. Allen, "Developments in Collective Bargaining in Construction in the 1980s and 1990s," North Carolina State University and Bureau of Economic Research, February 1993, p. 10.

28. The Business Roundtable, "More Construction for the Money," Summary Report of the Construction Industry Cost Effectiveness Project, New York, 1983, p. 3.

29. CPS Public Use Tapes, pp. 18–21.

Chapter 7

1. Interview with James Van Dyke, February 25, 1992.

2. "Construction Labor Rate Trends and Outlook," Construction Labor Research Council, February 1984.

3. 1984 Convention Proceedings, p. 35; 1988 Convention Proceedings, p.23.

4. 1984 Convention Proceedings, pp. 38.

5. 1988 Convention Proceedings, pp. 22–25.

6. The Business Roundtable, *Local Labor Practices, A Construction Industry Cost Effectiveness Project Report,* Report C–5, April 1992, p. 18.

7. Business Roundtable, *Constraints Imposed by Collective Bargaining Agreements, A Construction Industry Cost Effectiveness Project Report,* Report C–5, April 1982, p. 4.

8. *Cost Reducing Modifications to Construction Collective Bargaining Agreements,* "An Update of the Business Roundtable's CICE Study, Constraints Imposed by Collective Bargaining Agreements (Report C–4), A Report to the AGC-Basic Trades Committee by Construction Labor Research Council," August 1992, p. 3.

9. The Business Roundtable, *Local Labor Practices,* op. cit., p. 4.

10. Officers' Report to the 34th IUOE Convention, Chicago, IL, April 5, 1993, p. 8.

11. The Business Roundtable, *Training Problems in Open-Shop Construction,* A Construction Industry Cost-Effectiveness Project Report, New York, September 1982, p. 1.

12. The Business Roundtable, *More Construction for the Money,* Summary Report of the Construction Industry Cost Effectiveness Project, New York, January 1983, p. 60.

13. Herbert R. Northrup, *Open-Shop Construction Revisited,* Industrial Relations Unit, The Wharton School, University of Pennsylvania, Philadelphia, PA, 1984, pp. 46–56.

14. "High Wage Vs. Real Cost Analysis: Wage Rate Vs. Productivity Report Update," International Union of Operating Engineers, AFL-CIO, Washington, D.C., 1992.

15. "Analysis of Productivity of Highway Construction Workers in the Southern States Within the Jurisdiction of Local 5, IUOE" (report submitted to the IUOE), 1992.

16. 1984 Convention Proceedings, pp. 30–31.

17. RC Petition, Local 39, International Unit of Operating Engineers, NLRB, May 5, 1975.

18. Albert L. Lake, Assistant to the General President of the IUOE, "Statement before the National Labor Relations Board," August 17, 1987, p. 13.

19. Ibid., pp. 14–15.

20. 29 CFR Part 103, 54 FR No. 76, 284 NLRB 1580.

21. Employment Retirement Income Security Act of 1974 (ERISA).

22. Interview with Frank Hanley, January 9, 1992.

23. Interview with Rowland Hill, January 25, 1993.

24. Interview with Herb Ingram, January 25, 1993.

25. Telephone interview with Jim Biddle, November 9, 1993.

26. *Officers' Report, 34th Convention of the International Union of Operating Engineers*, April 5, 1993, Chicago, IL, p. 35.

Chapter 8

1. Interview with Dale Marr, March 27, 1992.

2. *Master Agreement for Northern California between Associated General Contractors of California, Inc. and Operating Engineers Local No. 3 of the International Union of Operating Engineers, AFL-CIO, 1986–1989*, p. 32.

3. Interview with Thomas Stapleton, March 26, 1992.

4. Ibid.

5. Interview with Dale Marr, March 27, 1992.

6. Ibid, note 3.

7. Ibid.

8. Ibid.

9. Interview with Ron De Juliis, January 15, 1993.

10. Ibid.

11. Ibid.

12. Ibid.

13. Interview with Fred Dereschuk, March 29, 1992.

14. Ibid.

15. Ibid.

16. Interview with Art Viat, March 26, 1992.

17. Ibid.

18. Interview with Robert Fox, March 23, 1992.

19. Ibid.

20. Ibid.

21. Ibid.

22. Ibid.

23. Interview with Lionel Gindorf, March 30, 1992.

24. Ibid.

25. Ibid.

26. Ibid.

27. Ibid.

28. Peter Babin, Jr., *1903–1988, 85 Years, History of Local 406, International Union of Operating Engineers, New Orleans, Louisiana*, the local union, 1988.

Chapter 9

1. *Report of the General Secretary-Treasurer to the 34th Convention of the International Union of Operating Engineers*, April 5, 1993, p. 83.

2. *Report of the General Secretary-Treasurer to the 34th Convention*, p. 76, and *Report of the General Secretary-Treasurer to the 33rd Convention*, p. 86.

3. *Officers' Report to the 34th IUOE Convention*, p. 68 (Central Pension Fund); *Report of the Pension Committee of the International Headquarters Pension and Beneficiaries Plan to the Officers and Delegates to the 34th IUOE*

Convention, p. 91; and *Report of the General Pension Plan to the 34th Convention,* p. 97.

4. *Officers Report to the 34th IUOE Convention, Chicago, IL,* April 5, 1993, p. 7.

5. The Business Roundtable, *Summary Report,* Construction Industry Cost Effectiveness Study, New York, 1983.

6. Ibid.

7. Ibid.

8. Theodore C. Kennedy, *Managing Change in the 21st Century,* Address before the Engineering and Construction Conference of the American Institute of Chemical Engineers, San Francisco, CA, 1992.

9. Ibid.

10. Ibid.

11. Ibid.

12. Ibid.

13. Interview with Hal Clyde, June 10, 1993.

14. *International Union of Operating Engineers Labor Market Analysis,* prepared for the U. S. Department of Labor, International Union of Operating Engineers, Washington, D.C., October 1991.

15. Ibid.

16. Ibid.

17. Daniel Quinn Mills, *Industrial Relations and Manpower in Construction,* The Massachusetts Institute of Technology Press, Cambridge, MA, 1972.

18. Herbert R. Northrup, *Open Shop Construction Revisited,* Industrial Research Unit, The Wharton School, University of Pennsylvania (Reprinted in 1986), p. 416.

19. Quotation in John Walsh and Garth Mangum, "Labor Struggles in the Post Office," in *Selective Lobbying and Collective Bargaining* (Armonk, NY: M.E. Sharpe, 1992), p. 233.

20. Jeff Faux, "EPI Links Economic Growth with Economic Justice," in *Challenge: The Magazine of Economic Affairs,* January–February 1992, p. 21.

INDEX

ABOUT THE AUTHORS

Garth Mangum is Max McGraw Professor of Economics and Management at the University of Utah. He is author and coauthor of thirty books and numerous monographs and articles on labor and employment, including *Capital and Labor in American Copper* and *The Operating Engineers: Economic History of a Trade Union.* In addition to teaching at several universities, he served the federal government as senior research analyst of the Eisenhower-appointed Presidential Railroad Commission, and research director of the Senate subcommittee on employment and manpower during the Kennedy administration and as executive director of the President's Committee on Manpower and executive secretary of the National Commission on Technology, Automation, and Economic Progress during the Johnson administration.

John Walsh is the author of four books and the coauthor with Garth Mangum of three others, *A Decade of Manpower Development and Training, What Works Best for Whom,* and *Labor Struggle in the Post Offoce.* His articles have appeared in the *International Journal of Social Economics* and several government periodicals. His twelve years of government service included posts in the U.S. Department of Labor and in the executive offices of President Lyndon Johnson. Outside the government, Walsh has served as a senior consultant with Arthur D. Little Co. and vice president of Olympus Research Corporation.